Probabilistic Metaphysics

Probabilistic Metaphysics

PATRICK SUPPES

Basil Blackwell

First published 1984
Reprinted 1985

Basil Blackwell Publisher Ltd
108 Cowley Road, Oxford OX4 1JF, UK

Basil Blackwell Inc.
432 Park Avenue South, Suite 1505,
New York, NY 10016, USA

British Library Cataloguing in Publication Data

Suppes, Patrick
    Probabilistic metaphysics
    1. Free will and determinism
    I. Title
    123 BJ1461

ISBN 0-631-13332-1

Library of Congress Cataloging in Publication Data

Suppes, Patrick, 1922 –
    Probabilistic metaphysics.
    Bibliography: p.
    Includes index.
    1. Probabilities. 2. Science—Philosophy. I. Title.
BC141.S86 1984   120   84 – 14657
ISBN 0-631-13332-1

Typeset by Fourjay Typesetters Ltd, Oxford

Printed by TJ Press Ltd, Padstow

To Christine

Contents

Acknowledgments   xi

1 INTRODUCTION   1

   Aristotle on metaphysics   3
   Being and matter   4
   Kant on method   7
   Metaphysics as presupposition   8
   Some metaphysical propositions   10

2 RANDOMNESS IN NATURE   12

   Common natural phenomena   12
     Babble of speech   13
     Smelling and seeing   13
   Adequacy of probabilistic laws   15
     Epicurus   15
     Laplace   17
   Stochastic retreat from determinism   19
     Radioactive decay   22
     Randomness in quantum mechanics   23
   What is randomness?   25
     Analogy of action at a distance   25
     Randomness and complexity   30
     Physical randomness and stability   32
   Summary   33

3 CAUSALITY AND RANDOMNESS   35

   Classical philosophical views   36
     Aristotle on luck and chance   36
     Hume   38
     Kant   41
     De Moivre and secret causes   41

Bayes	43
Laplace	44
Systematic definitions	47
Spurious causes	50
Varieties of probabilities	52
Alternative modern views	52
Ordinary experience	54
Conflicting intuitions	55
Simpson's paradox	55
Macroscopic determinism	57
Types and tokens	59
Physical flow of causes	63
Common causes	67
Appendix on Common Causes	71
General assumption	71
Two deterministic theorems	72
Exchangeability	73
4 UNCERTAINTY	76
Certainty of mathematical knowledge	77
Euler's three senses of certainty	79
Errors of measurement	82
Heisenberg's uncertainty principle	85
Quantum mechanics and classical probability theory	89
Meaning of probability statements	93
5 INCOMPLETENESS	100
Logical completeness	101
Incompleteness of arithmetic	102
Incompleteness in geometry	102
Incompleteness of set theory	103
Cartesian physics	104
Kant's metaphysical foundations of physics	107
Laplace	110
The unified field theory	111
Einstein–Podolsky–Rosen paradox	112
Incompleteness of probability spaces	114
What to expect	115

6 THE PLURALITY OF SCIENCE   118
  What is unity of science supposed to be?   118
  Unity and reductionism   120
    Reduction of language   120
    Reduction of subject matter   122
    Reduction of method   124
  N-body problem   125
  Information and computation   130
  Mental software and physiological hardware   132

7 LANGUAGE   135
  Speech production and reception   135
    Distinctive features   136
    Phonemes   137
    Syllables and words   138
  Grammar   139
  Competence versus performance   143
    A simple grammar   147
    Applications of probabilistic grammars   148
  Meaning and procedures   149
    Some general propositions about procedures   153
    A puzzle about responses   161
  Congruence of meaning   165
    Indirect discourse   168
    Grody to the max   170

  Appendix on Probabilistic Grammars   173
    Likelihood estimation   174
    French example   177
    Developmental models   179
    The all-or-none stage model   179
    Incremental model   180
    Empirical test of the two models   182

8 RATIONALITY   184
  The meanings of rationality   184
  Model of justified procedures   187
    Recipes as procedures   189
    Applications of procedures and probability   194
    Rational cooks and carpenters   196
    The practical and the theoretical   197

Expected-utility model   203
   Weakness of the expected-utility model   207
   Fantasy of intention   207
   Intentional randomness   210
   Fantasy of attention   212
   Matter of context and approximation   213
Place of judgment   215
   Positive theory of judgement   217
   Linear models for aggregating judgments   219
The Bayesian core   220

Appendix on Probability and Expectation   222
   Qualitative expectation structures   226
   Formal developments   228

References   231

Name Index   242

Subject Index   245

Acknowledgments

A first and partial draft of this book was given at the Hägerström Lectures in Uppsala, Sweden, in 1974. These lectures were circulated in mimeographed form through the University of Uppsala. I owe to Amartya Sen, another Hägerström lecturer, the suggestion of revising, extending, and publishing them in book form. Given the several intervening years in which to change my views and to extend at leisure many of the themes, the present manuscript is very different from the original lectures both in content and in length. The book is more than twice as long as the manuscript of the lectures. Chapters 6, 7 and 8 of the book overlap hardly at all with anything I said in 1974. I have added brief technical appendices to several of the chapters, but these can be ignored without any loss of continuity.

The original written lectures benefited considerably from criticism of their content and style by Nancy Cartwright and Diane Axelsen. Stig Kanger and other Swedish philosophers forced me by their remarks at the time of presentation in Uppsala to revise a number of passages. The present version has benefited from detailed and sometimes sharp criticism from Joseph Almog, Michael Bratman, John Dupré, Wilbur Knorr, Julius Moravcsik, John Perry, and Jean Roberts, all of whom along with Nancy Cartwright are colleagues of mine at Stanford. Specific criticisms of chapter 7 were also made by John Biro, Jens Erik Fenstad, Daniel Quesada, and Phillip Staines. Various historical, as well as systematic, errors and oversights in several chapters were pointed out by Jules Vuillemin.

My thanks to Marguerite Shaw for using the computer facilities available to us to produce with accuracy and good humor successive revisions of various chapters, some more numerous than I care to think about. My wife Christine has supported my ups and downs of manuscript completion far more than I deserve.

I have used passages from articles previously published or about to be published in various chapters. Permission to use them in this book is gratefully acknowledged. The last part of chapter 3 is being printed, with minor changes, as 'Conflicting Intuitions about Causality', Volume IX; of *Midwestern Studies in Philosophy, Causation and Causal Theories*, edited by Peter French, Theodore Yuehling, Jr, and Howard Wettstein (1984). The last section of chapter 4, 'The Meaning of Probability Statements', is reprinted from *Erkenntnis* (1983), **19**, 397–403. The first part of chapter 6 draws on 'The Plurality of Science', in P. Asquith and I. Hacking (eds), *PSA 1978* (Vol. 2), Lansing, Mich., Philosophy of Science Association (1981), pp. 3–16. Chapter 7 uses passages from three articles: 'Probabilistic Grammars for Natural Languages', *Synthese* (1970), **22**, 95–116; 'Procedural Semantics', in R. Haller and W. Grassl (eds), *Language, Logic, and Philosophy*, Vienna, Hölder-Pichler-Tempsky (1980), pp. 27–35; and 'A Puzzle about Responses and Congruence of Meaning', *Synthese* (1984), **58**, 39–50. Chapter 8 uses passages from 'The Limits of Rationality', *Grazer Philosophische Studien* (1981), **12/13**, 85–101, and also from *Logique du Probable*, Paris, Flammarion (1981).

1

Introduction

One way of quickly sketching the essence of what I shall be saying is to compare my criticism of what I term the new theology with Kant's criticism of the old theology. The central problems on which Kant focused were the celebrated triad: the existence of God, the immortality of the soul, and the freedom of the will. Kant has this to say about the history of these ideas in the final chapter of the *Critique of Pure Reason*:

> It is very remarkable, though naturally it could not well have been otherwise, that in the very infancy of philosophy men began where we should like to end, namely, with studying the knowledge of God and the hope or even the nature of a future world. However crude the religious concepts might be which owed their origin to the old customs, as remnants of the savage state of humanity, this did not prevent the more enlightened classes from devoting themselves to free investigations of these matters, and they soon perceived that there could be no better and surer way of pleasing that invisible power which governs the world, in order to be happy at least in another world, than good conduct. Thus theology and morals became the two springs, or rather the points of attraction for all abstract enquiries of reason in later times, though it was chiefly the former which gradually drew speculative reason into those labours which afterwards became so celebrated under the name of metaphysics. (A.852–853)

It would be surprising if I were to devote my own critique to 'studying the knowledge of God and the hope or even the nature of a future world'. Most philosophers do not take these ideas seriously today, at least not during professional hours, and certainly I do not.

It is my contention, however, that the old theology has been replaced by a metaphysics of philosophy and science that is equally fallacious and mistaken in character. Here are five of its basic tenets:

(1) The future is determined by the past.
(2) Every event has a sufficient determinant cause.
(3) Knowledge must be grounded in certainty.
(4) Scientific knowledge can in principle be made complete.
(5) Scientific knowledge and method can in principle be unified.

I am not concerned to make the historical case as to who does or does not adhere to these propositions, which collectively I shall label tenets of *neotraditional metaphysics*. They have been widely accepted in much of post-Kantian philosophy, in much of contemporary analytic philosophy, and, to varying extents, in contemporary versions of logical empiricism or logical positivism. It is my thesis that each of the tenets is false or, at least, that the best evidence at present is that they are false; consequently, we should be able to construct a general metaphysic or epistemology on other grounds. I shall devote a chapter to each of the five and, in the process, try to make clear what I think is the appropriate replacement. To push the argument for a probabilistic viewpoint of the world further, the last two chapters of this book are devoted to two additional topics. The first is concerned with probabilistic aspects of language, a citadel of determinism, at least as defended by many modern linguists and philosophers. The last chapter reviews the probabilistic grounds of rational belief and action, and stresses how seldom these grounds can be made either certain or complete.

I use concepts of probability to deal with metaphysical and epistemological matters, and I argue for replacing the concept of logical empiricism by that of probabilistic empiricism. But probabilistic empiricism is not meant to have a reductive bias as I conceive it. I shall claim that it is probabilistic rather than merely logical concepts that provide a rich enough framework to justify both our ordinary ways of thinking about the world and our scientific methods of investigation.

It is also not my intention in these pages to enter deeply into technical considerations. I shall assume that elementary probability concepts and elementary logical concepts, as well as certain parts of science of a general character, can be used and referred to without extensive exposition or explanation. I shall use repeatedly the concept of randomness. An informal theoretical account of this difficult and elusive notion is to be found at the end of chapter 2. A detailed analysis of the meaning of probability statements, which is intended to use aspects of both objective and subjective interpretations of probability, is given at the end of chapter 4. That randomness and probability are real phenomena, and therefore are not to be accounted for by our ignorance of true causes, is a proposition that I defend from a variety of perspectives. But as part of my irenic viewpoint I also defend the essential role of a Bayesian theory of subjective probability, especially in chapter 8.

ARISTOTLE ON METAPHYSICS

In the first book of his *Metaphysics*, Aristotle emphasizes how philosophy begins in wonder and moves to questions about the stars, about the origin of the universe, and about the character of knowledge itself. Speculations of this kind, he notices, are not for any direct ulterior purpose, but are pursued for their own sake. It is sometimes said that Aristotle's *Metaphysics* is a model of descriptive metaphysics, an attempt to organize the most general and at the same time the most significant aspects of experience. Such descriptive metaphysics is contrasted with the kind of speculative metaphysics that Kant was so concerned to criticize and eliminate from philosophy. The kind of probabilistic metaphysics I try to develop in these pages is meant to be descriptive rather than speculative. The conclusions I want to reach depend upon the science of our day in the same way that much of what Aristotle had to say depended upon the science of his time. However, I do not draw any Kantian distinction between necessary scientific knowledge and contingent empirical knowledge; there is, in my view, a continual progression from sophisticated common sense to the latest scientific developments. One of the most important roles of a descriptive metaphysics is to provide a synthesis of contemporary common sense and science.

The tenets of a properly formulated descriptive metaphysics that is also properly supported by the weight of scientific and commonsense evidence should form a broad conceptual framework for thinking about natural phenomena and human experience. The framework should always, however, be treated as tentative and subject to revision. Unfortunately, there has been a strong tendency, both in philosophy and in science, to build or to use a framework of concepts that seem unsupported by experience and that hamper the effort at improvement in the light of experience. The claim to have advanced some final version of the truth is perhaps the most egregious general error made by most of the past philosophers we all respect. Here, for example, is Kant in 1799, near the end of his life:

> Nevertheless the critical philosophy must remain confident of its irresistible propensity to satisfy the theoretical as well as the moral, practical purposes of reason, confident that no change of opinions, no touching up or reconstruction into some other form, is in store for it; the system of the *Critique* rests on a fully secured foundation, established forever; it will be indispensable too for the noblest ends of mankind in all future ages. (Open letter on Fichte's *Wissenschaftslehre*: Zweig, 1967, p. 254)

As is evident, modesty about the foundations he laid down is not a salient feature of Kant's view of himself. But what is more striking from a modern view is the naiveté of his assurance of the permanence of his intellectual structure.

Emphasis on the relation between metaphysics and science is not as explicit in Aristotle as the brief account that I have given above about his descriptive metaphysics might indicate, however. Before turning to the topics of main interest in this book, it will be useful to review some of the more general problems of traditional metaphysics and to remark how they fit in to the matters discussed here.

BEING AND MATTER

One traditional formulation is that Aristotle's main concern in the *Metaphysics* was the study of being *qua* being, that is, the most general principles that any existent thing must satisfy. In later times the issue has also been taken to be that the proper study of metaphysics is all possible forms of being. This leads us naturally into modern talk about logically possible worlds. Considering the weakness of this apparatus and the very detailed things that Aristotle and subsequent philosophers have had to say under the general banner of metaphysics, it is clear that a rigorous and systematic study of being *qua* being has not been the entire focus or indeed even the main focus of metaphysical writings. It could be claimed that only the modern work on logical possibility has offered an appropriate rigorous and systematic study.

Traditionally, the general talk about being and especially possible forms of being has rather rapidly veered off into the fundamental problem of the nature of substance as the primary carrier of being. Aristotle, for example, has an elaborate theory of substance, closely related to his theory of matter and form. It is important to recognize that the concept of matter (*hylē*) in Aristotle is very different from a modern physicist's conception of matter. In fact, what the modern physicist calls matter is closer to what Aristotle would think of as substance.

A brief summary of Aristotle's doctrine of matter and substance would go something like the following. Matter is the substratum of change. 'For my definition of matter is just this— the primary substratum of each thing, from which it comes to be without qualification, and which persists in the result' (*Physics*, 192a31). Matter *qua* matter is purely potential and without attributes (*Metaphysics*, 1029a19). A substance has both form and matter. The nature of a substance is complex. It is neither simply the form nor the matter (*Physics*, 191a10; *Metaphysics*, 1043a15). There is no principle of individuation for matter *qua* matter, for reasons that are obvious from what has already been said. The principle of individuation for substances does not require sameness of matter for sameness of substance. For example, an animal is both intaking and excreting substance, but we still speak of the identity of that animal through time. (For a more detailed discussion, see Suppes, 1974a).

It may be instructive to compare this sketch of Aristotle's theory of matter with modern scientific views and how Aristotle's theory might be reconciled with it. As the atomic theory of matter became the dominant scientific theory in the nineteenth century, it looked certain that the ancient atomic theories of matter were the conceptually correct ones and views such as those of Aristotle would be permanently put to the side. By the beginning of this century it was recognized that atoms have structure, and aspects of this structure were clearly identified so that the simple ancient talk about atoms as the ultimate simples was not appropriate. The concept of a nucleus with electrons in orbit around the nucleus was developed. The atom was now thought of on the lines of a small-scale solar system but electrons and protons were the building blocks so that simple atomic theories of matter in the ancient conceptual sense were once again saved. It seemed clear also that the elementary particles had constant fundamental properties, for example, the same mass for all electrons and similarly for all protons, the same electrical charge and the same negligible but definite size.

As quantum mechanics developed, it became apparent that the particles that make up an atom were not simply little balls bounding around in a small-scale world very much like the one we ordinarily move about in. The properties were stranger and more elusive than once thought. Of particular relevance here is the concept of intrinsic spin, a property that has certainly had very little satisfactory conceptual explication by quantum theoreticians. It was also recognized that matter was not indestructible, contrary to ancient ideas about atoms. All the same, the case for the atomic theory seemed to remain rather strong, and most physicists probably felt that some version of the atomic theory was basically the correct theory of how the universe was put together. There was the troublesome problem of fields, both electromagnetic and gravitational, but this did not disturb greatly the dominant atomic theory with a few simple particles like electrons and protons being the ultimate simples.

The pursuit of higher energy levels continued in experimental physics and it became apparent that the world was full of particles that are continually undergoing processes of generation and corruption, as Aristotle would put it. Methods for observing this generation and corruption were brought to a fine point by bubble chamber and other related apparatus. Moreover, the idea of the fundamental importance of fields came more and more to the fore, and much physics was done in terms of continuous properties of fields rather than singular properties of individual particles.

It should be clear how Aristotle's theory of matter can fit into this new and more complicated picture. In the first place, from an

Aristotelian standpoint the search for ultimate simples in terms of fundamental building blocks is a definite mistake. The empirical evidence both from macroscopic bodies and high-energy particles is that the forms of matter continually change. There is no reason to think that one form is necessarily more fundamental or ultimate than another. Cloud-chamber data, for example, which show so well the generation and decay of particles, support Aristotle's definition of matter. As we observe change there must be a substratum underlying that which is changing. What is the substratum underlying the conversion of particles into other particles, or the conversion of particles into energy? The Aristotelian answer seems attractive. We can adopt an Aristotelian theory of matter as pure potentiality. The proper aim of theoretical physics is determining the laws that describe these varied changes of form. In speaking so positively of the Aristotelian theory of matter and substance, I do not mean to suggest that we can get from Aristotle detailed guidance on the laws of physical phenomena. What is valuable is that his way of approaching the theory of matter and substance provides a conceptually important and valuable alternative to the atomic viewpoint that has been dominant for too long in modern science. In later chapters I shall indicate how probabilistic notions need to be added to the general view of matter and substance I have sketched here, in order to have a more realistic theory. But my conception of probabilistic metaphysics should be thought of as an extension of the Aristotelian metaphysics of matter and substance.

KANT ON METHOD

There are, of course, other problems that have occupied the center of the stage for metaphysicians of the past. Unfortunately, as Kant emphatically pointed out in his negative critique of traditional metaphysics, there is no single book like Euclid's *Elements* of which it can be said 'This is metaphysics, herein is to be found the chief end of the science, the knowledge of a Supreme Being and of a future world, demonstrated upon principles of the pure Reason' (*Prolegomena*, p. 17). Aristotle's *Metaphysics* is undoubtedly the closest thing to a definitive text, but it certainly has not played the role of Euclid's *Elements*. Kant, in fact, loved to make the point that his new critical philosophy stands to the old metaphysics as chemistry stands to alchemy, or as astronomy stands to astrology. It could be said more explicitly of Kant than of Aristotle that one of his missions was to lay the foundations of science in an appropriate metaphysical fashion within the flights of pure reason he so rightly criticized. Kant also loved to make the point that metaphysics will never disappear, that the giving up of metaphysical investigations is as improbable as that we should stop breathing. The problem is to stop bad metaphysics just as we should stop breathing bad air (*Prolegomena*, p. 117). It was Kant's mission above all to show how this could be done, how, in short, rigorous methods could be applied to metaphysics.

There is one other point about metaphysical methods. Kant has insisted that there is nothing so absurd as the use of probability in metaphysics. As he puts it:

> Nothing could be more absurd than in a system of metaphysics, a philosophy of pure Reason, to attempt to base judgments on probability and conjecture. All that can be known *a priori* is thereby given out as apodictically certain, and must be proved as such. A geometry or arithmetic might just as well be attempted to be founded on conjectures. (*Prolegomena*, p. 119)

Evidently, here again I am happy to disagree with Kant. As I point out later, Kant's avoidance of all systematic discussion of the theory of probability is, in historical perspective, one of the major failures of his conception of science.

I said at the beginning of this chapter which topics would be mainly criticized. It is possible to argue that the neotraditional metaphysics that I am criticizing has already faded from the scene, but, if so, I am afraid this is true only in very enlightened quarters. The critique I make of determinism, certainty, completeness, and unity in scientific or commonsense knowledge will surely not be accepted by many philosophers or scientists.

METAPHYSICS AS PRESUPPOSITION

An influential twentieth-century view of metaphysics has been that of R. J. Collingwood (1939/1972). He holds that metaphysics is the set of absolute presuppositions of scientific thinking of a given time. Several observations about his views will make clear how they are both similar to and very different from those I am developing in this book. First, there is great similarity in the stress on the relation of metaphysics to science at a given time. Second, there is similarity in recognizing that what is a metaphysical presupposition changes as science changes. Collingwood is as critical as I am of those who believe that an adequate metaphysics can be developed once for all just on the basis of the analysis of ordinary experience and our ordinary talk about that experience. Third, Collingwood uses a broad definition of science to include any systematic thinking, and in this I concur. On the other hand, our differences are several. I do not agree that metaphysics is the science of absolute presuppositions, which cannot as such be regarded as either true or false. In the spirit of Kant's critical philosophy, Collingwood has tried to reserve a special status for metaphysical statements. Kant retreated from the traditional metaphysics of his time by severely limiting the use of reason. But his aim was to establish a proper metaphysical foundation for science once for all, as the quotations I have cited make evident. Collingwood represents a retreat from Kant's position by recognizing the absurdity of trying to establish the metaphysical foundations of science once for all.[1] His emphasis is nothing if not historical. But he retains the Kantian view of metaphysics as having a special subject matter and a special methodology. The special subject matter is the set of absolute presuppositions of any given collection of thinkers during some historical period. The special methodology is that required for determining what is or is not an absolute presupposition. On this question of method Collingwood simply is not able to say much that is conceptually satisfactory, and the examples, especially those about causality, while interesting do not provide the kind of rich analytic details needed to make the case for the correctness of a special methodology.

My position is that there is no sharp delineation of the class of metaphysical assertions. It is as pointless to try to give a logically

[1] But Collingwood (1939/1972) is nearly as adamant as Kant about his ability to clear up once for all the past obscurities of metaphysics. 'A great deal of work has been done in metaphysics since Aristotle created it; but this work has never involved a radical reconsideration of the question what metaphysics is. A great deal of grumbling has been done about it, too, and a great many people have declared the whole thing to be a lot of nonsense; but this, too, has never involved a radical reconsideration of what the thing is. On that question Aristotle bequeathed to his successors a pronouncement containing certain obscurities; and from his time to our own these obscurities have never been cleared up. To clear them up is the task of the present essay' (p. 5).

airtight definition of metaphysics as it is to try to do the same for physics or musicology. Moreover, metaphysics currently has a bad name in many quarters, although its reputation has been improving once again for the past several decades as logical positivism has nearly faded from the scene. Still there are many philosophers—and probably more scientists—who become uneasy if asked to give their best examples of metaphysical assertions or propositions. I like the spirit of Kant's and Collingwood's willingness to commit themselves in detail to assertions they regard as genuinely metaphysical. In the same spirit, but with no illusion that I can clear up past or present obscurities in any definitive way, I end this introductory chapter with a list of metaphysical propositions that are argued in the remainder of the book.

SOME METAPHYSICAL PROPOSITIONS

(1) The fundamental laws of natural phenomena are essentially probabilistic rather than deterministic in character.
(2) Our conception of matter must contain an intrinsic probabilistic element.
(3) Causality is probabilistic, not deterministic, in character. Consequently, no inconsistency exists between randomness in nature and the existence of valid causal laws.
(4) Certainty of knowledge—either in the sense of psychological immediacy, in the sense of logical truth, or in the sense of complete precision of measurements—is unachievable.
(5) The collection of past, present, and future scientific theories is not converging to some bounded fixed result that will in the limit give us complete knowledge of the universe.
(6) The sciences are characteristically pluralistic, rather than unified, in language, subject matter, and method.
(7) Language learning and performance in their phonological, grammatical, semantical, and prosodic aspects are intrinsically probabilistic in character.
(8) The theory of rationality is intrinsically probabilistic in character.

My emphasis in this list and in this book is on general propositions that depend on probabilistic concepts, but this is because of their neglect or, in many cases, rejection, as metaphysical assertions by many philosophers just because of their probabilistic character. There are many other metaphysical propositions I accept as sound and important which do not involve probability in any way. Aristotle's *Metaphysics* is one of the best sources of examples.

It is, to say the least, uncommon to claim that probability should be regarded as a fundamental metaphysical concept. As already remarked, the traditional focus of metaphysics is on the nature of being, or the nature of substance, the nature of space and time, and similar concepts. One way of formulating my claim is that the probabilistic character of phenomena is almost as ubiquitous as their spatial or temporal character. Traditional metaphysics has ordinarily moved away from the concrete variety of actual experience to seek some underlying bedrock of permanence. There have been important past philosophers who have concentrated much more on the surface features of experience than on that which seems to underlie these surface phenomena. William James and John Dewey are good examples, but Charles Peirce is perhaps the most obvious predecessor I should acknowledge, because of his explicit emphasis on chance phenomena in nature. It is not my aim to give a point-by-point comparison of Peirce's and my views. I believe that I have widened the arena of phenomena considered by Peirce, especially with the emphasis on probabilistic features of language in chapter 7. In any case, I have organized my ideas without close historical attention to Peirce. Because of my effort to challenge traditional metaphysics, I have more historical references to classical philosophers, for example, Aristotle, Descartes, and Kant.

Descartes and Kant have almost nothing to say about chance or probability. I discuss Aristotle's rather restricted view of the role of chance (*tychē*) in chapter 3. But men everywhere, especially those who have reflected on the vicissitudes of politics and war, have from the beginning recognized the central place of chance in human affairs. In the opening lines of Pericles' first speech, as reported by Thucydides, he says: 'for sometimes the course of things is as arbitrary as the plans of men; indeed this is why we usually blame chance for whatever does not happen as we expected.'[2]

---

[2] For a detailed analysis of the concept of chance in Thucydides, see Edmunds (1975). I could as well have ended with these famous lines from Ecclesiastes (9: 11): 'I returned, and saw under the sun, that the race is not to the swift, nor the battle to the strong, neither yet bread to the wise, nor yet riches to men of understanding, nor yet favor to men of skill; but time and chance happeneth to them all.'

2

Randomness in Nature

The concept of determinism is a modern one. The intuitive notion is that phenomena are deterministic when their past uniquely determines their future. (Later on in the chapter I give a more explicit characterization.) The concept is not explicitly discussed even as late as the eighteenth century.[1] On the other hand, the antecedents are present in much earlier thought and the case for randomness in nature leads all the way back to Epicurus. I have divided my case against natural phenomena being wholly deterministic into three parts. First, I consider some of the ordinary natural phenomena that argue strongly against such a view. At any given period of science, and certainly not just the present, the weight of systematic evidence has always been against a thesis of determinism, but explicit examination of this evidence has not been a strength of either scientists or philosophers. Second, I examine some of the history of developments, and, third, I consider some of the most important scientific results at a fundamental level that seem to provide a decisive argument against determinism. Finally, I examine the question, what is randomness?

COMMON NATURAL PHENOMENA

Ordinary observation and participation in physical phenomena seem to argue decisively against nature being deterministic.

---

[1] Various historical counterexamples can be offered to this claim, but these earlier passages did not crystallize the concept of determinism for continued analysis and disputation. An early eighteenth-century instance is the section on liberty and necessity in Hume's *Treatise of Human Nature,* which is more or less repeated in *An Enquiry Concerning Human Understanding.* But what Hume says in these passages on the score of determinism is casual and unworked out, and above all, not the focus of his interest.

Casual attention to the way that a breeze moves the leaves on a tree would seem to make it quite unrealistic to think of having a theory that could predict their motion. Clouds forming in all their irregularity of shape, dust settling in the trail of an automobile, raindrops falling in a strong wind—almost any phenomena that involve simultaneous motion of many different things would seem to make the case for determinism a hopeless chimera. To think that one could actually predict these phenomena, that there would ever be a possibility to do so, seems on the surface quite mistaken. It would indeed take something close to theological commitment to think otherwise.

Babble of speech. It is also easy to pick human phenomena close at hand to make the case against determinism. My own favorite is the endless babble of human speech. That anyone at any time or place could ever have been so foolish as to think that he could deterministically analyze the endless flow of talk men engage in everywhere and for most of their lives seems on the face of it ridiculous. And what I have to say applies not only to the listener or the analyst, but also to the speaker. It is unusual indeed to formulate completely and explicitly any given sentence that we utter. In moments of complete deliberation or in an unusual state of reflection, we are capable of such total preformulation, but this is exceptional. Most of the talk between human beings flows on endlessly without prior thought. Talk and thought are simultaneous; even if we can paraphrase and anticipate the thought, we can never predict or hope to determine the actual sequence of words spoken, not to speak of the subtle and intricate details of the actual sound pressure waves we emit as speakers and receive as listeners.

I should emphasize, of course, that I do not hold the absurd thesis that speech is wholly random, a point on which I expand in chapter 7. Like other natural phenomena, ranging from radioactive decay to the collisions of molecules in a gas, there are causal constraints that are not sufficient to determine fully the phenomena, but that can lead to fruitful causal analysis, a matter to be explored in the next chapter.

Smelling and seeing. Among human phenomena the most obvious candidate that comes at once to mind beyond the example of speech is the quantum character of our highly sensitive sense of vision—sensitivity down to the level of a single photon. A second equally subtle example, but one that is less well understood, is the molecular level at which the sense of smell operates. A good sense of the enormous complexity of contemporary biochemical theories of the senses of smell and taste are to be found in the volume edited by Cagan and Kare (1981). The first treatise on the sense of smell was written by Aristotle's student Theophrastus, and he would probably be surprised at how much we still do not know about smell in spite of the rich scientific resources that have recently been brought to bear. There are literally hundreds of papers a year now being published on the biochemistry of smell, and there are two abstract publications alone listing the annual literature, *Odor Abstracts* and *Chemoreception Abstracts*. My point is that the more detailed the investigations become, the more complicated and difficult it is to understand the full story. It is doubtful that in this century we will have an adequate theory at all for the neural code for quality of smells. Much of this literature does not seem probabilistic in character because of the way it is written, and the casual observer might think that it is complex but that out of it will emerge a deterministic theory of the sense of smell. A deeper look at the literature makes it easy to disabuse anyone of this notion. The evidence on the activities of single cells, which can only be thought of in probabilistic terms, or the data on the absorption process of odorant molecules, which are only really discussed in statistical terms and are fundamental to the whole process, seem decisive. (A good reference on the history and a more general survey than the earlier reference on taste and smell is Carterette and Friedman, Volume VIA, 1978.) These scientific references should not divert us from the fact that the ordinary view of the sense of smell is not a hard and fast one. There is not a common-sense deterministic theory of smell that the detailed scientific developments are contravening. Either at a commonsense or a scientific level it seems ridiculous on the face of it to talk in terms of phenomena of smell being in any clear and constructively understandable way deterministic.

It may be useful to give some concrete examples of how unpredictable the phenomena of smell are. In controlled experimental conditions, individual threshold judgments of the presence of butanol varied by two orders of magnitude, i.e., 100 to 1 (Semb, 1968). Adaptation to smells shows similar, large variability;

familiarity, for example, promotes easy adaptation, as does distraction by other tasks. Still a different class of phenomena entirely are the effects almost certainly produced by odorous chemical messengers, e.g., the striking effects produced in the reproductive physiology of mice. At either a phenomenological or molecular level, development of a deterministic theory of such subtle phenomena seems hopeless.

The sorts of things that I have said about the sense of smell can be said in even greater detail about vision, but because the facts of vision are much more widely known I shall not enter into details. I do want to emphasize the almost universally accepted view that the physiological mechanism of vision is photochemical in character and is sensitive at the level of individual photons. When light reacts on a given molecule, the probability of absorption of an individual photon is a function of wavelength. The utterly probabilistic character of the fundamental phenomena is disputed by no one. (For a good modern overview of the sense of seeing, see Carterette and Friedman, Volume V, 1975.)

ADEQUACY OF PROBABILISTIC LAWS

I do not mean to suggest by my criticisms of the inadequacy of deterministic laws that there is any guarantee that we can find adequate probabilistic laws for any phenomena we consider. The exponential law of radioactive decay, which is discussed in some detail later, is an ideal positive example. A correspondingly satisfactory account of meteorological or much perceptual phenomena seems essentially impossible, at least with our present methods of probabilistic analysis. We must be content now, and possibly forever, with relatively crude probabilistic approximations in many domains.

Epicurus.   That our conception of the world should be in qualitative terms broadly probabilistic in character is as old as the conception of atoms and the void to be found in Epicurus. The scientific ideas are certainly modern. No progress from a scientific standpoint was made on atomic concepts in antiquity or even during the Renaissance. But the broad conception was arrived at early and its naturalness as a possible way of thinking about the nature of the universe was widely recognized. Thus here is a quotation from Epicurus' letter to Herodotus, written most likely in the fourth century B.C. (Oates, 1940):

> And the atoms move continuously for all time, some of them falling straight down, others swerving, and others recoiling from their collisions. And of the latter, some are borne on, separating to a long distance from one another, while others again recoil and recoil, whenever they chance to be checked by the interlacing with others, or else shut in by atoms interlaced around them. For on the one hand the nature of the void which separates each atom by itself brings this about, as it is not able to afford resistance, and on the other hand the hardness which belongs to the atoms makes them recoil after collision to as great a distance as the interlacing permits separation after the collision. And these motions have no beginning, since the atoms and the void are the cause. (p. 5)

Most of this passage sounds modern and highly sensible. Looked at more carefully, the physical notion of swerving does not make sense in the context of classical physics in contrast to the concept of collision. But this is a narrow framework for analyzing concepts of ancient science and philosophy. In any case, it is not to the point here to defend the detailed physics of the Epicureans, but to recognize the way in which already at this early date a central role for chance and uncertainty was recognized.

On this point of uncertainty here is a quotation from Lucretius' *De Rerum Natura*, written in the first century, B.C. (Oates, 1940):

> This point too herein we wish you to apprehend: when bodies are borne downwards sheer through void by their own weights, at quite uncertain times and uncertain spots they push themselves a little from their course: you just and only just can call it a change of inclination. If they were not used to swerve, they would all fall down, like drops of rain, through the deep void, and no clashing would have been begotten nor blow produced among the first-beginnings: thus nature never would have produced aught. (p. 95)

Again the untenable physical theory of swerving is called on, but what is important here is the emphasis on uncertainty in both time and place. This is very different from the fundamental physical theory of Plato or Aristotle.

It is not my point here to enter into these historical matters in depth. I do want to emphasize the constancy through time and the importance attached to the atomistic views of the Epicureans. There were few fundamental changes in the system in the three hundred years between Epicurus and Lucretius. (Epicurus was responsible for organizing and putting in much better systematic shape the earlier atomism of Leucippus and Democritus, which was deterministic in spirit—for the comparison, see Bailey, 1928.) It is worth noting, in view of some of my earlier remarks in chapter 1, that one of the main roles of the atomism of the Epicureans was the way in which they used the atomic theory to combat religious, oracular, and astrological views of the causes of human actions, although they did not deny the existence of gods. By the time of Cicero, their voices were the sanest to be heard, but unfortunately they were overwhelmed in time by views that appealed more deeply to the irrational aspects of human psychology.

Laplace. I now skip across the centuries to the most famous single passage on determinism. Contrary to what one might expect, it is found in the introduction to Laplace's treatise on probability, not in his great treatise on astronomy, *Celestial Mechanics* (1829–39/1966). He asserts that given a knowledge of the present state of the universe, an "intelligence", or as we might say in modern terminology, 'a computer adequate to the task', would be able to determine the entire past and future of the universe. Here are his words:

> We ought then to regard the present state of the universe as the effect of its anterior state and as the cause of the one which is to follow. Given for one instant an intelligence which could comprehend all the forces by which nature is animated and the respective situation of the beings who compose it—an intelligence sufficiently vast to submit these data to analysis—it would embrace in the same formula the movements of the greatest bodies of the universe and those of the lightest atom; for it, nothing would be uncertain and the future, as the past, would be present to its eyes. The human mind offers, in the perfection which it has been able to give to astronomy, a feeble idea of this intelligence. Its discoveries in mechanics and geometry added to that of

universal gravity, have enabled it to comprehend in the same
analytical expressions the past and future states of the systems of the world. Applying the same method to some other
objects of its knowledge, it has succeeded in referring to
general laws observed phenomena and in foreseeing those
which given circumstances ought to produce. All these
efforts in the search for truth tend to lead it back continually
to the vast intelligence which we have just mentioned, but
from which it will always remain infinitely removed. This
tendency, peculiar to the human race, is that which renders
it superior to animals; and their progress in this respect distinguishes nations and ages and constitutes their true glory.
(pp. 4–5)

The analysis of the idea so vividly expressed in this passage can
be taken in many different directions. I restrict myself at the
moment to considering the deterministic character of physical systems and of the physical universe. Without entering into technical
details, let me state a theorem of classical particle mechanics that
expresses Laplace's idea in explicit form. For this purpose I
characterize systems of particle mechanics in the sense of
McKinsey, Sugar, and Suppes (1953) or Suppes (1957), but only
in a very informal way. The theorem is this.

Theorem I.   *Let two systems of mechanical particles be such that
the particles have the same masses, the forces acting on the particles
are the same, and for some time* t *the positions and velocities of
identical particles of the two systems are the same. Then the trajectories of the particles in both systems must also be identical. In
other words, the trajectories of the particles throughout time are
wholly determined by their positions and velocities at some one instance and by the forces acting on them.*

It should be noted that the theorem just stated depends on the
absence of collisions. From a formal standpoint, the theorem is
correct if it is assumed that particles are penetrable, or that during
the period of time for which the analysis holds, no collisions
occur, either because of separation of distance or because of the
particular configuration of motion. It has been properly stressed
by several writers that the general thesis of Laplacean determinism does not hold once collisions are considered. There is in

fact a whole set of puzzling and fascinating problems about collisions or impacts and their relation to determinism, wholly within the framework of classical mechanics, but it is not appropriate here to pursue these matters.[2]

In contrast, let us look at the simplest probability process and notice how different the situation is. Suppose that we are going to flip two coins a thousand times, and that we use the same apparatus for each trial. We begin with the same initial conditions, which correspond to the identical positions and velocities at time t of the particles. We may ask ourselves then, what is the probability that the two coins will have exactly the same sequences of heads and tails? The answer is easy to compute. First, we can ask what is the probability on each trial that the two coins will either both show heads or both show tails? The answer is of course 1/2, and consequently the probability that the "trajectories" through the thousand trials of the two coins in terms of the sequences of heads and tails will be the same is the incredibly small number $1/2^{1000}$. Almost certainly, in other words the two coins will have different histories, and determinism, in the sense of identity of history following from identity of initial conditions, has a probability of almost zero, that is, is almost impossible. Physical realizations of this simple probability process can be constructed in many different ways. Their existence is scarcely to be doubted either on practical or theoretical grounds.

STOCHASTIC RETREAT FROM DETERMINISM

The high ground of Laplacean determinism as exemplified in the deterministic theorem of classical mechanics stated above is, in fact, occupied by no working branch of science. Before examining in some detail the question of whether even theoretically such determinism should be the ultimate ideal of science, it may be useful to examine the ways in which actual scientific practice

[2] As I try to bring out later in the discussion of randomness, in many ways what is thought of as determinism is confounded with stability. Classical dynamical systems that are sufficiently unstable—small variations in initial conditions lead to large differences in subsequent behavior—are not just practically but also theoretically unpredictable, for the initial conditions cannot be known exactly. Such unstable systems correspond to one ordinary notion of being indeterminate. The technical literature on these matters is large and complex. Some principal recent sources are Siegel and Moser (1971), Moser (1973), Ornstein (1974), and, for a very detailed set of references as well, Barrow (1982).

requires a retreat to analyses and theories of phenomena that are not deterministic in character.

The first and most important retreat, already found in classical Laplacean astronomy, is the recognition that measurements of spatial conditions and boundary conditions are subject to errors of measurement. When the underlying theoretical probability distributions of these errors are integrated into the deterministic differential equations of mechanics, the result is a theory of phenomena with randomness. There is an inevitable dispersion of accuracy over time so that intuitively the phenomena in question are less and less predictable as time progresses. Analyses of a variety of problems in which initial conditions are assumed subject to random variation are important not only in astronomy, but also in chemistry, in engineering mechanics, and in other areas of applied science. Traditionally, a determinist is not upset by admission that errors of measurement produce randomness of initial conditions and, therefore, a nondeterministic analysis of phenomena. The classical response is that the errors of measurement can in principle be eliminated. One of the unrealized ideals of classical physics was to perfect methods of measurement with the aim of ultimately eliminating all such errors.

A second source of randomness in actual scientific practice that does not disturb the thorough-going determinist is the random intrusion of effects from outside the system being analyzed. A paradigm case would be the intrusion of small amounts of matter and energy from outside the solar system, or the variations in density of matter in space through which the solar system is moving. The effects of these external intrusions are extraordinarily slight in terms of the motion of the main objects in the solar system, and consequently, even though it is recognized that they exist and that detailed calculation of their behavior is almost certainly out of the question, the attitude is one of serenity because of their relatively insignificant effects.

An example of a different sort is the following. From the standpoint of the fundamental dynamics of the earth's atmosphere, the science of meteorology can look upon the earth as a closed system and can attempt to solve an elaborate set of differential equations to predict the entire motion of the atmosphere. Although it is not really feasible to look at the whole atmosphere this way, it is sometimes considered an approachable ideal. What is not taken into account in the fundamental dynamical equations of meteorology are random disturbances caused by unpredictable disturbances on the surface of the sun. So far as I know, no fundamental analysis of the dynamical equations of the earth's atmosphere attempts to include equations that would account for the appearance of sun spots and other disturbances on the surface of the sun that affect the earth's atmosphere. (For evidence of a strong effect during the reign of Louis XIV, see Eddy, 1976; for a more conservative and somewhat skeptical view, see Evans, 1982). Even a phenomenon of this sort, however, is probably not too disturbing to the hard-line determinist, and he would probably be content to remain as firm as Kant in his conviction of the fundamental correctness of Newtonian physics—the fundamental dynamical equations of meteorology are, of course, squarely within the tradition of classical physics. He would simply regard these external influences or forces as difficult to deal with in detail, but not as conceptually surprising. Of course, I think this position is wrong, as I discuss in more detail later, but fortunately there are still deeper lines of attack.

A third and more fundamental kind of indeterminism arises when the equations of motion of a phenomenon are themselves stochastic equations, i.e., the evolution of the system is not deterministic at the level of the basic equations used for prediction. In phenomena subject to stochastic equations, there is no hope (within the given framework) of predicting or of being able to determine exactly the future or past course of events. Already in this third case, however, there is an important division to be made. In the first place, stochastic differential equations as the fundamental dynamical equations of a phenomenon can be used not because of any firm conviction that the phenomena in question are indeterministic in character, but rather, because of the complexity of the phenomena we can best approximate the actual course of events by using such random equations. Instances may be found even in the hydrodynamics or aerodynamics of fluids, for example, in considering wave propagations in inhomogeneous media; in chemical systems in which there exist small percentages of impurities; in economic systems whose underlying microanalysis either is unknown or involves too much data collection to make analysis feasible; and in biological systems that have the same character. For example, in biology we can believe that the fundamental physics and chemistry of cells can be understood at the level of classical physics and yet can apply to the study of the

motion of fluids and cells through porous media, etc.—stochastic
rather than deterministic equations. Again, it is the enormous
complexity of the situation that justifies the choice of analysis.
The philosopher sitting in detachment from the agony of the details in these cases can still maintain that the fundamental laws of
the universe are deterministic and that all is well with the broad
Laplacean or Kantian thesis. In the disdainful tradition of pure
science and thought, the philosopher may attribute the use of
concepts of randomness to the practical exigencies and demands
of applied science.

Apart from any attitude toward this disdain, to which I shall return, this is not the end of the story at the level of fundamental
theory. The third kind of indeterminism involving stochastic
equations also arises in the most fundamental areas of science,
and I now discuss the issues that arise in this context. I leave aside
for later consideration the close relation between randomness and
instability of classical dynamical systems.

Radioactive decay.   There are two natural lines of attack at the
level of fundamental laws of physics. First, within the framework
of classical physics there is evidence in favor of randomness in
radioactive decay. Second, there is the extensive literature on the
possibility of hidden-variable theories as a theoretical under-
pinning of quantum mechanics, theories formulated to restore determinism as conceived within the framework of classical physics.
I want to examine each of these lines of attack, because it seems
to me that the outcome of the analysis of either makes it extremely difficult to believe that the universe operates in a deterministic fashion.

We may begin by looking quickly at some of the historical
background of radioactivity. In the autumn of 1895, Roentgen,
professor of physics at Würzburg, accidentally discovered X-rays,
and through a beautiful series of experiments, demonstrated their
fundamental properties. (It is worth noting that as an example of
an immediate application of pure research it is harder to find a
better example. Only three months after Roentgen's accidental
discovery, X-rays were being used in at least one hospital in
Vienna in connection with surgical operations, and the worldwide
use of diagnosis in surgical cases spread rapidly.)

The discovery of radioactivity itself followed accidentally from
experiments connected with phenomena similar to those ob-

served in X-rays. Several investigators found that fluorescent bodies exposed to sunlight gave out a type of radiation similar to that of X-rays. Early in 1896, in trying an experiment of this kind, Henri Becquerel discovered that the specimen of uranium and potassium he was using emitted radiation even in the dark. Shortly thereafter, he found that the emission of radiation by uranium was more or less independent of its state of chemical combination with other substances and that there was no connection between this phenomenon of radiation and phosphorescence, the initial subject of his investigations. Also, he found that the radiation was more or less independent of the temperature of the uranium compound. Not too much later, radium was discovered by the Curies.

By 1905 at least, physicists were already questioning whether the emission of particles from radioactive substances was deterministic or probabilistic in character. In 1910, Rutherford and Geiger published a paper on this topic that contained an appendix by Bateman on the mathematical properties of Poisson processes, and over the next decade or so, a number of additional studies followed. An excellent review of the literature, including a detailed critique of the various studies, was given by Kohlrausch in 1926. Although methodological criticisms can be made of most of the studies from the standpoint of modern statistics, the weight of the evidence is certainly in favor of the statistical character of radioactive decay. There is no body of systematic evidence that a deterministic law holds, and it seems appropriate to interpret the large number of studies of these matters as directly supporting the thesis that randomness is in nature, and not simply in our ignorance of true causes as Laplace would have wanted it.

Randomness in quantum mechanics. I turn now to the case for randomness that can be made at a deeply theoretical level. It is undoubtedly true that the instance of radioactive decay can be treated as lacking in theoretical import, because the phenomenon in question and the probabilistic laws of decay that adequately describe the phenomenon do not have a deep theoretical reach; consequently, the possibility of a deeper theory to account in a deterministic way for the apparently random phenomena of decay remains open. In broad terms, it is well known that it was Einstein's view that a deeper deterministic theory would be found to subsume quantum mechanics. The search for such theories has come to be known as the search for hidden-variable theories. The term *hidden variables* is picturesquely descriptive of what is desired. The hope is that back of the probabilistic variables observed in quantum mechanics will be found deterministic causal variables that will account for the observed probabilistic phenomena, as is characteristic of classical statistical mechanics. It is part of classical statistical mechanics to postulate a determinant state for individual particles and to introduce randomness in proper Laplacean terms as an expression of our ignorance of the true state. (The problems for determinism arising from collisions have already been mentioned above and will not be reiterated.)

The analysis of hidden-variable theories has a complicated history in modern physics, beginning with the celebrated proof of von Neumann that dispersion-free states and, consequently, hidden variables are impossible in quantum mechanics. It is important to realize what the connection between dispersion-free states and hidden variables is. Dispersion-free states correspond intuitively to classical states in which position and momentum, for example, are definitely and exactly determined. The central idea is that hidden variables lead to the specification of such dispersion-free states. Various improvements that weaken the assumptions of von Neumann have been made subsequently in the literature.[3]

---

[3] The essential assumption of von Neumann's proof is that any linear combination of two quantum-mechanical Hermitian operators, e.g., position and momentum, represents an observable, and the linear combination of expectation values of the operators is the expectation value of the combination. From a conceptual standpoint, this assumption can be criticized as smuggling in unwarranted and rich assumptions about the results of quite different experiments. The point is that three different experiments would ordinarily be required—one for the first observable, a second for the second noncommuting variable, and a third for the linear combination of the two. Given the different experimental configurations required in the three cases, there is no reason to assume that the expectation values will hold for pure states as opposed to quantum-mechanical averages. The significance of this argument, stated most clearly, for example, in Bell (1966), is that the results for the linear combination of observables cannot be arrived at simply by computation. If this were the case, matters would be simple. What is important is the requirement that there be a third and distinct experimental arrangement for the measurement of the linear combination. Perhaps the most valuable work in this direction is due to Gleason (1957). As a result of his work on measures on Hilbert space, it follows that the additivity requirement for expectation values, when restricted only to commuting operators, cannot be met by dispersion-free states. It is not appropriate to enter into the details of Gleason's theorem, but it is useful to summarize Bell's criticism that, within this framework, it has been tacitly assumed that the measurement of one observable must yield the same value independently of what other measurements may be made simultaneously. Remember that in this case we are dealing with commuting operators, and thus the possibility of simultaneous measure-

In a beautiful series of papers beginning with Bell (1964 and 1966), a much more reasonable and intuitive treatment of hidden-variable theories has been given, and their impossibility has been demonstrated experimentally at a rather satisfactory level. Without entering into the details, essentially what Bell has been able to show is that if we start with the paradox of Einstein, Podolsky, and Rosen (1935), which argues for the incompleteness of quantum mechanics, which I consider again in chapter 5, and if we insist that a hidden-variable theory that removes the incompleteness must satisfy natural conditions of causality and locality, then by considering a simple system with two particles of spin one-half, these conditions cannot be satisfied. There can be no hidden-variable theory for such two-particle systems. Within the context of this analysis, Bell was able to derive an inequality that has come to be known as 'Bell's inequality', and this has been used by Clauser, Horne, Shimony, and Holt (1969) and Freedman and Clauser (1972) to show that by use of Bell's inequality the existence of local hidden variables imposes restrictions that are, as Bell originally showed, in conflict with quantum mechanics, and that, second, new experimental data are in agreement with quantum mechanics. Moreover, well within the accuracy of experimental error the data violate the restrictions required by local hidden-variable theories. (These ideas are also related to the analysis of the principle of a common cause at the end of chapter 3, including the discussion of deterministic and probabilistic causes.)

I think it is fair to say that the outcome of this whole sequence of papers, both theoretical and experimental, is to provide perhaps the conceptually most satisfying confirmation of the ultimately statistical character of quantum mechanics that we yet have. Furthermore, from a philosophical standpoint it provides one more blow against Laplacean or Kantian ideas of determinism as regulatory for the behavior of the universe.

WHAT IS RANDOMNESS?

Analogy of action at a distance. I would like to draw a historical analogy to current debates about the existence of randomness

---

ment is open to us. As Bell points out though, dependent on the choice of the different pairs of operators, different experimental arrangements are required, and there is no a priori reason to believe that the results will remain the same for an operator when it is paired with different commuting operators.

in nature. The analogy concerns the disputes about action at a distance in the seventeenth century. It is well known that Descartes was very much against action at a distance and partly introduced his famous vortex theory to account for the phenomena of the visible world in a way that did not require action at a distance. His fantasies about the way the phyical universe operates were spelled out in considerable detail in parts III and IV of his *Principia Philosophiae*. No doubt many of the ideas he proposes are no longer of physical interest, but I shall return to part III in chapter 5 for other reasons. The prestige of his view on other matters and the persuasiveness of many of his followers made his view about action at a distance the dominant one of the seventeenth century. Indeed, it was so dominant that Newton himself was reluctant to call his law of gravitation anything other than a mathematical hypothesis in order not to be in conflict with Cartesian physics.[4] At Newton's own university, Rohault's famous textbook on Cartesian physics was *the* textbook on physics for a number of years after Newton's *Principia* was published.

The Cartesian attitude toward action at a distance is similar to neo-Kantian and neo-Laplacean views about determinism. It may in some logically consistent way always be maintained that the unfolding of the universe in time is a deterministic phenomenon, and we simply do not have the clue to the details, but such a view is, if not logically inconsistent, highly improbable and not supported by the evidence. Unless a detailed view about the nature of physical phenomena can be supported in some fashion by organized and systematic evidence, it is unlikely to be taken seriously beyond a certain time. It seems to me that the weight of

---

[4] The actual phrase '*actio in distans*' does not, I believe, occur anywhere in Descartes' *Principia*. However, references to action at a distance can be found scattered throughout his other writings. Descartes was particularly concerned to give an explanation of gravity that would avoid any reference to occult forces, i.e., forces that either assume an inherent attraction between distant bodies or act in a manner similar to the action of the soul. A few examples are the following. In a letter to Mersenne, July 13, 1638, he examines three possible explanations of gravity and explicitly rejects attraction (*Oeuvres*, Adam and Tannery, eds, II, 223–224). In a letter to Princess Elizabeth, May 21, 1643, he asserts that gravity, heat, etc., are not substances distinct from body, and he does not see how attraction would work as a mechanism (*ibid.*, III, 667). In another letter to an unknown correspondent he asserts that the cause of gravity is neither a real quality nor some attraction of the earth (*ibid.*, I, 324). In yet another passage he says that to endow particles with the power of acting at a distance would make them 'vraiment divines' (*ibid.*, IV, 396).

the evidence, even apart from quantum mechanics, supports the existence of randomness in nature.

Claiming as I do that the occurrences of randomness in nature are legion, I would like to examine in somewhat greater detail the view that the universe is essentially probabilistic in character or, to put it in more colloquial language, that the world is full of random happenings. The most important point is to dispel the illusion that, because random happenings may be found everywhere, the analysis of phenomena somehow becomes too complex, too disorderly, and consequently too difficult to leave any hope for the development of systematic theory. It is part of the theme of this book that it is a return to realism, realism in the sense of realism of belief and not in the sense of ontological realism, to recognize how schematic any of our knowledge of the universe must be and that it is the character of commonsense knowledge itself to be schematic and probabilistic in character. It is mistaken and hopeless to think we can pursue to the bitter end a sequence of determinant events with the whole universe interlocked in one vast movement forward. Independence is also associated with randomness. The basic physical assumption of radioactive decay can be stated in a completely elementary and qualitative way, whereas, in contrast, if a deterministic theory of the orbits of electrons around nuclei were required as was once thought in classical physics, the details would be extraordinarily complicated and difficult.

Most of the experimental data using Geiger counters or similar measuring devices count the number of emissions from a measured mass of a radioactive substance in equal time periods, for example, in intervals of two seconds. If we look at the theory with respect to discrete and equal time intervals, we get an especially elementary formulation of the basic probabilistic law. It is just that the probability of decay in the next interval of any atom, given that it has not decayed up to interval n, is the same as its probability of decaying in the first interval. In other words, the atoms have no history, and this simple assumption of the absence of the effect of history permits us to derive directly the one-parameter geometrical (or exponential) distribution for the decay law. Notice how drastic and simplifying this assumption is (like the assumption of independence for each coin flip). It says that if a given atom has not decayed for a thousand years, the probability of its decaying in the next two seconds is the same as was the probability of its decaying in the first two seconds of the measurement period. (For a detailed discussion of this example from the standpoint of a propensity theory of probability, see Suppes, 1973b.)

We should note also how natural the tendency is to want to infer complicated effects from the history of the atom and to be psychologically unsatisfied with such a simple assumption. Surely, we are inclined to say, 'Something is going on in the atom during all this period, and the effect of these somethings should be cumulative and should affect the probability of decay.' This is the same kind of drastic simplification found when Newton's inverse square law of attraction replaced Descartes' complicated and unwieldy hypothesis of vortices. Surely, it was felt, gravitation could not be that simple. The same view transposed to our time is true of those who cannot accept randomness in nature. That such views are difficult to accept even by those who discover them is well illustrated by Newton's famous letter to Richard Bentley of February 25, 1692/3, in which Newton violently rejects the very conception of gravity acting at a distance. Let me quote the most important passage:

It is inconceivable, that inanimate brute matter should, without the mediation of something else, which is not material, operate upon and affect other matter without mutual contact, as it must be, if gravitation, in the sense of Epicurus, be essential and inherent in it. And this is one reason why I desired you would not ascribe innate gravity to me. That gravity should be innate, inherent, and essential to matter, so that one body may set upon another at a distance through a vacuum, without the mediation of anything else, by and through which their action and force may be conveyed from one to another, is to me so great an absurdity, that I believe no man, who has in philosophical matters a competent faculty of thinking, can ever fall into it. Gravity must be caused by an agent acting constantly according to certain laws; but whether this agent be material or immaterial, I have left to the consideration of my readers. (Bentley, 1838, pp. 211–212)

The deterministic idealizations of classical physics have been among the most misleading aberrations of philosophical thought since the pre-Socratics began their ruminations. That marvelous period of physics running from Newton to Maxwell is also a marvelous aberration in the main tendencies of human thought. Natural theology was replaced by celestial mechanics, and all seemed right once again with the world. But to take seriously as an account of the endless variety of natural phenomena the remarkably restricted theories of classical physics, especially classical mechanics, and not to appreciate simultaneously their real inability to explain most natural phenomena, is indeed a characteristic, I should hope, of religious rather than of scientific method at work. It is not just the quantum world that has an essential random component—it is almost every aspect of experience. The evidence supports the thesis that random or probabilistic phenomena are found in nature and not simply in our lack of knowledge.

A possible response to what I have said might be that it is metaphysically proper to hold that all phenomena are regulated by deterministic laws that govern their behavior completely. It is just an epistemological failure that the various scientific disciplines with merely probabilistic theories—if any theories at all— cannot do better. The universe is what it is, and it is not imaginable that events just happen. It is natural enough that we often cannot successfully determine the causes of events, but this widespread difficulty should not disturb our basic metaphysical views. There is, of course, nothing inconsistent about this position, but it is, I would claim, a good line to take to make metaphysics irrelevant to science and ordinary experience, as many people already believe it is.

A metaphysics subject to continual revision just like any branch of science should make every effort to fit well-developed scientific theories as well as well-substantiated features of ordinary experience. As I have already said several times, such a descriptive metaphysics does not find it difficult to make a place for randomness in nature.[5]

---

[5]Although the metaphysical status of the modalities of necessity and possibility has a history that is too complicated to examine here, placing randomness in nature does promote the candidacy of probability as an additional metaphysical modality. On the subjective view, the statement *It is probable that it will rain tomorrow* expresses a propositional attitude. On the other hand, on the view argued for here the statement *It is probable that this gram of radium will decay in less than x hours* is meant to be a physical statement on a par with *It is mechanically necessary that the center of mass of this mechanical system move uniformly in a straight line.*

Randomness and complexity. So far in this chapter I have written as if the dichotomy between deterministic phenomena and random phenomena is absolute. A difficulty of the exposition thus far is that I have not made an effort to define randomness. I did state informally, in the case of mechanics at least, a well-defined concept of determinism. It would be possible to have the division absolute and logically sound by simply saying that phenomena are random that are not deterministic. Formulated in a somewhat more satisfactory way, we would say that such phenomena have a random component if they are not deterministic.

Reference to standard theorems in mechanics about the past and future histories of particles' motions being determined once the forces are known and initial conditions of position and momentum are given is too simple. When the data that are given us do not lead to a determinant result, we may be able simply to say that we did not have all the information we should have had. In other cases, we may want to say that it is not sensible to try to formulate the phenomenon within a mechanical framework and thus a characterization of determinism within the framework of classical mechanics is too restrictive a concept. The many complexities that one can rapidly generate by going into these matters in detail cannot be dealt with here in proper fashion. On the other hand, the constructive mathematical efforts to define randomness lead to some interesting observations, I think, about the relation between determinism and randomness. Beginning with a paper of the Russian mathematician Kolmogorov (1963), which itself builds on the earlier efforts of Richard von Mises to define probability in terms of the limits of relative frequencies in infinite random sequences, a substantial literature has developed to characterize randomness for finite sequences. The central idea has been to make randomnes depend on complexity. The intuitive idea is that only sequences that are highly complex are random. Early important papers in addition to that of Kolmogorov have been those of Solomonoff (1964a and 1964b), Martin-Löf (1966), and

As these examples illustrate, particular modal statements can be about particular physical systems, for example, but the modalities themselves are metaphysical in nature because of their generality and wide applicability. (The opposition expressed in this footnote between subjective and objective views of probability is only for immediate purposes at hand. A reconciliation is attempted in the last section of chapter 4.) For a more extended discussion of probability and modality, see Suppes (1974b).

Chaitin (1969). A good general overview is to be found in chapter 5 of Fine (1973).

Complexity as a general notion seems even more vague than the intuitive notion of randomness. But a virtue of this recent work is to give a definition of complexity and thereby of randomness in a way that seems intuitively satisfactory and at the same time precise. First let us think just in terms of sequence of ones and zeros, for example, a sequence of flips of a coin. If the sequence consists only of ones, intuitively it is very simple. If it also follows some simple regular pattern, for example, that of alternation of ones and zeros, the complexity also seems very low. The way that this idea is caught formally is in terms of the length of a program it would require to describe the sequence on some fixed computer and in some fixed language, for example, BASIC, FORTRAN, PASCAL, or LISP. The longer the program in the given fixed language, the more complex the sequence. Thus, for example, it is easy to write a program to describe or generate a sequence consisting only of ones or an alternating sequence. A program, on the other hand, describing what we intuitively think of as a random sequence of zeros and ones will be roughly of the length of the sequence itself. Complexity is thus characterized in terms of the length of the program and it is only highly complex sequences that are random. When the sequences are finite, there is necessarily going to be some arbitrariness in the characterization of high complexity and therefore of randomness. It is also fair to claim that in working with real empirical data we are always dealing with finite sequences, never with infinite ones. Consequently it is straightforward to claim that there is not an absolute dichotomy between random phenomena and deterministic phenomena. The dividing line is not well defined. What we may have at best is a good comparative notion of when one kind of phenomenon is more random than another. The idea of not drawing an absolute line between deterministic and random phenomena is appealing in many ways. It is often a natural scientific response to complex data to say that if one just had the time to construct sufficiently complicated functions one could give an account of the data. There is also a whole lore of curve fitting in statistics and the issue of how many parameters it is reasonable to estimate in curve fitting. From still another standpoint, we might argue that the right way to think about the matter is in terms of prediction. The real test of determinism is predictability.

Phenomena that we cannot predict must be judged random. Most of us feel, however, that this is probably too stringent a criterion without qualifications of various kinds.

Subject to the reservations mentioned in the next paragraph, I think it is satisfactory to think of randomness in terms of high complexity and to take the position that there is not an absolute dichotomy between determinism and randomness. It is philosophically too artificial to have a totally sharp dichotomy. Thus, some of the statements that I have made earlier in the chapter in the spirit of much standard discussion of randomness need to be slightly qualified to take account of what I am saying here about complexity. But these ordinary ways of talking will continue to be used, even by those who accept the central point I have just been trying to make.

Physical randomness and stability. There are several unsatisfactory features of the complexity characterization of randomness. First, we intuitively think of certain physical processes as random. Without necessarily being very precise, we envisage these processes as having characteristics that make them intrinsically random. This view of processes as random contrasts with the external outcome-criterion in terms of complexity. Of course, this does not mean that the two ways of looking at randomness are not related. But the demand for an intrinsic characterization of random processes is natural, and needs to be met by an adequate theory.

Physical randomization of some sort is familiar to everyone with even a very superficial contact with games of chance. Shuffling cards, throwing dice against a vertical surface, and spinning a roulette wheel are three standard examples. Except in unusual circumstances we judge these randomizing processes by their symmetry and other features, and not by a careful study of the outcomes. Indeed, the willingness to judge the process without detailed attention to actual outcomes seems too prevalent. In spite of the widespread passion for gambling in the ancient Roman world, for example, there is no evidence that anybody analyzed sequences of outcomes with any real care.[6]

---

[6] The passion of the Roman emperors for gambling was well reported by Suetonius. Claudius wrote a book about gambling, which unfortunately has not survived. For a good discussion of these matters, including photographs of ancient gambling devices, see David (1962). The same absence of analysis is found in ancient and medieval China, in spite of the important use of dice in divination (cf. Needham, 1959, vol. III, p. 139).

Fortunately this process-orientated view of randomness so deeply built into our gambling heritage has in this century been supported by a significant body of mathematical work. This work is the source of my second point about the complexity definition of randomness. The analysis of randomness in classical dynamical systems, i.e., physical systems satisfying Newton's laws together with other more particular constraints such as the only forces being gravitational ones, has centered on the concept of stability, rather than determinism or complexity. As already mentioned, intuitively a dynamical system is stable if trajectories that are close in initial position remain so.[7] Dice and roulette wheels are good examples of unstable systems, and their instability is an essential property of their use as gambling devices. They also possess another important feature that is characteristic of most gambling devices, namely, certain properties of symmetry. Of course, instability does not imply symmetry, nor conversely, but the two features in association are almost universally a part of our thinking about gambling devices, which exemplify in a natural way the class of dynamical systems that generate random phenomena (for a good discussion of this point, see von Plato, 1983; for more detailed remarks on stability see the section on the N-body problem in chapter 6).

SUMMARY

Four classes of phenomena have been mentioned that exhibit randomness in nature. First and most ubiquitous is the class of

[7] There is more than one concept of stability. The classical Lyapunov condition for a system of ordinary differential equations is this, which formalizes the intuitive description in the text. Let a system of differential equations:

$$(1) \qquad \frac{\mathrm{d}x_i}{\mathrm{d}t} = f_i(x_1, \ldots, x_n, t) \qquad i = 1, \ldots, n$$

be given. A solution $y_i(t)$, $i = 1, \ldots, n$ of (1) with initial conditions $y_i(t_0)$ is a Lyapunov stable solution if for any real number $\epsilon > 0$ there is a real number $\delta > 0$ such that for each solution $x_i(t)$, $i = 1, \ldots, n$, if

$$|x_i(t_0) - y_i(t_0)| < \delta \qquad i = 1, \ldots, n$$

then

$$|x_i(t) - y_i(t)| < \epsilon \qquad i = 1, \ldots, n$$

for all $t \geq t_0$.

ordinary phenomena, especially but not exclusively centering on human perception of sights, sounds, and smells. The second class consists of various classical dynamical systems for which there is considerable theoretical development. The third consists of statistical mechanics still in the framework of classical physics. Again, there are significant theoretical developments including the theory of Brownian motion, which is in many ways the theory of perfect random processes. Fourth, and finally, there are the atomic and subatomic phenomena of quantum mechanics. Without expecting agreement from all quarters I defend each of the four classes as making the case for randomness in nature, but quantum mechanics, obviously, provides the firmest ground on which to base an argument.

On the basis of a wide variety of physical phenomena and many particular human phenomena, I defend the following view. *The fundamental laws of natural phenomena are essentially probabilistic rather than deterministic in character.*

3

Causality and Randomness

To affirm, as I did in the second chapter, the fundamental probabilistic character of many basic laws of science and of ordinary experience is for some tantamount to denying the applicability of causal concepts to the phenomena governed by probabilistic laws. The claim that probabilistic or statistical laws, if taken as fundamental, make a proper causal analysis of phenomena impossible is a mistaken view that has permeated much of western philosophy from Aristotle to the present. The notion that every event has a sufficient determining cause is one of the most salient remnants of neotraditional metaphysics to be found in contemporary philosophy of science. Unfortunately, the remnant still stands, and I am under no delusion that what I have to say will persuade those who are firmly tied to it. Unlike some modern metaphysicians, however, I do not have an ecumenical spirit about these matters.

Without any attempt at completeness, it seemed desirable to begin the detailed discussion with a look at some of the classical philosophical views. I begin with Aristotle and his theory of luck or chance. I then move directly to the eighteenth century and Hume's famous analysis of causality, much of which I commend, but I find wanting an appropriate attention to chance phenomena. After Hume I consider Kant, who also pays no real conceptual attention at all to probability—in fact even less than Hume. The related but different analyses of causality of Hume and Kant have dominated much of modern philosophy. I then turn back in the spirit of what I said in chapter 1 to a more scientific view of causality. I go back to de Moivre, who is slightly earlier than Hume in the eighteenth century, and then on to Bayes and Laplace. As part of my analysis of the concepts of de Moivre, Bayes, and Laplace, I claim that ignorance of the development of probability theory in the eighteenth century had disastrous consequences for the subsequent history of philosophical thinking about causality.

I next turn to systematic definitions of causal concepts, but in a spirit that is highly sympathetic to the much earlier work of Bayes and Laplace. I end the chapter with an analysis of five instances from the recent philosophical literature of conflicting intuitions about causality.

CLASSICAL PHILOSOPHICAL VIEWS

Aristotle on luck and chance. Aristotle's commitment to a sophisticated version of the doctrine of design kept him from providing a deeper analysis of chance phenomena. I have in mind the central place assigned to notions of intention or purpose in Aristotle's analysis of natural phenomena, and the fact that he began such analysis almost always by considering human or animate behavior and not by considering inanimate physical phenomena. Contrary to the view that I am advocating, Aristotle reduced the notions of luck and chance to the concept of incidental causation and left no separate place for chance distinct from causation in the scheme of things. This aspect of Aristotle, it seems to me, is something that is adhered to in continuous fashion by all major philosophers from Aristotle to Kant, including Descartes, Locke, Hume, and even Berkeley. Because of this strong historical continuity, it will be worthwhile to examine the major passages in Aristotle on these matters. The most important ones may be found in the second book of the *Physics*, especially chapters 4–6, and the texts that I cite are drawn from these chapters (Loeb edition).

Aristotle's concept of luck or fortune [*tychē*] is illustrated by the example of the man who goes to the marketplace and by chance meets there a debtor who pays his debt (196b36). In the case described, Aristotle says:

> He would in fact be said to have come there 'by luck'; whereas, if that had been the purpose he contemplated or if he always went to the market, or if he generally recovered a debt when he did, we should not say that the result came by luck. Clearly then, luck itself regarded as a cause, is the name we give to causation which incidentally inheres in de-

liberately purposeful action taken with respect to some other end but leading to the event we call fortunate. (197a5)

It is important to emphasize that luck is connected closely with intention. As Aristotle puts it, 'thus since choice implies intention, it follows that luck [*tychē*] and intention are concerned with the same field of objects' (197a8). In other words, only an actor faced with choices can be subject to luck. A stone, a cloud, or a river cannot. Aristotle construes the class of such actors quite narrowly, as he says later in chapter 6, 'that is why neither inanimate things nor brute beasts nor infants can ever accomplish anything by tychē, since they exercise no deliberate choice' (197b7).

A broader notion for Aristotle is that of automaton or chance.[1] Again in a characteristic example, Aristotle says:

We attribute it to chance [*automaton*] if a horse escapes a danger by coming accidentally to a place of safety. Or again, if a tripod chances to fall on its feet for a man to sit down upon this is due to chance [*automaton*], for though a man would put it on its feet with a view to its being a seat, the forces of nature that controlled its fall had no such aim. (197b15)

Although for Aristotle the stone that falls and hits a man does not fall for the purpose of hitting the man, there is a completely natural account of the causation—what Aristotle would term *incidental causation*—just as there is an analysis in terms of incidental causation of the man's meeting his debtor in the marketplace when he goes there for another reason.

Two points in Aristotle's analysis are worth noting. The first that is evident is an opposition between actions performed deliberately and events that occur as the result of luck [*tychē*] or chance [*automaton*]. There is no integration of the two; in fact, they are to be regarded as separate lines of explanation in terms of causes. When a causal account can be given for an action in

---

[1] In *Physics*, book 2, 197b20–25, Aristotle explicitly discusses the etymology of *automaton*, and he puts the matter this way: 'so then *automaton*, as the form of the word implies, means an occurrence that is in itself (*auto*) to no purpose (*maten*)'. It is sometimes claimed that Aristotle's etymology is incorrect and that the root meaning is that of *think*; thus, an automaton would be one who thinks and acts for himself, which is, of course, closer to the usage in contemporary theory of automata.

terms of reasons or purpose, there is no need—in fact it would be inappropriate—to give an account in terms of luck or chance.

Second, Aristotle emphasizes that luck [*tychē*] cannot be calculated, for, as he says 'we calculate only from necessary or normal sequences and luck acts outside such' (197a20). Regarding this last point, it is important to note that because luck cannot be calculated it does not mean that an analysis in terms of causation cannot be given after the fact. In other words, nowhere in Aristotle's analysis of *tychē* or *automaton* is there an introduction of randomness.[2]

Hume. In one sense, it is easy to modify Hume's famous analysis of causality in order to obtain a probabilistic characterization of causes. Hume claimed that the relation between cause and effect has three essential characteristics, namely, contiguity in space, succession in time, and constant conjunction. For the moment, let us set aside considerations of contiguity and succession, and look only at what he has to say about constant conjunction.

The most important single passage on constant conjunction is probably the following.

'Tis therefore by EXPERIENCE only, that we can infer the existence of one object from that of another. The nature of experience is this. We remember to have had frequent instances of the existence of one species of objects; and also remember, that the individuals of another species of objects have always attended them, and have existed in a regular order of contiguity and succession with regard to them. Thus we remember to have seen that species of object we call *flame*, and to have felt that species of sensation we call *heat*. We likewise call to mind their constant conjunction in all past instances. Without any farther ceremony, we call the one *cause* and the other *effect*, and infer the existence of the one from that of the other. In all those instances, from which we learn the conjunction of particular causes and effects,

[2] In the last paragraph of chapter IX of *On Interpretation*, at the close of the famous discussion of future contingencies, Aristotle does say 'For one half of the said contradiction must be true and the other half false. But we cannot say which half is which. Though it may be that one is more probable, it cannot be true yet or false' (19a36–39, Loeb edn). But this idea of the probable is not developed, and it does not suggest that, contrary to the other passages cited, Aristotle came close to holding that there is randomness in nature.

both the causes and effects have been perceiv'd by the senses, and are remember'd: But in all cases, wherein we reason concerning them, there is only one perceiv'd or remember'd, and the other is supply'd in conformity to our past experience.

Thus in advancing we have insensibly discover'd a new relation betwixt cause and effect, when we least expected it, and were entirely employ'd upon another subject. This relation is their CONSTANT CONJUNCTION. Contiguity and succession are not sufficient to make us pronounce any two objects to be cause and effect, unless we perceive, that these two relations are preserv'd in several instances. (1888, pp. 86–87)

Note in this passage the casualness of Hume's actual use of the concept of constant conjunction. If we replaced *constant conjunction* by *frequent conjunction*, we would get something that would be more faithful to the facts and that would do little violence to Hume's analysis. Moreover, even a casual reader of Hume is impressed by the total lack of serious examples in his discussion of causality. By *serious* examples I mean ones that are subjected to detailed analysis and not simply described in a sentence or two as in the passage quoted above. There is in Hume no extended discussion of how we use specific methods of investigation to discover causes and what practical problems we encounter if we try to apply his three essential characteristics in the identification of causes.

To find Hume asking for constant conjunction when it would have been very much in the spirit of his general views to ask for frequent conjunction is disappointing. But there are many good reasons why Hume did what he did. It is sometimes said that he was the first to work out the full implications of empiricism, and, in so doing, he transformed it into what is sometimes called radical empiricism; however, it is clear enough that Hume was seriously concerned neither with radical empiricism as a philosophy of science nor with the connection between his general philosophical ideas and the science of his time.

My summary remarks about Hume are not entirely fair. In part III of book I of the *Treatise of Human Nature*, Hume discusses probability extensively; section XII in fact is entitled 'Of the Probability of Causes'. In an occasional passage here and there he does discuss frequent conjunction rather than constant conjunction, and he has numerous sensible things to say about the relation between probability and cause. Still I would insist that the main force of my criticisms remain: his central idea is that of constant conjunction, not frequent conjunction, and he does not attempt any detailed analysis of actual causes in complex cases, especially as these matters were undertaken in the more sophisticated parts of eighteenth-century science. In addition, the realism of his analysis is vitiated by an unswerving allegiance to the doctrine that probability is the proportion of favorable possibilities to total possibilities, a view also enunciated by Laplace, but quickly abandoned once real work was undertaken.

In the previous chapter I drew a historical parallel between the lack of acceptance of action at a distance in the seventeenth century by Newton and the lack of acceptance of randomness in nature in the twentieth century, even after the detailed experimental test of statistical fluctuations in radioactive decay. What I want to emphasize in the present context is that the systematic development of probability theory in the eighteenth century made it possible to hold that chance or randomness is actually in nature and not simply due to our ignorance of true causes. The view that unfortunately dominated the eighteenth century is put succintly by Hume in the following passage in the section of the *Treatise* dealing with the probability of causes:

> What I have said concerning the probability of chances can serve to no other purpose, than to assist us in explaining the probability of causes; since 'tis commonly allow'd by philosophers, that what the vulgar call chance is nothing but a secret and conceal'd cause. (p. 130)

Hume's philosophy would have been all the deeper had he stood this passage on its head and said that it is the vulgar who seek always for secret and concealed causes and that it is good philosophy to recognize that in many cases no true determinate causes are to be found. But he was not sufficiently serious about these matters to be led to such a radical stand, so contrary to the general view. This lack of seriousness becomes evident enough in the broad banality of his rules for judging causes and effects (sec. XV, part III, book I), which stand in such contrast to the powerful and original methods of analysis developed by Bayes and Laplace.

Kant. Starting from a different point and with a much deeper knowledge of science, Kant shared Hume's conviction about constant conjunction, but went far beyond the Humean position to a view of causality that aims at restoring the necessity Hume so severely criticized. In spite of the many differences between Hume and Kant, each in his own way provides comfort to those who insist that every event has a determinant cause.

In Kant's representation of all synthetical principles of the pure understanding in the *Critique of Pure Reason*, he is firm on the following point. The proposition that nothing happens by blind chance is an a priori law of nature. It is a consequence of the principle of production, the second analogy of experience. In the *Metaphysical Foundations of Natural Science*, Kant generalizes Newton's first law of motion to: Every change of matter has an external cause (proposition 3 of chapter 3). Nowhere in Kant is there a detailed analysis of physical examples of causality; especially lacking is a discussion of how causes in nature are to be identified for the first time. He too readily accepts Newtonian mechanics as the final story on the nature of the universe.

De Moivre and secret causes. The thrust of much of the eighteenth-century thinking about probability by those devoted to it was to stand the quotation from Hume on its head and to demonstrate that the vulgar way of thinking was always to find secret and concealed causes. It would have been consistent with Hume's philosophy, but not with Kant's, and in broad philosophical terms, nothing demonstrates better Kant's lack of appreciation of fundamental scientific developments of the eighteenth century than his almost total disregard of probabilistic concepts.

Throughout the seventeenth and eighteenth centuries the elitist or aristocratic segments of society had an intense and widespread interest in gambling and games of chance. Given their general ignorance of scientific matters and the relatively low level of the development of probability theory, it is not surprising that their conceptions of luck, chance, and concealed causes were full of superstition and mistaken views. One of the important theses of analysis and one of the most important forces behind the development of probability theory was the attempt to understand what, purely on the basis of chance, might be expected in games of cards and dice. I quote from the introduction to the most important predecessor in many ways to Laplace's treatise, namely, de

Moivre's *The Doctrine of Chances.* (The first edition appeared in 1718 and the third edition, from which I am quoting, appeared in 1756, shortly after the author's death.)

> *The Doctrine of Chances* may likewise be a help to cure a Kind of Superstition, which has been of long standing in the World, viz. that there is in Play such a thing as *Luck*, good or bad. I own there are a great many judicious people, who without any other Assistance than that of their own reason, are satisfied that the Notion of *Luck* is merely Chimerical; yet I conceive that the ground they have to look upon it as such, may still be farther inforced from some of the following Considerations.
>
> If by saying that a Man has had good Luck, nothing more was meant than that he has been generally a Gainer at play, the Expression might be allowed as very proper in a short way of speaking: But if the Word *Good Luck* be understood to signify a certain predominant quality, so inherent in a Man, that he must win whenever he Plays, or at least win oftener than lose, it may be denied that there is any such thing in nature.
>
> The Asserters of *Luck* are very sure from their own Experience, that at some times they have been very Lucky, and that at other times they have had a prodigious Run of *ill Luck* against them, which whilst it continued obliged them to be very cautious in engaging with the Fortunate; but how Chance should produce those extraordinary Events, is what they cannot conceive.

The point to be clear about in this passage is that the traditional concept of luck is not a concept of chance in the sense of randomness, but a concept of causation. The lucky man in the traditional concept is not one who fortuitously benefits from randomness in nature, but one who by some mysterious influence or cause is able to sway the course of events. As de Moivre points out, there is a proper concept of luck, namely, just benefiting fortuitously from randomness in nature, but this is not the vulgar concept.

A few paragraphs later, de Moivre also contrasts chance and design:

> Further, the same Arguments which explode the Notion of Luck, may, on the other side, be useful in some Cases to es-

tablish a due comparison between Chance and Design: We may imagine Chance and Design to be, as it were, in Competition with each other, for the production of some sorts of Events, and may calculate what Probability there is, that those Events should be rather owing to one than to the other.

As this last passage especially of de Moivre's indicates, it would have been perfectly consistent with the glorious developments in probability theory in the eighteenth century to have assigned a proper place to design and a proper place to chance, thereby moving rapidly away from the framework of classical mechanics to a broader conception of natural phenomena. So far as I know, this significant and workmanlike attack on the superstitions about luck and design in games of chance did not receive at the hands of anyone its proper philosophical application, just as the important work of Laplace on the use of probability analysis to identify unknown causes was not generalized to a probabilistic conception of causality that would have fitted so well with assigning a proper place to chance in the scheme of the universe.

Perhaps the major aspect of these eighteenth-century developments is that broad, ill-defined notions of chance were converted into an exact calculus, and only by means of such a calculus could contrary notions of superstition or luck be combated effectively. It is of course the case that earlier philosophers had useful and sane things to say about chance or luck and certainly were not swept up by the superstition of the gambler. What is important to contrast, however, and what is a critical turning point in intellectual and scientific history is the development of the explicit calculus of chance. The passages from de Moivre I have cited are a preface to an elaborate mathematical and quantitative development.

Bayes.   The important memoir of Bayes directly relevant to the analysis of causes was published in the *Philosophical Transactions of the Royal Society* in 1764. Bayes develops a general philosophy of causation that is considerably subtler than Hume's. Instead of using constant conjunction to infer the existence of causes and to give the account in terms of habit that Hume does of our future anticipations, Bayes sets forth an empirically sounder and more sophisticated approach. I quote an important passage:

What has been said seems sufficient to shew us what conclusions to draw from *uniform* experience. It demonstrates, particularly, that instead of proving that events will always happen agreeably to it, there will be always reason against this conclusion. In other words, where the course of nature has been the most constant, we can have only reason to reckon upon a recurrency of events proportioned to the degree of this constancy; but we have no reason for thinking that there are no causes in nature which will *ever* interfere with the operations of the causes from which this constancy is derived, or no circumstances of the world in which it will fail. And if this is true, supposing our only *data* derived from experience, we shall find additional reason for thinking thus if we apply other principles, or have recourse to such considerations as reason, independently of experience, can suggest. (1764, pp. 410–411)

Bayes goes on to discuss in some detail, indeed at some considerable length, a lottery example. There are three important points he makes in the process of discussion of this example. First, that without calculation it is very hard to judge correctly the probability of an event and thus a calculus of probability is essential, not just for theoretical work. Second, it is often impossible to discover the exact probability of an event and we have to be prepared to accept some reasonable limits. This is a point to which I return in chapter 8. Third, he is very explicit on the concept of particular causes operating in a probabilistic fashion. I quote a short paragraph on this point:

By calculations similar to these may be determined universally, what expectations are warranted by any experiments, according to the different number of times in which they have succeeded and failed; or what should be thought of the probability that any particular cause in nature, with which we have any acquaintance, will or will not, in any single trial, produce an effect that has been conjoined with it. (p. 417)

Laplace. All the same, real applications of the viewpoint that was probably first clearly enunciated by Bayes were made by

Laplace, and constitute in my judgment one of the most important contributions ever made to the tangled history of the theory and methodology of causal analysis.

Laplace's memoir of 1774 is of fundamental importance because it is the first to offer a definite methodology for estimating the probabilities of the causes that have produced an observed event. In the memoir itself Laplace gives several substantive examples, and in his famous treatise on the subject of probability, he turns to these matters again and extends his discussion. Because of the much greater availability of the treatise on probability (1820), I shall refer to some of the examples considered there.

One method that Laplace emphasizes is the use of detailed probabilistic considerations to infer whether or not data are to be accounted for in terms of a *constant cause* or are simply to be explained as being due to random fluctuations or errors in measurement. In the introduction to his treatise on probability, Laplace claimed to have used this method of constant causes to make some of his more important discoveries in astronomy. His explanations of a number of these phenomena for which a constant cause is inferred represent some of the most profound applications of mathematics in the history of science. Examples are (a) his derivation of the secular equation of the moon from the gravitational attraction of the sun and the secular variation of the eccentricity of Earth's orbit, (b) his explanation of the irregularities in the motion of Jupiter and Saturn as being due to their mutual interaction, (c) his recognition and explanation of the mean movements of the first three satellites of Jupiter, and (d) his elaborate theory of the tides.

Because these substantive examples involve complicated considerations, Laplace gives a simple methodological example to illustrate the method of constant causes. The example concerns diurnal fluctuations in a barometer measuring the pressure of the atmosphere. Suppose observations are made for 400 days, and during this period the height of the barometer does not vary more than four millimeters (an unrealistic assumption except for locations very close to the equator). We observe diurnal fluctuations with the maximum height occurring around nine o'clock in the morning and a minimum height occurring around four o'clock in the afternoon. Suppose, further, that the sum of the heights at nine o'clock in the morning exceeds the sum of the heights at four o'clock in the afternoon by 400 millimeters. We want to estimate the probability that this excess is due to a constant cause. By detailed calculations that I shall not enter into, Laplace shows that the probability that such a constant cause exists is extremely close to one. In other words, we cannot attribute the diurnal variation simply to random fluctuations or errors in measurement.

A possible rejoinder to my attempt to separate the probabilistic thinking of Laplace on the one hand from the deterministic viewpoint of Hume and Kant on the other is that Laplace in his own basic philosophy was just as deterministic in his ultimate view of causes as either Hume or Kant. Laplace is extremely clear in stating that for him probability arises from ignorance of true causes, and in that light, rather than being something in nature, probability is an epistemological concept expressing our ignorance of natural processes. It thus might be affirmed that Kant and Laplace, for example, can easily be made to stand together in their fundamental viewpoint that every event has a determinant cause. Moreover, the basis from which they adopt this viewpoint is the same. Kant, on his side, is impressed above all by the magnificent edifice of classical mechanics, and Laplace is the greatest contributor to that edifice since Newton.

I am not, however, deterred in conceptually separating the important ideas developed by Bayes and Laplace from the general philosophical ideas of constant conjunction or necessity of Hume and Kant. There is, it seems to me, a standard historical delay of intellectual traffic in both directions. What I have in mind is this. Laplace is swept up in philosophical ideas that are natural in the framework of classical mechanics, but they do not reflect profound changes in viewpoint that arise from the fundamental developments in probability theory in the eighteenth century. Kant, on the other hand, is not aware in any deep sense, as far as I can tell, of these mathematical developments, and he thinks of science as primarily reflected in classical mechanics and not in the development of probabilistic concepts, which is as original a contribution of the eighteenth century as the development of classical physics.

If one asks which philosophers of the eighteenth century, or indeed which modern philosophers from the seventeenth through the nineteenth centuries, had the most influence on our thinking about causality, almost everyone would respond immediately that either Hume or Kant should be given first place. Without denying their importance as philosophers, there is much that is distorted in this standard history. Laplace has a strong claim to be assigned first place, at least from the standpoint of developing an actual methodology for the investigation and identification of causes. As is so often the case in philosophy, what is happening at the same time in the best and newest science is not absorbed into the philosophy of the time nor does any proper dialogue take place. This was certainly true of the latter part of the eighteenth century. Hume has nothing to say about detailed concepts of probability; there is, for example, no mention of de Moivre's work, in spite of the prominence of his *Doctrine of Chances* (1718). Kant gives no indication of being familiar with the important memoirs being written in the period just preceding the publication of the first edition of the *Critique of Pure Reason*. I have not examined the evidence in detail, but I doubt that Kant had a knowledge of Laplace's memoir of 1774. Once again we have evidence of the way in which a communication gap between philosophy and science can have unfortunate repercussions, unfortunate in the present case for the theory of causality.

SYSTEMATIC DEFINITIONS

I have lingered over these historical matters, reaching in the discussion all the way back to Aristotle, in an attempt to emphasize the historical depth of the philosophical commitment to a determinist view of causality that allows no place for randomness in nature, and that in basic conceptual structure is implicitly inconsistent with randomness in nature. I have also tried to make the point that as early as the eighteenth century important scientific and mathematical developments made possible the advancement of quite a different philosophical viewpoint. This viewpoint assigned a proper place to causality and a proper place to randomness; indeed, it did not make the claim that every event must have a fully determinant cause.

Although I have terminated the historical analysis with Kant, it would be possible to continue this analysis through the nineteenth century into present times. It is still the case that a good many philosophers would not accept the thesis of a theory of causality that assigns a proper and an irreducible place to randomness in nature. General arguments can only be persuasive to a certain degree. For this reason, I now turn to the more systematic aspects of a probabilistic theory of causality and show, both in terms of systematic concepts and in terms of specific examples, how natural and useful such a viewpoint toward causality is, and how well it fits in with ordinary experience. The full developments of the theory require consideration of a large body of concepts and techniques from modern probability theory and mathematical statistics. I shall try to thread an elementary route through these concepts, but what I have to say must be extended in specific technical ways for real scientific use of the theory. Also, to keep matters simple, I shall retrogress from Laplace and consider qualitative rather than quantitative phenomena in order to make conceptual developments less technical. In this context then, I define the three notions of prima facie cause, spurious cause, and genuine cause. The technical details are worked out in an earlier monograph (Suppes, 1970b) and are not repeated.

Definition 1.   *An event* B *is a prima facie cause of an event* A *if and only if* (i) B *occurs earlier than* A, (ii) *the conditional probability of* A *occurring when* B *occurs is greater than the unconditional probability of* A *occurring.*

Here is a simple example of the application of definition 1 to the study of the efficacy of inoculation against cholera (Greenwood and Yule, 1915, cited in Kendall and Stuart, 1961). I also discussed this example in my 1970 monograph. The data from the 818 cases studied are given in Table 1.

Table 1   Incidence of cholera among inoculated and noninoculated populations

	Not attacked	Attacked	Totals
Inoculated	276	3	279
Not inoculated	473	66	539
Totals	749	69	818

These data clearly show the prima facie efficacy of inoculation, for the mean probability of not being attacked is 749/818 = 0.916, whereas the conditional probability of not being attacked, given that an individual was inoculated, is $276/279 = 0.989$. Here A is the event of not being attacked by cholera and B the event of being inoculated. This kind of medical example is in my own judgment a paradigm of qualitative causal inference of importance and significance.

In many areas of active scientific investigation the probabilistic data are not so clearcut, although they may be scientifically and statistically significant. I have selected one example concerning vitamin A intake and lung cancer to illustrate the point. The results are taken from Bjelke (1975). The sample of Norwegian males 45–75 years of age was drawn from the general population of Norway but included a special roster of men who had siblings that had migrated to the United States. In 1964 the sample reported their cigarette smoking habits. More than 90 percent of those surviving in 1967 completed a dietary questionnaire sufficiently detailed to permit an estimate of vitamin A intake. On January 1, 1968, of the original sample, 8,278 were alive. Their records were computer-matched against the records of the Cancer Registry of Norway as of March 1, 1973.

The sample was classified into two groups according to an index of vitamin A intake as inferred from the dietary questionnaire, with 2,642 classified as having low intake and 5,636 as not low—I am ignoring in this recapitulation many details about this index. There were for the sample, as of March 1, 1973, 19 proven cases of carcinomas other than adenocarcinomas, which we ignore for reasons too detailed to go into here. Of the 19 proven cases, 14, i.e., 74 percent, occurred among the 32 percent of the sample— the 2,642 who had a low intake of vitamin A. Only 5 cases, i.e., 26 percent, occurred among the 68 percent of the sample who had a high intake of vitamin A. Let C be the event of having a lung carcinoma and let L be low intake of vitamin A. Then for the sample in question

$$P(C) = 0.0023 < P(C|L) = 0.0053$$

Using definition 1, we infer that low intake of vitamin A is a prima facie cause of lung cancer. The probabilities in question are small, but the results suggest further scientific investigation of the proposition that high intake of vitamin A may help prevent lung cancer.

It is now widely accepted that cigarette smoking causes lung
cancer, but as the present data show, the incidence of lung cancer
in the general population is so small that it is a primary medical
puzzle to explain why so few smokers do get lung cancer. This
study is meant to be a contribution toward solving this puzzle.
The study, as already indicated, did look at the cigarette smoking
habits of the sample. I remark on this part of the data below, in
the discussion of spurious causes.

An important feature of this study is that the results are fragile
enough to warrant much further investigation before any practical
conclusion is drawn—such as the admonition to heavy smokers to
eat lots of carrots. In my view, perhaps a majority of scientific
studies of causal connections have a similar tentative character. It
is mainly science far from the frontiers, much worked over and
highly selected, that has clear and decisive results.

Spurious causes.   A common argument of those who oppose a
probabilistic analysis of causality is to claim that it is not possible
to distinguish genuine prima facie causes from spurious ones. This
view is mistaken. Because in my sense spuriousness and genuine-
ness are opposites, it will be sufficient to define spurious causes,
and then to characterize genuine causes as prima facie causes that
are not spurious.

For the definition of spurious causes, I introduce the concept of
a partition at a given time of the possible space of events. A partition is just a collection of incompatible and exhaustive events. In
the case where we have an explicit sample space, it is a collection
of pairwise disjoint, nonempty sets whose union is the whole
space. The intuitive idea is that a prima facie cause is spurious if
there exists an earlier partition of events such that no matter
which event of the partition occurs the joint occurrence of *B* and
the element of the partition yields the same conditional probability for the event *A* as does the occurrence of the element of the
partition alone. To repeat this idea in slightly different language,
we have:

Definition 2.   *An event* B *is a spurious cause of* A *if and only if* B
is a prima facie cause of A, *and there is a partition of events earlier
than* B *such that the conditional probability of* A, *given* B *and any
element of the partition, is the same as the conditional probability
of* A, *given just the element of the partition.*

The history of human folly is replete with belief in spurious causes. One of the most enduring is the belief in astrology. The better ancient defenses of astrology begin on sound empirical grounds, but quickly wander into extrapolations that are unwarranted and that would provide, upon deeper investigation, excellent examples of spurious causes. Ptolemy's treatise on astrology, *Tetrabiblos*, begins with a sensible discussion of how the seasons, the weather, and the tides are influenced by the motions of the sun and the moon. But he then moves rapidly to the examination of what may be determined about the temperament and fortunes of a given individual. He proceeds to give genuinely fantastic explanations of the cultural characteristics of entire nations on the basis of their relation to the stars. Consider, for example, this passage:

> Of these same countries Britain, (Transalpine) Gaul, Germany, and Bastarnia are in closer familiarity with Aries and Mars. Therefore for the most part their inhabitants are fiercer, more headstrong, and bestial. But Italy, Apulia, (Cisalpine) Gaul, and Sicily have their familiarity with Leo and the sun; wherefore these peoples are more masterful, benevolent, and co-operative. (63, Loeb edition)

Ptolemy is not an isolated example. It is worth remembering that Kepler was court astrologer in Prague, and Newton wrote more about theology than physics. In historical perspective, their fantasies about spurious causes are easy enough to perceive. It is a different matter when we ask ourselves about future attitudes toward such beliefs current in our own time. In any case, we cannot pass from genuine causes and the elimination of spurious causes to the consideration of ultimate causes. The belief that this can be done is another one of the aspects of theology that has been difficult to eliminate and that retains its place as a kind of wan substitute for belief in the omniscient action of God.

In the study of the relationship between level of vitamin A intake and incidence of lung cancer described earlier, the usual positive correlations between amount of cigarette smoking and incidence of lung cancer were found. More to the point here, at each level of cigarette smoking (four were used) the negative correlation between vitamin A intake and lung cancer was found. This shows that the causal character of vitamin A as an inhibitor of lung cancer is genuine, relative to the framework of this investigation. The partitioning of the sample into four levels of smoking did not render spurious the vitamin A effect.

Varieties of probabilities.   The sense of probability used in the characterization of causes need not be univocal. As I have pointed out earlier (Suppes, 1970b), there are at least three senses in which probability can be used in making a probability claim. One is in the sense of a theoretical probability, as for example when one analyzes the formal character of a theory that is formulated as a class of stochastic processes. A second is when data are analyzed from a particular experiment, and restricted relative frequencies are considered together possibly with some prior probabilities highly relevant to the experiment. A third concerns the most general sense of the expression of beliefs. Each of these cases has its appropriate and proper place in the expression of causal claims. (For a more detailed discussion of the meaning of probability statements see the end of chapter 4.)

Alternative modern views.   Consideration of this example is a good occasion to examine some major alternative views of simple causal relations. One standard alternative view is the lawlike view of causality, which runs as follows in relation to the events A and B identified above. Let A be represented by the proposition P and B by the proposition Q; then A is caused by B if and only if there are a set of scientific laws and a set of particular facts such that the conjunction of these two sets with Q implies P. Moreover, it is also ordinarily required that the laws are necessary to the implication. A more elaborate formal statement of the lawlike view of causality can be given, but it is not essential here.

In the kind of application I have just cited, it is clear that there are no appropriate scientific laws from which the efficacy of the inoculation can be derived. In such medical experimentation a relatively surface empiricism must replace a deeper theoretical approach; yet no one in ordinary circumstances would doubt the causal efficacy of the inoculation when there are data of the kind just presented or at least when similar data of still greater magnitude are collected. It is in my mind merely a fantasy of philosophers to think that the lawlike view of causality is the one that is dominant, either in empirical science or in ordinary experience. The number of established laws is not that great and the net of logical connections is not that dense.

A second popular view (among philosophers) is to give a counterfactual analysis of causality. A good example of this approach may be found in an article by David Lewis (1973). Many conceptual and technical criticisms may be made of Lewis's counterfactual analysis and similar analyses by other people, but in the context of the present example there is an objection that I think is overwhelming. Lewis's analysis makes use of the concept of comparative similarity of possible worlds. He says that one world is closer to actuality than another if the first resembles our actual world more than the second does. A counterfactual is then nonvacuously true if it takes less of a departure (in the sense of the similarity relation) from actuality to make the consequent true along with the antecedent than it does to make the antecedent true without the consequent. The virtue of Lewis's analysis is to make explicit the undefined and uncharacterized concept of similarity of possible worlds. But it seems to me evident that too little is said about this relation to make it feasible as an explication of the way in which we use causal concepts either in empirical science or in ordinary experience. It is not that the idea Lewis proposes is farfetched—it is just that the basic idea is much too undeveloped to be persuasive as an explication of the concept.

I cannot emphasize too strongly the difference between a counterfactual analysis and a probabilistic analysis of causality. The probabilistic analysis has an extensively developed methodology and is widely used in actual science. In contrast, the counterfactual analysis does not have a developed methodology and is not used in practice, for good reason. There are, of course, conceptual similarities between the two approaches. For example, it is possible to impose a relation of similarity between possible worlds by using the probability measure on the set of possible outcomes, and it is also possible to use the measure to talk about similarity between events rather than between worlds. I shall not attempt to develop these considerations, but rather to emphasize the natural and practical applicability of the probabilistic concept of causality.

There is an important other variety of causality special to the physical sciences which is not in conflict with the probabilistic definition given but goes beyond it in highly significant ways in postulating additional causal structure. I have in mind all those concepts in physics and chemistry that we ordinarily think of as causal. Perhaps the ideal example is to be found in mechanics in the concept of force. Certainly it is completely natural as an extension of ordinary experience and ordinary language always to think of forces in physics as causal, and in spite of some rhetoric to the contrary by some philosophers and some physicists, I think that matters very much continue to be the same as before: forces are special kinds of causes. Indeed, from a physical standpoint, forces are the primary causes of any phenomena. Our intuitive thinking about forces seems to me clear and straightforward. On the other hand, the way in which we think of transfers of momentum or energy as being causal in character is more complicated and subtle, less attuned to ordinary thought about the world. There are a host of additional processes in chemistry that we think of as causal in character—oxidation, for example. To account for such cases, a fully developed theory of casuality would need to provide a detailed analysis, and at the same time provide for the plurality of causal concepts that arise in different sciences. There is no significant reason to try to reduce them to any small number. The point of the kind of probabilistic causal structure introduced is that it has considerable generality. It provides a framework for analysis of many different kinds of causes, and especially so for those for which we do not have a well-developed scientific theory.

Ordinary experience.   It will be said by some that a probabilistic view of causality runs contrary to the use of causal concepts in ordinary language to reflect ordinary experience. This is not the occasion to argue a thesis on these matters, but I do not accept this view. The open context of most statements about ordinary experience makes a probabilistic framework the appropriate one for causal claims. In previous writing (Suppes, 1970b), I attempted to make this case in detail. I now take a more pluralistic view of the many different kinds of causal structures encountered even in ordinary experience and our analysis of it.

Much discussion has revolved around the role of reasons as causes and the extent to which a reason can be a cause of an action. The giving of a reason as the cause of an action fits in well with probabilistic analysis. If I ask someone 'What are you going to do today?' and he responds 'I am going to San Francisco', and I then ask 'Why?', an appropriate response on his part might be 'Because I want to buy a marble table at Cellini's'. In terms of the analysis of prima facie causes given earlier (definition 1), the verbal reason can be taken as an event that raises the probability of his going to San Francisco, even if it is not a genuine cause. On the other hand, it would be foolish to accept the fact that he is going to San Francisco as a certainty; all kinds of things could interfere, ranging from an accident to an emergency call or a preemptive demand from a colleague. Let me emphasize again that the open-textured character of most causal statements about ordinary experience makes a probabilistic framework a natural one.

CONFLICTING INTUITIONS

The concept of causality has so many different kinds of applications and is at the same time such a universal part of the apparatus we use to analyze both scientific and ordinary experience that it is not surprising to have a variety of conflicting intuitions about its nature. I examine in the remainder of this chapter 5 examples of such conflict, but the list is in no sense inclusive. It would be easy to generate another dozen just from the literature of the last ten years.

Simpson's paradox. Simpson (1951) showed that probability relationships of the kind exemplified by definition 1 for prima facie causes can be reversed when a finer analysis of the data is considered. From the standpoint of the framework of this chapter, this is just a procedure for showing that a prima facie cause is a spurious cause, at least in the cases where the time ordering follows the definitions given. In Simpson's discussion of these matters and in the related literature, there has not been explicit attention to temporal order, and I shall ignore it in my comments on the "paradox". There is an intuitively clear and much discussed example of sex bias in graduate admissions at Berkeley (Bickel, Hammel, and O'Connell, 1975). When data from the university as a whole were considered, there seemed to be good evidence that being male was a prima facie cause for being admitted to graduate school. In other words, there was a positive bias toward the admission of males and a negative bias toward the admission of females. On the other hand, when the data were examined department by department it turned out that a majority of the departments did not show such a bias and in fact had a very weak bias toward female admission. The conflict in the data arose from the large number of female applications to departments that had a large number of rejections independent of the sex of the applicant. As is clear from this example, there is no genuine paradox in the problem posed by Simpson. There is nothing inconsistent, or in fact even close to inconsistent, in the results described, which are characteristic of the phenomena.

Cartwright (1979) proposes to meet the Simpson problem by imposing further conditions on the concept of one event being a cause of another. In particular, she wants to require that the increase in probability characteristic of prima facie causes defined above is considered only in situations which are 'otherwise causally homogeneous with respect to' the effect. I am skeptical that we can know when situations are causally homogeneous. In the kind of example considered earlier concerning high intake of vitamin A being a potential inhibitor of lung cancer, it is certainly not possible to know or even to consider causally homogeneous situations, even experimental ones. I am also skeptical at a conceptual or philosophical level that we have any well-defined notion of homogeneity. The search for homogeneity seems as quixotic and metaphysically mistaken as the search for ultimate causes. Consider, for example, the data from Berkeley just described. There is no reason that we could not also pursue additional hypotheses. We might want to look at partial data from each department where the data were restricted just to the borderline cases. We might test the hypothesis that the female applicants were more able than the males but that at the borderline there was bias against the females. So far as I know, such a more refined analysis of the data has not been performed, but there is no reason conceptually that we might not find something by entertaining such additional questions. My point is that there is no end to the analysis of data in a practical sense. We can, of course, exhaust finite data theoretically by considering all possible combinations, but this is only of mathematical significance.

A conflict of intuition can arise about when to stop the refinement of data analysis. From a practical standpoint, many professional situations require detailed rules concerning such matters. The most obvious example is in the definition of classes for actuarial tables. What should be the variables relevant to fixing the rates on insurance policies? I have in mind here not only life insurance but also automobile insurance, property insurance, etc. I see a conflict at the most fundamental level between those who think there is some ultimate stopping point that can be determined in the analysis and those who do not. Where I stand on this issue should be clear enough from what I have already said.

There is another point to be mentioned about the Simpson problem. It is that if we can look at the data after collection and if the probabilities in question are neither zero nor one, it is then easy to define artificially events that render any prima facie cause spurious. Of course, in ordinary statistical methodology it would be regarded as a scandal to construct such an event after looking at the data, but from a scientific standpoint the matter is not so simple. Certainly, looking at data that do not fit desired hypotheses or favorite theories is one of the best ways to get ideas about new hypotheses or new theories. But without further investigation we do not take seriously the *ex post facto* artificial construction of concepts. What is needed is another experiment or another set of data to determine if the hypotheses in question are of serious interest. There is, however, another point to be made about such artificial concepts constructed solely by looking at the data and counting the outcomes. It is that somehow we need to exclude such concepts in order to avoid the undesirable outcome of every prima facie cause being spurious, at least every naturally hypothesized prima facie cause. One way to do this is to characterize the notion of genuine cause relative to a given set of concepts that may be used to define events considered as causes. Such an emendation and explicit restriction on the definition given above of genuine cause seems appropriate.[3]

Macroscopic determinism.   Even if one accepts the general argument that there is randomness in nature at the microscopic level, there continues to be a line of thought that in analysis of causality in ordinary experience it is useful and, in fact, in some cases almost mandatory to assume determinism. I have tried to state in chapter 2 many examples of ordinary experience that argue against this viewpoint, but it is useful to examine once again in the context of specific causal investigations the arguments that are

---

[3] As Cartwright (1979) points out, it is a historical mistake to attribute Simpson's paradox to Simpson. The problem posed was already discussed in Cohen and Nagel's well-known textbook (1934), and according to Cartwright, Nagel believes that he learned about the problem from Yule's classic textbook of 1911. There has also been a substantial recent discussion of the paradox in the psychological literature (Hintzman, 1980; Martin, 1981).

given for such determinism. I will not try to summarize all the literature here but will concentrate on the arguments given in Hesslow (1976 and 1981), which attempt to give a deep-running argument against probabilistic causality, not just my particular version of it. (In addition to these articles of Hesslow the reader is also referred to Rosen, 1978, and for a particularly thorough critique of deterministic causality, Rosen, 1982/3.)

As a formulation of determinism which avoids the global character of Laplace's, both Hesslow and Rosen cite Anscombe's (1975, p. 63) principle of relevant difference: 'If an effect occurs in one case and a similar effect does not occur in an apparently similar case, then there must be a relevant further difference'. Although statistical or probabilistic techniques are employed in testing hypotheses in the biological and social sciences, Hesslow claims 'there is nothing that shows that these hypotheses themselves are probabilistic in nature. In fact one can argue that the opposite is true, for statistics are commonly used in a way that presupposes determinism, namely, in various kinds of eliminative arguments.'

Hesslow's intuitions here are very different from mine so there is a basic conflict that could best be resolved by extensive review of the biological, medical, and social science literature. I shall not attempt that here, but merely state what I think is wrong with one of Hesslow's ideal examples. He says that these kinds of eliminative arguments all have a simple structure. He takes the case of Jones, who had a fatal disease but was given a newly discovered medicine and recovered. We conclude, he says, that the cause of his recovery was M, the event of taking medicine. Now he says at the beginning that Jones had a 'universally fatal disease'. The first thing to challenge is the use of the adverb *universally*. It seldom applies to the diseases of interest. Almost no diseases that are the subject for analysis and study by doctors are universally fatal. It is a familiar fact that when medicine is given we certainly like to attribute the recovery to medicine. But ordinarily the evidence is not overwhelming, because in the case of almost all diseases there is evidence of individuals' recovering who were not treated by the medicine. This is true of all kinds of diseases, from the plague to pneumonia. In making this statement, I am certainly not asserting that medicine is not without efficacy, but only that Hesslow's claim is far too simple. The actual data do not support what he says.

Hesslow's claim that this is a case of determinism is puzzling because in his own explicit formulation of the argument he says 'Thus, (probably) M caused R', where R is the event of recovery. He himself explicitly introduces the caveat of probability. What he states is 'because something caused the recovery and, other causes apparently being scarce, M is the most likely candidate'. Determinism comes in the use of *something*, but the conclusion he draws is probabilistic in character and could just as well have been drawn if he had started with the view that in most cases an identifiable agent caused the recovery but that in the remaining cases the recovery was spontaneous. Moreover, I would claim that there is no powerful argument for the determinism of the kind Hesslow was trying to give. One could look from one end of the medical literature to the other and simply not find the kind of need for the premises he talks about.

There is a point to be clear about on this matter. Because one is not endorsing determinism as a necessary way of life for biological and social scientists, it does not mean that the first identification of a probabilistic cause brings a scientific investigation of a given phenomenon to an end. It is a difficult and delicate matter to determine when no further causes can be identified. I am not offering any algorithms for making this determination. I am just making a strong claim that we do get along in practice with probabilistic results and we do not fill them out in an interesting deterministic fashion.

Types and tokens. There are many conflicting intuitions about whether causality should mainly be discussed in terms of event types or event tokens, and also how the two levels are related. I restrict myself here to two issues, both of which are fundamental. One is whether cases of individual causation must inevitably be subsumable under general laws. The second is whether we can make inferences about individual causes when the general laws are merely probabilistic.

A good review of the first issue on subsumption of individual causal relations under general laws is given by Rosen (1982/3), and I shall not try to duplicate her excellent discussion of the many different views on this matter. Certainly, nowadays probably no one asserts the strong position that if a person holds that a singular causal statement is true then the person must hold that a certain appropriate covering law is true. One way out, perhaps most ably defended by Horgan (1980), is to admit that direct covering laws are not possible but that there are at work underneath precise laws, formulated in terms of precise properties that do give us the appropriate account in terms of general laws. But execution of this program certainly is at present, and in my own view will forever be, at best a pious hope. In many cases we shall not be able to supply the desired analysis, but I shall not go over my arguments again, which have already been stated in chapter 2 and which I return to in chapter 4.

There is a kind of psychological investigation that would throw interesting light on actual beliefs about these matters. Epistemological or philosophical arguments of the kind, for example, given by Horgan do not seem to me to be supportable. It would be enlightening to know if most people believe that there is such an underlying theory of events and if somehow it gives them comfort to believe that such a theory exists. The second and more particular psychological investigation would deal with the kinds of beliefs individuals hold and the responses they give to questions about individual causation. Is there a general tendency to subsume our causal accounts of individual events under proto-covering laws? It should be evident what I am saying about this first issue. The defense that there are laws either of a covering or a foundational nature cannot be defended on philosophical grounds, but it would be useful to transform the issue into a number of psychological questions as to what people actually do believe. The point is not to convert metaphysical into psychological questions, but rather to broaden the scope of metaphysics to encompass more about the structure of thought—chapters 7 and 8 represent a sustained effort in this direction.

The second issue is in a way more surprising. It has mainly been emphasized by Hesslow. It is the claim that inferences from generic statistical relations to individual causal relations are necessarily invalid. Thus, he concludes 'if all generic causal relations are statistical, then we must either accept invalid inferences or refrain from talking about individual causation at all' (1981, p. 598). It seems to me that this line of argument is definitely mistaken and I would like to try to say why as clearly as I can. First of all, I agree that one does not make a logically or a mathematically valid argument from generic statistical relations to individual causal relations. It is in the nature of probability theory and its applications that the inference from the general to the particular is not in itself a mathematically valid inference. The absence of such validity, however, in no way prohibits using generic causal relations that are clearly statistical in character to make inferences about individual causation. It is just that those inferences are not mathematically valid inferences—they are inferences made in the context of probability and uncertainty. I mention as an aside that there is a large literature by advocates of a relative frequency theory of probability about how to make inferences from relative frequencies to single cases. Since I come closer to being a Bayesian than a relative frequentist, I shall not review these arguments, but many of the discussions are relevant in arguing from a different viewpoint than mine about Hesslow's claims.

First, though, let me distinguish sharply between the generic relations and the individual relations and what I think is the appropriate terminology for making this distinction. The language I prefer is that the generic relations are average or mean relations. The individual relations at their fullest and best depend upon individual sample paths known in great detail. An individual sample path is the continuous temporal and spatial path of development of an individual's history. There is in this history ordinarily a great deal of information not available in simple mean data. I can say briefly and simply what the expected or mean life span is of an adult who is now 45 years old and is living in the United States, but if I consider some single individual and examine him in terms of his past history, his ancestors, his current state of health, his employment, etc., I may come to a very different view of his expected number of remaining years. Certainly it would be ludicrous to think that there is a logically valid inference from the mean data to the individual data.

But for a Bayesian or near Bayesian like myself the matter has a rather straightforward solution. First of all, probabilities as matters of belief are directly given to individual events and their individual relationships. Second, by the standard theorem on total probability, when I say that a given individual has an expected lifetime of twenty years, I have already taken account of all knowledge that I have about him. Of course, if I learn something new, the probability can change, just on the basis of the theorem on total probability. Now the central point is that ordinarily much of what I know about individuals is based upon generic causal relations. I simply do not know enough to go very much beyond generic relations, and thus my probabilistic estimate of an individual's expected remaining lifetime will very much depend on a few generic causal relations and not much else.

The absence of logical validity in relating the generic in the individual in no way keeps me from talking about individual causation, contrary to Hesslow's claim. In fact, I would say that what I have said is just the right account of how we do talk about individual causation in the cases where we know something about generic probabilistic causal relations. We know, for example, that heavy clouds are a good sign of rain, and when accompanied by a drop in atmospheric pressure an even better sign. We know that these two conditions alone will not cause rain with a probability of one, but there is a strong probabilistic causal relation. We go on to say that rain is likely sometime this afternoon. We are quite happy with our causal views of the matter based on a couple of generic causal relations. Intimate details of the kind available to meteorologists with the professional responsibility to predict the weather are not available, let us say, in the instance being discussed. The meteorologist faced with a similar problem uses a much more complex theory of generic relations in order finally to issue his prediction for the afternoon. It is also important to note, of course, that on the kind of Bayesian view I am describing here there is no algorithm or simple calculus for passing by probability from generic causal relationships to individual ones, even for the trained meteorologist. It is a matter of judgment as to how the knowledge one has is used and assessed. The use of the theorem on total probability mentioned above depends on both conditional and unconditional probabilities, which in general depend on judgment. In the case where there is very fine scientific knowledge of the laws in question it might be on occasion that the conditional probabilities are known from extensive scientific experimentation, but then another aspect of the problem related to the application to the individual event will not be known from such scientific experimentation except in very unusual cases, and judgment will enter necessarily.

The link between judgment and causal attribution to individual events should be clear in what I am saying. The estimates of probabilities of individual events depend almost always on an element of intuitive judgment, and causal attributions to such events depend on the probability estimates. A notable modern tendency, reflected in the daily weather and economic forecasts in many newspapers, is the move from crude qualitative estimates to refined quantitative ones, but the dominant commonsense view that individual events can be identified as causes with or without explicit knowledge of covering laws remains constant.

Physical flow of causes.   In his excellent review article on probabilistic causality, Salmon (1980) puts his finger on one of the most important conflicting intuitions about causality. The derivations of the fundamental differential equations of classical physics give in most cases a very satisfying physical analysis of the flow of causes in a system, but there is no mention of probability. It is characteristic of the areas in which probabilistic analysis is used to a very large extent that a detailed theory of the phenomena in question is missing. The examples from medicine given earlier in this chapter are typical. We may have some general ideas about how a vaccine works or about the mechanisms for absorbing vitamin A, but we do not have anything like an adequate detailed theory of these matters. We are presently very far from being able to make any kind of detailed theoretical predictions derived from fundamental assumptions about molecular structure, for example. Concerning these or related questions we have a very poor understanding in comparison with the kinds of models successful in various parts of classical physics about the detailed flow of causes. I think Salmon is quite right in pointing out that the absence of being able to give such an analysis is the source of the air of paradox of some of the counterexamples that have been given. The core argument is to challenge the claim that the occurrence of a cause should increase the probability of the occurrence of its effect.

Salmon uses as a good example of this phenomenon the hypothetical case made up by Deborah Rosen and reported in my 1970 monograph. A golfer makes a birdie by hitting a limb of a tree at just the right angle, not certainly something that he planned to do. The disturbing aspect is that if we estimated the probability of his making a birdie prior to his making the shot and we added the condition that the ball hit the branch, we would ordinarily estimate the probability as being definitely lower than that he would have made a birdie without this given condition. On the other hand, when we see the event happen we have an immediate physical recognition that the exact angle that he hit the branch played a crucial role in the ball's going into the cup. In my 1970 discussion of this example I did not take sufficient account of the conflict of intuition between the general probabilistic view and the highly structured physical view. I now think it is important to do so and I very much agree with Salmon that the issues here are central to a general acceptability of a probabilistic theory of causality. I therefore want to make a revised response, and expand upon what I said earlier in this chapter about the importance of such physical processes.

There are at least three different kinds of cases in which what seem for other reasons to be prima facie causes in fact turn out to be negative causes, i.e., the conditional probability of the effect's occurring is lowered given the cause. One sort of case involves situations in which we know a great deal about the classical physics. A second kind of case is where an artificial example can be constructed and we may want to make claims about observing a causal chain. Salmon gives a succinct and useful example of this kind, which I discuss. Third, there are the cases in which we attribute without any grounds some surprising event as a cause of some significant effect. In certain respects the ancient predilection for omens falls under this category, but I shall not expand upon this view further.

In the first kind of case there is a natural description of the event after the fact that makes everything come out right. Using the golf ball example as typical, we now describe the event as that of the golf ball's hitting the branch at exactly the right angle to fall into the cup. Given such a description we would of course make the conditional probability close to one, bu it is only after the fact that we could describe the event in this fashion. On the other hand, it is certainly too general to expect much to come out of the event described simply as the golf ball's hitting the limb of the tree. From what I have said about other matters my views should be clear. It is not really feasible to aim before the event at a detailed description of the event adequate to make a good physical prediction. We will not be given the values of parameters sufficiently precisely to predict that the golf ball will hit the limb of the tree at an angle just right for bouncing into the cup. Consequently, in such cases we cannot hope to predict the effects of such surprising causes, but based upon physical theories that are accurate to a high degree of approximation we understand that this is what happened after we have observed the sequence of events. Another way of putting the matter is that there is a whole range of cases in which we do not have much hope of applying in an interesting scientific or commonsense way probabilistic analysis, because the causes will be surprising. As we shall see in chapter 6, even in cases of extraordinary conceptual simplicity, e.g., the N-body problem with only forces of gravitation acting between the bodies, extended prediction of behavior for any length of time is not in general possible. Thus, although a Bayesian in such matters of individual events as the golf ball example. I confess to being unable to make good probabilistic causal analyses of many kinds of individual events. In the same fashion, I cannot apply to such events, in advance of their happening, detailed physical theories. The possibilities of application in both cases seem hopeless as a matter of prediction. This may not be the way we want the world to be, but this is the way it is. The limited applicability of most theories to most naturally occurring events is a fact about contemporary science that is not stressed enough.

Salmon also gives an example that has a much simpler physical description than the golf ball example. It involves the eight ball and the cue ball on a pool table with the player's having a 50–50 chance of sinking the eight ball with the cue ball when he tries. Moreover, the eight ball goes into the corner pocket, as Salmon says 'if and almost only if his cue ball goes into the other far corner pocket'. Let event A be the player's attempting the shot, B the dropping of the eight ball in the corner pocket, and C the dropping of the cue ball into the other corner pocket. Under the hypotheses given, B is a prima facie cause of C, and Salmon is concerned about the fact that A does not screen B off from C, i.e., render B a spurious cause of C. Salmon expresses his concern by saying that we should have appropriate causal relations among A, B, and C without having to enter into more detailed physical theory. But it seems to me that this example illustrates a very widespread phenomenon. The physical analysis, which we regard as correct, namely, the genuine cause of C, i.e., the cue ball going into the pocket, is in terms of the impact forces and the direction of motion of the cue ball at the time of impact. We certainly believe that such specification can give us a detailed and correct account of the cue ball's motion. On the other hand, there is an important feature of this detailed physical analysis. We must engage in meticulous investigations; we are not able to make in a commonsense way the appropriate observations of these earlier events of motion and impact. In contrast, the events A, B, and C

are obvious and directly observable. I do not find it surprising that we must go beyond these three events for a proper causal account, and yet at the same time we are not able to do so by the use of obvious commonsense events. Aristotle would not have had such an explanation, from all that we know about his physics. Why should we expect it of untutored common sense?

The second class of example, of which Salmon furnishes a very good instance, is when we know only probability transitions. The example he considers concerns an atom in an excited state. In particular, it is the fourth energy level. The probability is one that it will necessarily decay to the zeroeth level, i.e., the ground state. The only question is whether the transitions will be through all the intermediate states three, two, and one, or whether some states will be jumped over. The probability of going from the fourth to the third state is 3/4 and from the fourth to the second state is 1/4. The probability of going from the third state to the first state is 3/4 and from the third state to the ground state 1/4. Finally, the probability of going from the second state to the first state is 1/4 and from the second state directly to the ground state 3/4. It is required also, of course, that the probability of going from the first state to the ground state is one. The paradox arises because of the fact that if a decaying atom occupies the second state in the process of decay, then the probability of its occupying the first state is 1/4, but the mean probability whatever the route taken of occupying the first state is the much higher probability of 10/16. Thus, on the probabilistic definitions given earlier of prima facie causes, occupying the second state is a negative prima facie cause of occupying the first state.

On the other hand, as Salmon emphasizes, after the events occur of the atom going from the fourth to the second to the first state, many would say that this sequence constitutes a causal chain. My own answer to this class of examples is to meet the problem head-on and to deny that we want to call such sequences causal sequences. If all we know about the second state remains a negative prima facie cause of occupying the first state. The fact of the actual sequence does not change this characterization. In my own constructive work on causality, I have not given a formal definition of causal chains, and for good reason. I think it is difficult to decide which of various conflicting intuitions should govern the definition.

We may also examine how our view of this example might change if the probabilities were made more extreme, i.e., if the mean probability of occupying the first energy state comes close to one and the probability of a transition from the second to the first state is close to zero. In such cases when we observe the sequence of transitions from the fourth to the second to the first state, we might be inclined to say that the atom decayed to the first state in spite of occupying the second state. By using such phrases as *in spite of* we indicate our skepticism that what we have observed is a genuine causal chain.

Common causes.   It was a virtue of Reichenbach to have recognized that a natural principle of causality is to expect events that are simultaneous, spatially separated, and strongly correlated, to depend upon some common cause to generate the correlation. There are a variety of controversial questions about the principle of common cause, and the source of the controversy is the absence of clear and widely accepted intuitions about what we should expect of such causes. Should we expect such causes to exist? Thus, when we observe phenomenologically simultaneous events strongly correlated, should we always be able to find a common cause that eliminates this phenomenological correlation in the sense that when we condition on the common cause the new conditional correlation is zero? Another question concerns the determinism of common causes. Ought we to expect such causes to be deterministic, or can we find common causes that are strictly probabilistic? In a recent essay, Van Fraassen (1982) expresses the view that the causes must be deterministic in the following way.

> But a belief in the principle of the common cause implies a belief that there is in the relevant cases not merely a compatibility (so that deterministic hidden variables could be introduced into models for the theory) but that all those hidden events which are the common causes, are real, and therefore, that the world is really deterministic. (p. 208)

In his reply to Van Fraassen, Salmon (1982) suggests that the principle of common cause is sometimes used as an explanatory principle and sometimes as a principle of inference. Also he implicitly suggests a third and different use, considered as well by Van Fraassen as a maxim of rationality: search for a common cause whenever feasible to explain simultaneous events that are strongly correlated. Using the principle as a maxim does not guarantee any explanations nor any inferences, but can be important in the strategy of research. The dialogue between Salmon and Van Fraassen in the two articles mentioned contains a number of useful points about common causes, but rather than consider in detail their examples, counterexamples, arguments, and counterarguments to each other, I want to suggest what I think is a reasonable view of the principle of common cause. In doing so I shall avoid references to quantum mechanics except in one instance. I shall also generalize the discussion to more than two events, because in many scientific applications it is not adequate to consider the correlations of only two events.

First let me say more explicitly what I shall mean by common cause. The exposition here will be rather sketchy. The technical details of many of the points made are given in the appendix to this chapter.

Let A and B be events that are approximately simultaneous and that are correlated, i.e., $P(AB) \neq P(A)P(B)$. Then the event C is a *common cause* of A and B if:

   (i) C occurs earlier than A and B;
  (ii) $P(AB|C) = P(A|C)P(B|C)$;
 (iii) $P(AB|\bar{C}) = P(A|\bar{C})P(B|\bar{C})$.

In other words, C renders A and B conditionally independent, and so does $\bar{C}$, the complement of C. When the correlation between A and B is positive, i.e., when $P(AB) > P(A)P(B)$, we may also want to require:

  (iv) C is a prima facie cause of A and of B.

I shall not assume (iv) in what follows. I state in informal language a number of propositions that are meant to clarify some of the controversy about common causes. The first two propositions follow from a theorem about common causes proved in Suppes and Zanotti (1981).

Proposition I. Let events $A_1, A_2, \ldots, A_n$ *be given with any two of the events correlated. Then a necessary and sufficient condition for it to be possible to construct a common cause of these events is that the events* $A_1, A_2, \ldots, A_n$ *have a joint probability distribution compatible with the given pairwise correlations.*

An important point to emphasize about this proposition is its generality and at the same time its weakness. There are no restrictions placed on the nature of the common causes. Once any sorts of restrictions of a physical or other empirical kind are imposed, then the common cause might not exist. If we simply want to know whether a common cause can be found as a matter of principle as an underlying cause of the observed correlations between events, then the answer is not one that has been much discussed in the literature. All that is required is the existence of a joint probability distribution of the phenomenological variables. It is obvious that if the candidates for common causes are restricted in advance then it is a simple matter to give artificial examples which show that among possible causes given in advance no common cause can be found. The ease with which such artificial examples are constructed makes it obvious that the same holds true in significant scientific investigations. When the possible causes of diseases are restricted, for example, it is often difficult for physicians to be able to find a common cause among the given set of candidates.

Proposition II.   *The common cause of proposition* I *can always be constructed so as to be deterministic.*

Again, without restriction, determinism is always open to us. On the other hand, it is easy to impose some natural principles of symmetry that exclude deterministic causes when the correlations are strictly probabilistic, i.e., the correlations between the events at the phenomenological level are not themselves deterministic. Explicit formulations of these principles of symmetry are given in the appendix.

Proposition III.   *Conditions of symmetry can easily be imposed such that strictly probabilistic correlations between phenomenologically observed events must have as a common cause one that is strictly probabilistic.*

This last proposition is special in nature, of course. It refers to principles of symmetry discussed in the appendix. The conditions are sufficient but not necessary. It would be desirable to find significant necessary and sufficient conditions that require the common cause to be probabilistic rather than deterministic in character.

Finally, I state one application to quantum mechanics.

Proposition IV.   *There are correlated phenomenological data that cannot have a common cause that is theoretically consistent with quantum mechanics, because there can be no joint probability distribution of the data, as described in proposition* I.

The existence of joint probability distributions in quantum mechanics is discussed in some detail in chapter 4.

I end the chapter with this summary statement: *In general, causality is probabilistic, not deterministic in character, and consequently no inconsistency exists between randomness in nature and the existence of valid causal laws.*

APPENDIX ON COMMON CAUSES

In this appendix I present a number of theorems about inferences from phenomenological correlations to common causes. In the framework of quantum mechanics, the theorems are mainly theorems about hidden variables. Most of the proofs will not be given, but references will be cited where these proofs may be found. The content of this appendix follows closely the first part of Suppes and Zanotti (1984).

To emphasize conceptual matters and to keep technical simplicity in the forefront, I consider only two-valued random variables taking the values ± 1. We shall also assume symmetry for these random variables in that their expectations will be zero and thus they will each have a positive variance of one. For emphasis we state:

GENERAL ASSUMPTION

The phenomenological random variables $X_1, \ldots, X_N$ *have possible values* ± 1, *with means* $E(X_i) = 0$, $1 \leq i \leq N$.

We also use the notation X, Y, and Z for phenomenological random variables. We use the notation $E(XY)$ for covariance which for these symmetric random variables is also the same as their correlation $\rho(X, Y)$.

The basic meaning of *common cause* that we shall assume is that when two random variables, say X and Y are given, then in order for a hidden variable λ to be labeled a common cause, it must render the random variables independent, that is,

$$(1) \qquad E(XY|\lambda) = E(X|\lambda)E(Y|\lambda)$$

TWO DETERMINISTIC THEOREMS

We begin with a theorem asserting a deterministic result. It says that if two random variables have a strictly negative correlation then any cause in the sense of (1) must be deterministic, that is, the conditional variances of the two random variables, given the hidden variable λ must be zero. We use the notation $\sigma(X|\lambda)$ for the conditional standard deviation of X given λ, and its square is, of course, the conditional variance.

Theorem 1 (Suppes and Zanotti, 1976b). *If*:

  (i) $E(XY|\lambda) = E(X|\lambda)E(Y|\lambda)$
  (ii) $\rho(X,Y) = -1$

then:

$$\sigma(X|\lambda) = \sigma(Y|\lambda) = 0$$

The second theorem asserts that the only thing required to have a common cause for N random variables is that they have a joint probability distribution. This theorem is conceptually important in relation to the long history of hidden-variable theorems in quantum mechanics. For example, in the original proof of Bell's inequalities, Bell (1964) assumed a causal hidden variable in the sense of (1) and derived from this assumption his inequalities. What theorem 2 shows is that the assumption of a hidden variable is not necessary in such discussions—it is sufficient to remain at the phenomenological level. Once we know that there exists a joint probability distribution, then there must be a causal hidden variable and in fact this hidden variable may be constructed so as to be deterministic.

Theorem 2 (Suppes and Zanotti, 1981). *Given phenomenological random variables $X_1, \ldots, X_N$, then there exists a hidden variable λ, a common cause such that*

$$E(X_1, \ldots, X_N|\lambda) = E(X_1|\lambda) \ldots E(X_N|\lambda)$$

if and only if there exists a joint probability distribution of $X_1, \ldots, X_N$. Moreover, λ may be constructed as a deterministic cause, i.e., for $1 \leq i \leq N$

$$\sigma(X_i|\lambda) = 0$$

EXCHANGEABILITY

We now turn to imposing some natural symmetry conditions both at a phenomenological and at a theoretical level. The main principle of symmetry we shall use is that of exchangeability. Two random variables X and Y of the class we are studying are said to be exchangeable if the following probabilistic equality is satisfied:

$$(2) \qquad P(X=1, Y=-1) = P(X=-1, Y=1)$$

The first theorem we state shows that if two random variables are exchangeable at the phenomenological level, then there exists a hidden causal variable satisfying the additional restriction that they have the same conditional expectation if and only if their correlation is nonnegative.

Theorem 3 (Suppes and Zanotti, 1980). *If X and Y are exchangeable, then there exists a hidden variable λ such that*

(1) *λ is a common cause of* X *and* Y
(2) $E(X|\lambda) = E(Y|\lambda)$

if and only if

$$\rho(X,Y) \geq 0$$

There are several remarks to be made about this theorem. First, the phenomenological principle of symmetry, namely, the principle of exchangeability, has not been used in physics as explicitly as one might expect. In the context of the kinds of experiments ordinarily used to test hidden-variable theories the requirement of phenomenological exchangeability is uncontroversial. On the other hand, the theoretical requirement of identity of conditional distributions does not have the same status. We emphasize that we refer here to the expected causal effect of λ. Obviously the actual causal effects will in general be quite different. We certainly would concede that in many physical situations this principle may be too strong. The point of our theorems about it is to show that once such a strong theoretical principle of symmetry is required then exchangeable and negatively correlated random variables cannot satisfy it.

Theorem 4 strengthens theorem 3 to show that when the correlations are strictly between zero and one then the common cause cannot be deterministic.

Theorem 4 (Suppes and Zanotti, 1984). *Given the conditions of theorem 3, if* $0<\rho(X,Y)<1$ *then* λ *cannot be deterministic, i.e.,* $\sigma(X|\lambda)$, $\sigma(Y|\lambda) \neq 0$.

Proof. We first observe that under the assumptions we have made:

$$\text{Min}\{P(X=1, Y=-1), P(X=1, Y=1), P(X=-1, Y=-1)\}>0$$

Now, let Ω be the probability space on which all random variables are defined. Let $\mathcal{A}=\{A_i\}$, $1\leq i\leq N$ and $\mathcal{H}=\{H_j\}$, $1\leq j\leq M$ be two partitions of Ω. We say that $\mathcal{H}$ is a *refinement of* $\mathcal{A}$ *in probability* if and only if for all i and j we have:

$$\text{If } P(A_i\cap H_j)>0 \text{ then } P(A_i\cap H_j)=P(H_j)$$

Now let λ be a causal random variable for X and Y in the sense of theorem 3, and let λ have induced partition $\mathcal{H}=\{H_j\}$, which without loss of generality may be assumed finite. Then λ is deterministic iff $\mathcal{H}$ is a refinement in probability of the partition $\mathcal{A}=\{A_i\}$ generated by X and Y, for assume, by way of contradiction that this is not the case. Then there must exist i and j such that $P(A_i\cap H_j)>0$ and

$$P(A_i\cap H_j)<P(H_j)$$

but then $0<P(A_i|H_j)<1$.

We next show that if λ is deterministic then $E(X|\lambda)\neq E(Y|\lambda)$, which will complete the proof.

Let, as before, $\mathcal{H}=\{H_j\}$ be the partition generated by λ. Since we know that

$$\sum_j P(X=1, Y=-1, H_j)=P(X=1, Y=-1)>0$$

there must be an H_j such that

$$P(X=1, Y=-1, H_j)>0$$

but since λ is deterministic, $\mathcal{H}$ must be a refinement of $\mathcal{A}$ and thus as already proved

$$P(X=1, \ Y=-1|H_j)=1$$

whence

$$P(X=1, \ Y=1|H_j)=0$$
$$P(X=-1, \ Y=1|H_j)=0$$
$$P(X=-1, \ Y=-1|H_j)=0$$

and consequently we have

(3)
$$P(X=1|H_j)=P(Y=-1|H_j)=1$$
$$P(X=-1|H_j)=P(Y=1|H_j)=0$$

Remembering that $E(X|\lambda)$ is a function of λ and thus of the partition $\mathcal{H}$, we have from (3) at once that

$$E(X|\lambda) \neq E(Y|\lambda).$$

4

Uncertainty

The third dogma of neotraditional metaphysics I listed in chapter 1 is the possibility of certain knowledge. From Descartes to Russell, a central theme of modern philosophy has been to set forth a method by which certainty can be achieved and at the same time to find a basis of knowledge that is adequate for the remaining superstructure. The introduction of the concept of sense data and the history of the development of the use of this concept are the history of the search for certainty in knowledge, especially in the empirical tradition, as an alternative to direct rational knowledge of the universe. I applaud the criticism of rationalism and the justifiable concern not to accept the possibility of direct knowledge of the world without experience. But it was a desire to compete with the kind of grounding that rationalism offered that motivated the mistaken additional step of attempting to ground knowledge in experience in a way that guaranteed certainty for the results.

Within this tradition of modern philosophy, there have been two kinds of knowledge about which claims of certainty have been prominent. One kind is the claim about sense data just mentioned. I may, for example, not be able to say with certainty that I am looking at a red apple, but I can claim with certainty I am perceiving a red patch.

The second kind of knowledge concerns logical or a priori knowledge. Claims of certainty have often been made about logical truths or truths of arithmetic. For example, it is claimed that one knows for certain that $7+5 = 12$ or that either it is going to rain or it is not going to rain tomorrow.

Both of these views seem to me to be mistaken, but it is not very original on my part to say this. Criticisms of both the doctrine of immediacy of knowledge and the doctrine of a priori certainty for logical truths are now widespread. On the one hand, it is claimed from the standpoint of perception that there is no such thing as immediate knowledge. The general psychological literature on perception certainly tends to support the view that perceptual knowledge is never immediate but depends upon a conceptual framework of interpretation. In a similar vein, the hope of drawing any sharp distinction between logical and empirical truths has been severely challenged, and the special status classically assigned to logical or mathematical knowledge is considered of a dubious character.

This chapter is organized along the following lines. I first challenge the traditional doctrine about the a priori certainty of mathematical knowledge. I next discuss Euler's three senses of certainty and then errors of measurement. The latter topic permits a natural move to quantum mechanics and the Heisenberg uncertainty principle. I end with a section on the meaning of probability statements.

CERTAINTY OF MATHEMATICAL KNOWLEDGE

There is a point about the problem of certainty of mathematical knowledge that seems to me not to have been sufficiently emphasized. It concerns the prevalence of the publication of corrections to mathematical articles. If the truths of mathematics are known a priori, it seems absurd to find that corrections to mathematical articles are more prevalent than corrections to articles in any other domain of science. Without giving the matter further thought, one would anticipate that in the publication of empirical articles dealing with complex experiments and observations of matters of fact one would expect errors to be made and corrections to those errors to be published. Of course, I have the clear distinction in mind between different people performing the "same" experiment and therefore attempting to replicate the experimental results, and a given individual publishing a statement of errors made in the performance of an experiment. Any of us familiar with the complex problems of performing anything should be suspicious, indeed skeptical, of the fact that so seldom are errors corrected in connection with the actual performance of experiments. On the other hand, this is common in mathematics, and it is part of my analysis of certainty to inquire why this is so.

The answer lies near at hand. The working criterion for judging a piece of mathematics is really a radically empirical criterion. Whatever is to be said about the status of mathematical truths, in actual fact the correctness of a given piece of mathematics is judged empirically by the evidence directly presented in the doing of the mathematics, and consequently is the reason for labeling mathematics radically empirical. Because the evidence is presented with a completeness not characteristic of any other area of empirical science, it is possible to detect errors and to bring these errors forcefully to the attention of the author.[1]

The canon on which errors are detected is a clear one. The proof as given either satisfies a particular criterion of proof, or defects are found. This criterion of proof is not wholly formal; yet a case can be made that if an argument persists about the correctness of a proof, the tendency is to resolve the issue by an ever-increasing approximation to a formal proof. As the kind of published correction I am referring to indicates, there is in a practical sense no realistic way to claim that truths of mathematics have a special status and a certainty not characteristic of truth claims about other domains of experience.

It could be said that in so strongly endorsing a radical empiricism for mathematics I am in fact strongly endorsing a particular philosophy of mathematics, namely, some variant of formalism. This does not seem to be the case, however, because for better or worse approximately the same canon of proof is applied in evaluating a published piece of mathematics, whatever the underlying philosophy of mathematics of the author or reader. Any concern about the foundational philosophy of the author is almost irrelevant to the actual evaluation of the correctness of the proof. There can, of course, be disagreements about exactly what principles of inference are acceptable, for example, the well-known disagreements about accepting the axiom of choice, but the published corrections never hinge on such matters. The errors that are corrected occur within the framework of principles accepted by the author.

---

[1] I undertook a small investigation to support the view of mathematics as radically empirical in comparison with experimental disciplines. For this purpose I compared for the year 1980 the number of published corrections in Volumes **27** and **28** of *Perception and Psychophysics*, a primarily experimental journal, and Volume **8** of *The Annals of Statistics*, a primarily mathematical journal. No corrections were published in *Perception and Psychophysics*. In contrast, seven notes correcting errors were published for the same period in *The Annals of Statistics*.

I shall try to make my point in another way. Whatever the claims may be about mathematical intuition, the correspondence between the notion of logical consequence and the syntactical notion of derivation is used to convert the criterion of correctness of proof from a general intuitive and semantical notion, if you will, to a syntactical and empirical notion, checkable ultimately in a completely finitistic empirical fashion. I claim that this ultimate empirical check is the real test of the correctness of a piece of mathematics, and the necessity of publishing the important part of the evidence makes it correct for me to claim that mathematics is the example of a radically empirical subject par excellence. The certainty we find in mathematics arises not from any intuitive or a priori consideration but simply from the discreteness and easily exhibited character of the evidence offered in support of a particular (empirical) claim.

EULER'S THREE SENSES OF CERTAINTY

Among Euler's letters to a German princess, the one dated April 14, 1761, is concerned with three senses of certainty. The first, which we would probably call perceptual certainty, is what Euler calls *la certitude physique*. It corresponds to what I have identified earlier as the seeing of a red patch, although Euler does not connect it to sense data but with the seeing of physical events. His example is seeing that the Austrians have been in Berlin and have created a great deal of havoc. His second sense of certainty, which is the sense of mathematical proof I was just discussing, is that of *certitude logique ou démonstrative*. Euler's examples of demonstrative certainty are, as you might expect, the truths of geometry demonstrated from Euclid's axioms. Finally, his third sense, which is what we know based on what we are told by others, is that of *certitude morale*. Our faith in their truthfulness leads us to call this a sense of moral certainty. His examples of moral certainty are our knowledge of the existence of Julius Caesar or Augustus, or our moral certainty that the Russians have been in Berlin. In general, his examples are historical facts.

These three senses of certainty have a strong basis in common sense. Although my remarks have tended to draw together Euler's physical and demonstrative certainty, a distinction definitely exists. I have tried to make a distinction that I think is

appropriate by calling mathematics the radically empirical subject, because it is the only scientific discipline that does not describe empirical data in summary terms, but actually publishes the
relevant bulk of the data, namely, the mathematical proofs themselves. The mere fact that the proofs can be published, thereby
offering the data directly, is an important distinction. If we compare any report of a complicated physical experiment, we see how
much our acceptance of the experimental results is a matter of
Euler's moral certainty. We must believe that the account of the
investigator is a faithful one. If we have reasons for serious doubt
or skepticism, we have no direct way to check the correctness of
the experimental report, except to look for another instance of
the experiment reported in the literature or, to undertake, if we
are competent, a replication of the experiment.

Another sense in which the radical empiricism of mathematics
can be separated from the empiricism of the rest of science is that
the empirical criterion for the correctness of a proof ultimately
depends on a purely syntactic criterion applied to the words and
symbols of the proof. This is not the case in the reporting of scientific experiments. On the other hand, it must be recognized that in
practice this distinction is not so sharp as I would like it to be. I
am pressing the viewpoint of radical empiricism toward mathematics in order to provide a basis for criticism of one of the classical foundations of nonempirical thought, and I think the case is
still good for insisting that the criterion of correctness of proof is
ultimately syntactical. Syntax, however, only makes sense in
terms of semantic interpretation. In practice it is usually the
meaning of the words used and not their precise syntactic form
that is used to evaluate the correctness of a proof.

I need to be careful in formulating this point about meaning. In
the case of scientific experiments there is also much common
agreement about meaning expressed in facts that are used as an
understood framework for an experiment. It is assumed that
many of these basic facts can be checked by repetition of past experiments when required. The same is characteristic of
mathematical proofs. There is a considerable assumption of understood meaning in the formulation of proofs, but it is also
understood that a challenge to any of these understood meanings
and the use of informal language can be checked by a breakdown
into simpler meanings that are agreed upon. This breakdown into
simpler meanings can ultimately be referred to a syntactical

criterion, and satisfying the syntactical criterion is then a direct empirical task. In practice, corrections to mathematical proofs do not resort to a pure syntactic criterion, just as replications of experiments that obtain different results do not investigate at the most primitive level all aspects of the assumed framework. What is important, however, is to recognize in both cases the possibility in principle of such reduction to elementary or primitive components.

For those not comfortable with my ultimate syntactic view of proofs—and many mathematicians will not be—the radical empiricism of mathematics can rest on an analysis of its practice. Much more of the relevant data are published than is the case for scientific experiments. This is the source of the many corrections to mathematical publications, which are not found in the experimental sciences (see p. 78, n. 1).

Surprisingly, an empirical view about mathematics is tacitly recognized by Kant in his reflection on the nature of metaphysical certainty in *An Inquiry into the Distinctness of the Principles of Natural Theology and Morals* (1764). Here are the pertinent passages:

> Mathematics in its inferences and proofs considers its universal knowledge as concretely in its signs, while philosophy considers its as continuing astractly alongside its signs. This makes a noteworthy difference in the way each attains certainty, for, since the signs of mathematics are sensuous instruments of knowledge, we can, with the same assurance we have in that which we see, also know that we have left no concept out of sight, that each individual comparison is made according to simple rules, etc. Attention herein is greatly facilitated by not having to consider the things in their universal sense but rather signs in the individual cognition we have of them.
> . . . In geometry, where the signs have in addition a similarity to the designated things, the evidence is even greater, though in calculations with letters the certainty is just as dependable. (Beck edn, pp. 276–277)

In this discussion I have acknowledged the ordinary distinction between mathematical proofs and scientific experiments; however, I have argued that both are empirical in character but with the most radical empirical claim being for mathematical proofs rather than for scientific experiments, contrary to the usual view. In practice, Euler's third sense of moral certainty is the one we use most extensively in accepting the results of mathematical or scientific work by others. Interestingly enough, this sense of certainty has received much less systematic analysis, undoubtedly because it has been felt in the classical philosophical tradition alluded to earlier that the two sources of genuine certainty are immediate perception and a priori truths. In this classical tradition a similar place is not assigned to knowledge obtained from communication with other individuals. The thrust of what I have said, however, is to argue that in many cases the first two senses actually reduce to the third. This third sense requires trust and cooperation among a community of persons with common interests. The psychological and social aspects of such communities have been almost entirely neglected in traditional philosophical analyses of certainty, which have emphasized a Robinson Crusoe approach to knowledge.

Euler's three senses of certainty introduce a useful set of distinctions and one that we all recognize in practice. I want to be clear that I do not accept the elevation of the distinctions he introduces to a fundamental epistemological status. All three senses are varying senses of empirical certainty which are fallible and subject to continual correction.

I now turn to more specific methodological remarks about certainty. This has been an important topic in the methodology of physics and more generally in the methodology of measurement. I first review some of the methodological issues and then reflect on their philosophical significance.

ERRORS OF MEASUREMENT

As scientific methodology and probability theory developed together in the burst of intellectual activity that occurred in the eighteenth century, it was recognized not only that errors in measurement occur, but also that a systematic theory of these errors can be given. Fundamental memoirs on the analysis of errors in observation were written by Simpson, Lagrange, Laplace, Gauss, and others. What is important about these memoirs, however, is that there was no examination of the question of the existence or nonexistence of an exact value for the quantity being measured. It was implicit in these eighteenth-century developments, just as it was implicit in Laplace's entire philosophy, that probabilistic considerations, including errors, arise from ignorance of true causes, and that the physical universe is so constituted that in principle we should be able to achieve the exact true values of physical quantities we desire to measure.

This same attitude persisted in the nineteenth century, and there was an atmosphere of confidence in being able to measure true values exactly, so that in important treatises (for example, Laplace's *Celestial Mechanics* or Maxwell's *Electricity and Magnetism*) little attention was given to the analysis of errors. In particular, there occurred no detailed quantitative or mathematical analyses of errors. It was implicitly assumed that it was simply a matter of tedious and time-consuming effort to refine the values reported to one more significant digit. The assumption that the fixed true value of a physical measurement can be found is conceptually linked to the attitude of strict determinism enunciated by Laplace and also to the view that every event has a strict determinant cause.

But there is no hope of actually carrying out a program of strict certainty in the sense of obtaining the exact and true value of a continuous physical quantity because of the subtlety and complexity of the interacting causes. From a working standpoint, there is little doubt that this was Laplace's attitude. Yet it would be a mistake to emphasize the primacy of this working attitude of Laplace and other astronomers and physicists, for the theoretical attitude that with sufficient effort a next significant digit can always be obtained is constantly implicit in nineteenth-century science. A curious and conceptually interesting fact is that hardly anyone enunciated the sensible thesis that this was all a mistake— that there were continual random fluctuations, and that the concept of an exact value had no clear meaning. A notable and philosophically important exception was C. S. Peirce (1891 and 1892).[2] The almost overwhelming adoption of the possibility of

---

[2] After citing Epicurus approvingly, Peirce says 'For we now see clearly that the peculiar function of the molecular hypothesis in physics is to open an entry for the calculus of probabilities' (1892, p.322). A few pages later Peirce has these wise words to say about errors of observation or measurement: 'Try to verify any law of nature, and you will find that the more precise your observations, the more certain they will be to show irregular

achieving certainty in science seems from the vantage point of the latter part of the twentieth century naive and unsupported by the evidence. The development of statistical mechanics and the kinetic theory of heat provided the right setting for sound views like those of Peirce to become dominant, but nothing of the sort happened. Certainly about the true value of a continuous quantity requires infinite precision of measurement, and the issues about certainty in classical physics all involve such quantities. The hegemony of theory over practice is reflected in the faith that there were no barriers to approaching asymptotically such precision.

The development of quantum mechanics in the first three decades of the twentieth century finally mustered strong enough evidence against this fantasy of certainty to dislodge it. It was reluctantly, but conclusively, recognized that it did not make sense to claim that any continuous physical quantity could be measured with arbitrary precision in conjunction with the simultaneous measurement of other related physical quantities. Thus, in the strict determinism of Laplace, to predict the deterministic course of events, we require the simultaneous exact measurement of the position and momentum of each particle. It is precisely the point of the fundamental facts of quantum mechanics, however, that such a simultaneously precise measurement of position and momentum is not possible, and, most important, it is not possible in principle. The inability to make exact measurements is not due to technological inadequacies of measuring equipment; rather, it arises from the fundamental principle of uncertainty first enunciated by Heisenberg about half a century ago.

Before turning to the uncertainty principle, there is a remark that needs to be made about the relation between inexact measurement and apparently certain qualitative statements. I discuss this matter more closely at the end of the chapter, but I want to mention here that I have no quarrel with the ordinary use of the word 'certain' and its other forms in ordinary talk, as when, for example, I say 'Of course, it is certain that Abraham Lincoln was once President of the United States', or any of the other stan-

departures from the law. We are accustomed to ascribe these, and I do not say wrongly, to errors of observation; yet we cannot usually account for such errors in any antecedently probable way. Trace their causes back far enough, and you will be forced to admit they are always due to arbitrary determination, or chance.' (1892, p. 329).

dard examples of *certitude morale* given by Euler.[3] It is just that when it comes to detailed and quantitative knowledge the search for certainty is bound to be frustrated in principle. I will not say more now—I expand upon this point later—but it is worth emphasizing that I do not intend that there be a direct application of Heisenberg's uncertainty principle to the qualitative statements of certainty so often made in ordinary discourse. Quantum-mechanical principles cannot be used to prove as much as some people would like about ordinary experience and about the incorrect character of ordinary talk. On the other hand, the philosophical search for certainty does necessarily run up against the central features of the most important scientific theory of the twentieth century. If, in the grand tradition of Aristotle, Descartes, and Kant, we want to ground our knowledge of the physical world in a detailed theory, then the kind of certainty asked for above all by Descartes is mistaken. On the other hand, if we look at Descartes and others from a psychological standpoint, not from the standpoint of our quantitative knowledge of the physical world, we run up against a similar set of difficulties. The more detailed we get in our phenomenological effort at certainty, the more that certainty recedes in front of us. But it would be a digression to explore these psychological matters in further detail at this point.

HEISENBERG'S UNCERTAINTY PRINCIPLE

Even though I shall argue that the Heisenberg uncertainty principle is congruent with commonsense experience, it is worth examining somewhat more carefully its meaning, because it represents such a conceptual departure from classical physics. There are several different ways of stating the principle, but perhaps the one easiest to explain is that pairs of conjugate variables, of which position and momentum are an example, must have the product of their variances greater than some positive constant. By *variance* I mean the variance of a probability distribution, and thus I have implicitly required in this formulation that the physical variables considered be random variables in the

[3] Compare this passage from Wittgenstein (1969, p. 6): 'Certainty is *as it were* a tone of voice in which one declares how things are, but one does not infer how things are from one's own certainty.'

sense of probability theory. (A random variable is some—measurable—function defined on an unknown sample space that takes real numbers as values.) The distribution of a random variable is merely the probability distribution that tells us for each real number the probability that the random variable will have a value equal to or greater than that real number. In most work in probability theory, random variables and not sample spaces are the objects studied, and we can look upon our physical variables, for example, position and momentum, as such random variables. Put in these terms, the point of Heisenberg's uncertainty principle is that the distribution of position and momentum cannot be made arbitrarily sharp or peaked at a point of "true" value.

Several aspects of the uncertainty principle are surprising from the standpoint of the way probabilistic ideas are used in other parts of science. To examine the principle in some detail will give us a deeper feeling for the novel way in which quantum mechanics has retreated from certainty and, in my judgment, has thereby returned scientific matters closer to the conceptual framework of ordinary experience, paradoxical as this may sound when thought of in light of the history of classical physics.

The first point to note about the uncertainty principle is that, looked at simply as a statement about the probability distribution of two physical quantities or variables, it may not seem surprising. Consider, for example, the parallel situation with measurements of height and weight of the present population of the United States. Intuitively we expect variation in the height and weight of members of a population, and it has nothing to do with our conception of certainty to find this variation. We know that the estimated distributions of height and weight in the American population will have variances or standard deviations such that their products are greater than a very large positive constant.

The difference, however, in the case of quantum mechanics is that such variation is found in "identical" particles submitted to "identical" experimental preparations. Two criteria of identity are at work here. One is the criterion concerning the macroscopic experimental equipment, which says that the equipment remains the same when different particles pass through it. The second criterion of identity is that as particles are prepared to pass through the measuring equipment, the only difference in the particles is one of numerical identity. For example, if two electrons are passed through the equipment, it is assumed that these electrons have the same mass and charge and, in fact, have no physical difference except one of numerical identity. The retreat from certainty expressed in the Heisenberg uncertainty principle is within this framework of the only difference being one of numerical identity. Deterministically, we should expect exactly the same phenomena upon repetitions of the experiment, that is, upon successive particles going through the apparatus, but this is not what occurs.

I emphasize again that if we take a commonsense viewpoint the results are not at all surprising. When we measure characteristics of the population of a country, look at the agricultural production of a given piece of land from year to year, or measure essentially any ordinary variables, we find variation in their values from one occasion to another or from one place to another. Of course, we explain this variation by assuming there are some features or properties that are different in the two situations. However, it is important to note that even though we have a kind of "stock" explanation—by the principle of sufficient reason, the difference is due to difference on some features—we are in ordinary experience not committed to identify the source of the difference, and we simply accept it as a fact of life. This is indeed the theory of chance that Hume identifies as the vulgar theory.

It is also worth noting that there is considerable variation in the attitude toward explaining differences in similar phenomena occurring in ordinary experience. For example, if the production of wheat on a piece of land varies drastically from one year to the next, an attempt will be made to explain the variation as being due to the weather. On the other hand, if we contemplate the three offspring of a man and a woman and notice the physical variation in the three offspring we do not ordinarily attempt to explain in any refined way the source of the difference. I would in fact claim that we are using something close to a "vulgar theory of chance". If we were to ask individuals how they would explain the variation in children of common parentage, on many occasions we would get remarks about random combinations of genes, even though current detailed theory of how genes combine to determine hereditary features would not be well understood by the individual giving this response. In other words, I am saying that the extension of strict determinism to ordinary experience is an unwarranted philosophical extension, and we already have in the warp and woof of ordinary talk implicit distinctions concerning what can be given a further explanation and what cannot.

Keeping in mind these ordinary examples, it is conceptually easy to see why there has been a search for hidden variables in the case of quantum-mechanical phenomena. If electrons that are identical, except in numerical identity, are passed through the same apparatus but different results are obtained, then there must be hidden causal variables that account for these differences. I will not review again the recent work on hidden variables mentioned in chapter 2. The thrust of that discussion was to claim that the effort to find an appropriate theory of hidden variables was currently deemed unsuccessful. We are faced with accepting a different attitude toward certainty, reflected, I am claiming, in parts of ordinary experience other than those that have led naturally to the extension to strict determinism. We are thus currently in the position of saying that particles that are identical, except in numerical identity, do perform differently in interaction with measuring equipment, and we simultaneously have an argument against strict determinism, strict causality, and strict certainty.

I have tried to present the principle of uncertainty so far in the discussion as if it represents a rather natural extension of ordinary experience, but an extension that takes a different fork in the road than that taken in the past by classical physics. It is, I am claiming, as much a part of ordinary experience to find variation as to find uniformity in what appear to be initially identical circumstances. I have given as examples the appearance of children of common parentage, and the productivity of adjacent pieces of land that are sowed with seed in the same fashion. This experience of variation under identical circumstances is at least as common as success in the search for concealed causes.

I would, however, be making a serious mistake if I tried to persuade you that quantum mechanics at its most basic conceptual level represents simply a return to enlightened common sense, especially enlightened common sense toward fantasies of strict determinism or strict certainty. There are some fundamentally new conceptual twists and turns in quantum mechanics, and I would like to describe these qualitatively before returning to their relation to common sense to see if once again we can muster a consistent picture of an attitude toward certainty, running all the way from quantum mechanics to the enlightened but scientifically casual talk of most of us, most of the time.

QUANTUM MECHANICS AND CLASSICAL PROBABILITY THEORY

From the standpoint of a methodology of probability and statistics that has been evolving since the eighteenth century and that I have described in part, especially in chapter 3, there is a natural way to formulate the problems of quantum mechanics as we accept the principle of uncertainty. The natural probabilistic question is simply to ask for the joint distribution of random variables of interest—the joint distribution of position and momentum, the joint distribution of spin and position, and so forth. As we pose the problem this way, two rather separate questions arise at once. First, can we actually calculate within the framework of ordinary quantum mechanics such joint distributions? And second, more or less independent of the first question, can we start from scratch and formulate the theory *de novo* as a probabilistic theory with the appropriate distributions of the random variables of interest? If probability theory is to have its natural and classical place in quantum mechanics, it would seem that the answers to both questions should be affirmative, even if the constructive details of calculation prove onerous and difficult.

As it turns out, the story is more subtle and interesting. By taking the expectation of the appropriate quantity, we can calculate in classical quantum mechanics what corresponds to the characteristic function of the joint distribution. Then, by classical mathematical methods, in particular the method of Fourier inversion, we can obtain what should be the joint distribution corresponding to the characteristic function. Unfortunately, it is a well-known mathematical fact that not every characteristic function generates a proper distribution, so that when we calculate, say, the characteristic function of what should be a joint distribution of position and momentum, we find upon Fourier inversion that the distribution is not a proper one. The problem is not at all complicated in many cases and has a simple intuitive interpretation. The joint probability distribution obtained for position and momentum, for example, will not be nonnegative for all regions of space and time. And of course, from a conceptual standpoint, we have no natural or direct way of interpreting negative probabilities. It makes no sense in terms of our standard concepts to talk about the probability of an event being $-1/4$.

Unfortunately, the difficulties that arise here are not easily avoided by taking the second route suggested earlier, that is, by formulating the theory *de novo* as a proper probabilistic process. Such attempts have been unsuccessful—unsuccessful in the sense that they have not been able to reproduce the important phenomena that are characteristic of quantum mechanics and that are the touchstone of its empirical validity.

For this reason, let us consider in more detail these peculiar joint distributions that are not proper probability distributions and the broad view of the physical world they lead us to.

In early work on interpretation of quantum-mechanical probabilities, I have been led to the conclusion that the appropriate interpretation of the improper joint distributions is that no joint measurement is possible. The Heisenberg uncertainty principle under this view is misleading because it suggests that we can have joint measurement but that the results will satisfy the uncertainty relationship as expressed in the product of the standard deviations or variances of the two measurements. It is worth noting the rather peculiar way in which the Heisenberg uncertainty relation has a genuine probabilistic interpretation, even though no joint distribution exists. From the improper joint distributions, we obtain proper marginal distributions for individual variables. From an ordinary statistical or probabilistic standpoint, the peculiarity of this situation must be emphasized. The uncertainty relation is never the kind of relation that would arise naturally from probabilistic considerations of processes or phenomena. The first question one would ask would be about the covariance of the two variables, that is, how they relate to each other in terms of their covariation. Only after much search in other directions would one ever come upon an expression in terms of the product of the variances. From a broad statistical standpoint, two random variables could satisfy the requirements of an uncertainty relationship in terms of the product of the variances and yet be completely deterministically dependent upon each other, that is, given the value of one, we would know exactly the value of the other. For example, two identically distributed random variables for which there is total dependence would have such a deterministic relation to each other.

Consequently, it is easy to move to the argument that no measurement is possible, because precise point values of position and momentum cannot be assigned simultaneously. According to this view, then, it is not possible to give a meaningful interpretation to the joint measurement. Therefore the real meaning of the

uncertainty principle under closer analysis is simply the categor-
ical statement that the two physical variables cannot be jointly
and simultaneously measured.

From this inability to make simultaneous measurements and
thus to observe the joint events defined in terms of position and
momentum, I have argued that we get the most direct and
straightforward argument for the nonclassical logic of quantum
mechanics. Let me quote the formulation of the argument I have
used in the past (Suppes, 1966b).

Premise 1: *In physical or empirical contexts involving the
application of probability theory as a mathematical discipline,
the functional or working logic of importance is the logic of
the events or propositions to which probability is assigned,
not the logic of qualitative or intuitive statements to be made
about the mathematically formulated theory.* (In the classical
applications of probability theory, this logic of events is a
Boolean algebra of sets.)

Premise 2: *The algebra of events should satisfy the
requirement that a probability is assigned to every event or
element of the algebra.*

Premise 3: *In the case of quantum mechanics, probabilities may be assigned to events such as position in a certain
region or momentum within given limits, but the probability
of the conjunction of two such events does not necessarily
exist.*

Conclusion: *The functional or working logic of quantum
mechanics is not classical.*

Given this conclusion, one can work out in a positive constructive
fashion the logic of quantum mechanics and end up with an
algebra of events that is not closed under arbitrary intersections
or unions because, in general, such events are not observable
according to premise 3. There are, however, a number of reasons
for moving very slowly to the adoption of a new logic, especially a
logic that is clearly weaker than classical logic. Those who have
rushed pell-mell into the advocacy of a nonclassical logic for
quantum mechanics of the kind just described have been guilty of
passing rapidly through the zone of uncertainty to a new kind of
certainty, namely, a certainty of not being able to make measurements at all. There were clear signposts along the way to make

one suspicious of such a rapid passage through the territory. Anyone who has spent some time on the history of physics is very much aware of the fact that it is important to trust the intuitions of physicists, even if matters are not put in a polished logical or mathematical fashion. Moreover, anyone who has listened to physicists talk about quantum mechanics for an extended period realizes how special and arcane are not only their concepts, but also their ways of using and thinking about these concepts. On the other hand, one cannot fail to be impressed by the powerful way they can bring this battery of concepts to bear on a subtle and complex physical problem. Without question, quantum mechanics is *the* intellectual achievement of the twentieth century in terms of empirical science and possibly in terms of all science, including pure mathematics. The signpost that was not heeded in my own previous thinking about these matters was the Heisenberg uncertainty relationship.

The program of revision is to examine in much greater detail the probabilistic features of quantum mechanics. I think it will remain true that a revision in the classical algebra of events will be required, but it would be interesting to have the new algebra reflect more of the peculiar features of quantum mechanics than do partial Boolean algebras or arbitrary orthocomplemented partial orderings, the current leading candidates. Here is a simple example of what I mean. If we compute the marginal probability distributions of either position or momentum for the ground state of the one-dimensional linear harmonic oscillator, we find they each have normal or Gaussian distributions, and for the higher energy levels somewhat more complex but continuous distributions closely related to the normal. The point I want to focus on here is the implicit implication that each of these theoretical marginal distributions can be tested against empirical histograms made up of arbitrarily precise measurements. This arbitrary precision of measurement for individual variables seems unrealistic and is not in practice reflected in any of the data actually reported in the experimental literature. Similar considerations apply to variables like those of wavelength or frequency, and suggest a similar discussion of precision.

To summarize the point, there is currently a conceptual discrepancy between the theoretical results derivable by mathematical argument from basic assumptions about the expectation of a quantum-mechanical quantity and the empirical and informal talk of physicists about the Heisenberg uncertainty relation. From the standpoint of probability theory there remains an ambiguity about the concept of precision of measurement that has not yet been properly analyzed. Is there lurking in the background, as yet unanalyzed mathematically, a family of probability distributions that can replace the familiar classical distributions and have as their domains a coarser set of objects than the real numbers?

I have lingered over this example of uncertainty from quantum mechanics in some detail to illustrate how deeply embedded the concept is in the most fundamental physical science, and consequently how improbable and unlikely it is that we shall ever return to a concept of certainty close to that associated with classical physics and the philosophical tradition of both British empiricism and Kantian idealism.

MEANING OF PROBABILITY STATEMENTS

Because defense of certainty has come from another quarter, namely, from adherents of subjective probability, I end this chapter by examining more carefully the meaning of probability statements and saying what I think is the proper way to think about them in comparison with physical statements about mass, etc. In one sense the aim of this section is to find a middle way between purely subjective and purely objective theories of probability, but most of the technical issues dividing the various schools of thought on these matters are not discussed here. I am more concerned to challenge the existence of a sharp distinction between subjective and objective claims, for the pure form of either one does not leave a proper place for uncertainty. If we hold, as does the distinguished Italian mathematician and statistician Bruno de Finetti (1970/1974, pp. x–xi), that probability is entirely a subjective matter, then we should expect that, in ideal cases at least, we learn from experience how to eliminate probability and probabilistic considerations and replace them with certainty. Are we left in the end with probabilistic kinds of statements about the weather, our future health, and the state of the nation, or should we expect to have convergence to objective statements of certainty? Let us first consider the way such matters are expressed in ordinary talk. It will be wise to begin with a similar distinction between subjective and objective aspects of statements that are not about probability but about other physical properties. (I do not entirely like the bald distinction "subjective versus objective" but because it has been so widely used in the literature I shall continue to use it for the moment; for general background on the topics discussed in this section, see Stegmüller, 1973.)

Suppose I say in casual conversation with a friend 'A 1980 compact Chevrolet weighs somewhere between 2,000 and 3,000 pounds. In fact, I believe it weighs about 2,800 pounds.' The first sentence is not formulated in such a way as to make the expression of a propositional attitude clearly evident, but together with the second sentence, which is explicit on this point, it becomes so. My friend says in return 'Well, I think your estimates are about right, but I happen to have some current literature here and let's look up the data.' He gets a report, which shows that a 1980 Chevrolet Citation in the two-door hatchback model has a curb weight of 2,595 pounds. He then says 'Your estimate of 2,800 pounds was not too far off.'

It seems to me there are several things to be said about this hypothetical exchange—and although it is hypothetical I think it is rather typical of what does occur in much ordinary talk. First, we do not talk about beliefs, ordinarily, but about estimates. There are occasions when one would say 'I believe so and so', but it is at least as common and natural to talk about estimates. But I take this to be simply an explicit way of making clear that one does not believe that one knows the exact weight. The second point is that there is no really easy way to draw a sharp line in such talk between that which is subjective and that which is objective, and I am suspicious of the distinction at this level of discourse. In ordinary talk, we do not make anything like a firm distinction between the two, just as there is no firm distinction between deductive and inductive reasoning.

In such contexts, as in more scientific ones, the important distinction is whether more is to be learned from experience, that is, whether we believe that more information is available to improve our estimates of weight. Here again, a distinction is to be made. In one set of cases we are not really satisfied with our estimates, but we do not believe that information is currently available that can improve a current estimate that is rather crude from the standpoint of what one would really like to know. For example, suppose I would like to have a good estimate of how much Aristotle weighed when he was 17 years old. I think there is an extremely small chance we will ever be able to make an estimate that is accurate within a kilogram or a pound or two.

On the other hand, in the other kind of case, the information we have is quite sufficient for the purposes at hand. The data I just cited on a 1980 Chevrolet Citation are as accurate as we would want. In fact, it is not clear that it would be useful at all to refine the estimate to, for example, the nearest one-hundredth of a pound. The variation between cars of the same design would be greater that this precision, and I can think of no purpose, in the context of that earlier hypothetical discussion, when such more refined data would be of any use.

This distinction between being satisfied or not with the estimate introduces, I think, the basis for still another one. When we are not satisfied with an estimate, we can be in one of two situations. In the matter of the young Aristotle's weight, it is simply a historical accident that the appropriate information is not available to us. By some lucky chance there could be records yet to be found in some now unknown site in Greece that would give us such information. The other sort of case is one in which we are psychologically unsatisfied with the answer but have systematic scientific evidence that nothing better can be expected. There is a certain form of naive object realism, and I emphasize the word *object*, that seems to entail the view that individual objects have a fixed and rigid presence in the world. Under this view, it is psychological disappointment that biological objects, like ourselves, for example, do not have a constant weight. It does not make any sense to talk about my weight or your weight with any detailed accuracy because it will vary from day to day and even according to the time of day. It is only a kind of physical fiction to talk about one's weight as a definite amount. Of course, we could try to talk about the instantaneous weight at some given point in time, but this is not an interesting concept. The romantic view generated by naive object realism is bound to be disappointed. More subtle examples of physical objects' having an obvious loss of molecules, as reflected in our ability to detect their odor, show that there is no idealized constant weight in terms of a fixed number of molecules.

Our naive way of thinking so naturally tends to constants that it makes us uneasy to realize how much fluctuation there is in the real world, even in what we regard as constant objects. For example, when we reflect upon the most elementary physical facts, we all recognize that such a prominent object as the sun has a mass that in any given moment can only be known in grossest terms. It is a nonsensical sort of question, we realize, to ask for the weight of the sun, even at a given instant, to the nearest gram.

I emphasize again that I do not think there is any clear division between the subjective and objective character of statements about weight. Going back to my original example, I can even see the claim being made that the first statement that the weight of a 1980 Chevrolet is between 2,000 and 3,000 pounds is an "objective" statement, whereas the second estimate of the exact amount being about 2,800 pounds is subjective. What is at work in this example is often at work: we can give crude bounding estimates that are scarcely disputable and we can follow these crude bounding estimates by exact estimates that both the speaker and any listener know are not highly accurate and are, therefore, rather subjective, although it seems strange to put it that way.

The point I am driving at in the case of weight or mass, which applies to other familiar physical properties, should be clear. There is not really an interesting and strong metaphysical distinction between subjective and objective, or between belief and knowledge. Here I am saying something that is probably rather close to de Finetti. The important distinction is between the information being complete in practice or in principle and being incomplete with the possibility of learning more. In the same spirit I avoid a sharp distinction between epistemic and metaphysical proposition.

The direct application of these ideas to probability leads me to diverge from de Finetti. What I have been saying about weight or mass, and implicitly about other standard physical properties, applies to statements about probability.

In the first place, there is the distinction between having complete or incomplete information, that is, putting it now in probabilistic terms, whether or not there is additional information we can condition on that will change the probability. There is a point here that I did not sufficiently emphasize earlier, namely, the point in time at which such considerations arise. This is especially true for properties of events as opposed to properties of objects. There are many events about which I can know more after they have occurred than I can at any time prior to their occurrence. Therefore, in talking about completeness of information it is important to stress at what point in time the matter is being discussed.

Many examples from physics illustrate completeness of information combined with a residue of uncertainty. Prior to the actual decay of a radioactive atom, I can do no better than to predict its decay according to an exponential law. The best that past experience can do for me is to let me, on the one hand, identify the nature of the atom—for example, is it an atom of radium, uranium etc.—and, on the other, to provide an extremely accurate estimate of the single parameter of the exponential distribution characteristic of that particular substance. Given the identification of the substance in pure form, for present simplified purposes, and the parameter of the exponential distribution prior to decay, nothing more can be said. Completeness of information has been attained in terms of current physical theory. A variety of other examples of a similar sort can easily be described on the basis of quantum-mechanical considerations.

The second distinction applies to probability in the same way that it applies to weight or mass. It is a matter of either being satisfied or not with the estimate given. In the case of radioactive decay, on best current theoretical grounds the information may be complete, but hard-line determinists are unsatisfied and disappointed in the character of the world as they find it. As I have sometimes put in other contexts, faced with radioactive decay such determinists have seen the truth and found it wanting. On the other hand, probability estimates, like weight estimates of large objects, can be rather crude, incomplete, and yet still be satisfactory for the purposes at hand. For example, in deciding to fly on a commercial airline one does not expect three-significant-digit estimates of the probability of a crash but only information that leads to an estimate that the probability of a crash is quite small. An even better example of a more general sort is deciding whether to take an umbrella or raincoat as one leaves home. One does not expect to have a really accurate estimate of the probability of a rainfall in the next six hours. From experience, tradition, and habit we are used to rather crude estimates and do not expect more, even if in principle we would readily admit that better forecasts would be desirable.

There is a philosophical wedge that someone might try to drive between the case of mass and the case of probability. It is this. It might be maintained that for a very large number of probability cases we should hold that the phenomena in question are deterministic and that the incompleteness of information is only a practical matter. In contrast, so it may be said, in the case of mass nothing corresponds to the determinist's ideal of everything that is possible having been learned from experience. I do not accept this distinction as being of major importance, for there is another distinction working the other way, representing a similar idealization but one that is in terms of mass rather than probability and that already has been alluded to. This is the assumption that many objects have masses that are constant in time. With probability this does not occur in the same way because ordinarily we are talking about the probability of events. We might, in an Aristotelian spirit, accept the difference here, namely, that the idealization in the case of mass is constancy in time, whereas the idealization in the case of probability is determinism of occurrence under conditions of complete information. Certainly there is a difference, and I accept it, but the similarity is also evident: theoretical idealization useful for the purposes of elementary physics classes but totally unrealistic as a theory of the world, and necessary to modify in many refined applications. What I have been concerned to do is to argue that probability statements are, at bottom, not very different from other physical statements. An important part of the view I have tried to express is to make the view of probability statements as physical statements compatible with the subjective view of probability statements as expressions of belief.

There is perhaps one other remark to be made about the reasons for my differences with de Finetti. Reading de Finetti's famous monograph (1937), one is struck by the extent to which he seems to have been driven by strong positivistic and operationalistic views. He cites with approval, for example, the American physicist Percy Bridgman, famous in earlier days for his operational approach to the meaning of concepts. Such positivistic views have properly run their course and no longer occupy a very important position in current philosophies of science—and for good reason, too. It is hard to think of anyone who set forth a more muddled set of ideas about physical concepts than Bridgman did. This is an aspect of de Finetti's thought from years past that I find mistaken and must demur from. This strongly positivistic tenor has infected his insistence on the purely objective character of all probability statements. His search for a strict operational interpretation of the meaning of probability statements has led him astray.

The longing for certainty has indeed not been easy to escape. The kinds of probabilistic considerations I have introduced are sometimes used to advance the argument that although certainty has escaped us at the first level of empirical knowledge of individual events, it returns at the second level of knowing exactly the probability distribution for the occurrence of events. Because this issue is interwined with the characterization of rationality of belief and behavior, I delay its deeper consideration until the final chapter.

I end the chapter with this tenet: *Certainty of knowledge—either in the sense of psychological immediacy, in the sense of logical truth, or in the sense of complete precision of measurement—is unachievable.* It is the responsibility of a thoroughly-worked-out empiricism to include an appropriate concept of uncertainty at the most fundamental level of theoretical and methodological analysis. Probabilistic methods provide a natural way of doing so.

5

Incompleteness

Ordinarily accompanying the explicit doctrines of strict determinism, strict determinant causality, and asymptotic certainty of knowledge is an implicit doctrine of completeness for knowledge and science. Underlying this view are such postulates as the one about the uniformity of nature. (The most famous discussion of this principle is found in John Stuart Mill's, *A System of Logic*, 8th edn, 1893.) There are, of course, in many situations impediments to complete knowledge, but these impediments, it is held, are only practical in character and do not exist in principle. When a strong thesis of strict determinism like that of Laplace is accepted, the concept of completeness seems otiose, because from a detailed specification of the current configuration of fundamental particles of the universe, the entire past and future of the universe is determined, and completeness of knowledge automatically follows.

In contrast, strict causality narrowly construed does not imply such completeness. For example, if the determinant cause of an event is not required to be contiguous in space and time but can act remotely, as in the case of gravitation or action-at-a-distance theories of electromagnetic phenomena, then completeness may not follow from strict causality because we may be caught in a potentially infinite regress. Thus, in order to find the fully determinant cause of a given event, we must make an unbounded search of past time and outer space. Incompleteness of any given finite physical system would then be compatible with strict causality in the sense that incompleteness would follow from the unbounded character of causal connections in space and time. On the other hand, if we add to the doctrine of strict causality the doctrine of contiguity in space and time for determinant causes, then we are closer to an implicit doctrine of completeness.

The interesting things to be said about completeness are not intertwined with broad doctrines of strict determinism or strict causality, but rather with more local issues in particular disciplines and their individual character, as I try to illustrate later. Whatever may be our philosophical tendency to affirm broad and deep cosmological theses about determinism, it is clear that in practice our theories are more limited and partial in character. Still, the push for completeness can be misleading and unattainable. As in the cases of determinism, strict causality and certainty, the thrust toward completeness characteristic of so many different kinds of investigations in science and mathematics is still another remnant of neotraditional metaphysics that remains from the ruins of earlier thought, especially the fantasy of an omniscient and omnipotent God. The naive tendency is to reach at once for completeness and to be dismayed at the inability to achieve it. The proper attitude of empiricism, as I see it, is to expect incompleteness and to be surprised by its opposite. A sophisticated empiricism should investigate the limits of completeness and attempt to understand why individual naive conceptions of completeness break down on detailed examination.

I examine in this chapter a number of individual cases of conceptual importance in which an original desire for completeness has been definitively established as untenable on either conceptual or empirical grounds. I begin with logic and mathematics, and then move on to the empirical sciences, with some historical consideration of the views of Descartes, Kant, and Laplace.

LOGICAL COMPLETENESS

The one area of experience in which a really satisfactory theory of completeness has been developed is that of logic. The facts are too familiar to require a detailed review. The fundamental result is Gödel's completeness theorem that in first-order logic a formula is universally valid if and only if it is logically provable. Thus, our apparatus of logical derivation is adequate to the task of deriving any valid logical formula, that is, any logical truth. What we have in first-order logic is a happy match of syntax and semantics.

More generally, the modern logical sense of completeness for theories of standard formalization, that is, theories formalized within first-order logic, provides a sharp and definite concept that did not exist in the past. The characterization of completeness in this context is that a theory is complete if and only if every sentence of the theory is either valid in the theory or inconsistent with the theory, that is, its negation is valid in the theory.

Even in the case of elementary logic, however, the ultimate sense of completeness does not obtain; that is, we do not have a decision procedure for determining whether a formula is logically true or not. We have only the recursively enumerable completeness result, but not a recursive decision procedure for logical truth. Of course, recursive procedures giving the fully satisfactory form of completeness can be found for special classes of theories, for instance, Tarski's decision procedure for elementary algebra and geometry (1951).

INCOMPLETENESS OF ARITHMETIC

On the other hand, the most famous incompleteness result occurs at an elementary level, namely, at the level of arithmetic or elementary number theory. In broad conceptual terms, Gödel's result shows that incompleteness will be characteristic of any relatively rich mathematical theory whose deductive resources are those of classical logic. A much earlier example, equally important historically, is the following incompleteness result.

INCOMPLETENESS IN GEOMETRY

The three classical construction problems that the ancient Greeks could not solve by elementary means (use of straightedge and compass only) were those of trisecting an angle, doubling a cube, and squaring a circle, that is, finding a square whose area is equal to that of a given circle. It was not until the nineteenth century that these constructions were shown to be impossible by elementary means, thereby establishing a conceptually important incompleteness result for elementary geometry.

A related and important sense of incompleteness for geometry was also established in the nineteenth century. This was the proof that the parallel postulate could not be derived from other postulates, and that non-Euclidian geometries of a wholly consistent kind could be constructed. This latter sense of incompleteness of geometry leads me to my next example.

INCOMPLETENESS OF SET THEORY

In the latter part of the nineteenth century, on the basis of the work of Frege in one direction and Cantor in another, it seemed that the theory of sets or classes was the natural framework within which to construct the rest of mathematics. Frege's principle of abstraction, that for any property there exists a set of elements having this property, together with the principle of extensionality, seemed to provide a complete basis for arithmetic. Only the axiom of choice or some similar principle would need to be added to obtain more nonconstructive parts of mathematical analysis. Russell's paradox dashed these hopes, and the discovery of additional paradoxes by Burali-Forti and others indicated that no simple complete foundation could easily be obtained. Put in terms of the intuitive notion of incompleteness, it was shown decisively that a complete principle of abstraction for sets led at once to contradiction.

Research in the twentieth century on the foundations of set theory, some of it quite recent, has shown that there is a still deeper sense of incompleteness in set theory. The continuum hypothesis as well as the axiom of choice are independent of other principles of set theory, and as in the case of geometry, a variety of set theories can be constructed. The results of these various investigations in the foundations of mathematics show unequivocally that the hope for some simple complete foundation of mathematics beyond that of elementary logic is not likely to be attained.

In spite of these results in the foundations of mathematics, ranging through arithmetic, geometry, set theory, and analysis, many of them classical and known for a long time, there has continued to be a naive desire for completeness in empirical scientific theories which seems wholly unwarranted by the careful results obtained in closely related parts of mathematics. This theological thrust for completeness is not easy to turn aside. Rather than concentrating on the familiar and classical examples from the foundations of mathematics, I want to examine some of the scientific cases of conceptual interest. A proper philosophy of empiricism should have a realistic attitude toward completeness and not be beguiled into a search for that which is not possible.

Behind the well-defined logical and mathematical analysis of completeness is a long history of discussions in physics that are less sharply formulated, but that have a similar intuitive content. It is these views that I now examine.

CARTESIAN PHYSICS

A good place to begin to look at the problem of completeness in physics is in Descartes' *Principia Philosophiae,* already mentioned in chapter 2. Part I is concerned with the general principles of human knowledge and is not considered here. In part II the field is narrowed to the general principles of material things that can be known clearly and distinctly. In this part are established a large number of general propositions regarding the nature of body, the nonexistence of atoms, the laws of motion, etc. Generally speaking, this part is meant to contain the first principles or laws of nature. Part III is entitled 'Of the Visible World' and deals primarily with what we would today call the subject matter of astronomy and astrophysics. In part IV, 'Of the Earth', Descartes deals with the major terrestrial phenomena: the nature of fire, water, air, earth, heat, gravity, light, and magnetism. As is well known, Descartes attempts to describe and explain the physical world in terms of nothing but extension and motion. The fundamental characteristic of matter or body is extension (I, §53; II, §4), for this property of extension is the only clear and distinct idea about a body that we can have (I, §54, §63; II, §1). All the variety and diversity of matter is to be explained by motion (II, §23), which, in contradistinction to Aristotle and Scholastics, is strictly local motion.

What is interesting here is the fundamental epistemological distinction between the statements of part II and part III, but before entering into this distincion, one preliminary problem must be clarified. Descartes makes a definite distinction in his theory between those assertions which are a priori and those which are a posteriori, but the similar distinction between analytic and synthetic is not explicit. Descartes enunciates a large number of a priori principles. The problem is: are they meant to be analytic or synthetic? Ayer (1946, p. 46), for instance, has used them as examples of analytic statements, and there is some ground for claiming that the contradictory of a sufficiently clear and distinct principle is self-contradictory.

Rule XIV of the *Regulae ad Directionem Ingenii* contains an interesting passage in which Descartes distinguishes between statements such as 'Pierre is rich' and 'a body is extended'. In the first, he says, there are two distinct ideas, but in the latter only one. This is similar to Kant's analysis of 'all bodies are extended' as analytic. On the other hand, in the *Meditations,* particularly the second and fourth, where Descartes discusses clear and distinct ideas along with truth and falsity, no hint is given that he considers the negation of a statement involving only clear and distinct ideas as self-contradictory. This is also generally true of the many references to clear and distinct ideas in part I of the *Principia*. Certainly the proofs given of the a priori assertions of part II use statements that do not seem analytic under any ordinary interpretation. For instance, the proposition that the quantity of motion in the world is conserved logically follows from the nature of God and His simple and invariant mode of action. The important point is that the principles of part II are a priori. Whether they are synthetic or analytic is almost an anachronistic question in terms of distinctions clearly drawn in the seventeenth century.

What is important is that the list of general principles of material things stated in part II, which are all meant to be a priori in character, is surprisingly large. The nature of body is extension. A vacuum is not possible in nature. Indivisible atoms do not exist in nature. The extension of the world is indefinite. The earth and the stars are made of the same matter. Three laws of nature pertaining to motion are set forth, one of which is the law of inertia. Seven rules are given for determining the movements of colliding bodies. The nature of hard and liquid bodies is explained. For the validation of these many principles no appeal to experience is required. In fact, we must be careful not to be deceived by our senses, for 'the perception of the senses do not teach us what is really in things, but merely that whereby they are useful or hurtful to man's composite nature' (II, §3). The procedure is to 'rely upon the understanding alone, by reflecting carefully on the ideas implanted therein by nature' (II, §3). The results of part II rest upon clear and distinct ideas and are therefore certain.[1] No evidence of our senses could be used to disprove

---

[1] Cf. rules II and IX, *Regulae ad Directionem Ingenii* and first and second Meditations.

them; no experiments could be performed to refute them.[2] The last article (§64) of this part declares that no principle has been received into the author's physics that cannot also be used in mathematics and geometry. The principles I have listed are thought of by Descartes as related by an intricate set of demonstrations. They are not to be taken as independent, but it is far too complex and subtle a matter to spell out their deductive dependencies, as envisaged by Descartes and as objectively assessed, and to consider them here. But certainly there is no rigor of development comparable in any sense to that found in Descartes' *La Géométrie* (1637/1954), one of the most important mathematical treatises of the seventeenth century.

When Descartes turns in part III to consideration of the visible world, he admits that pure deduction from the certain principles developed in part II is not sufficient to account for the actual phenomena of experience, for example, the motion of the heavens. Specifically, in article 4 of part III, Descartes admits that the principles of part II are necessary but not sufficient to account for these phenomena, because from these general principles one is able to deduce a great many more things than can be seen in the world or even conceived in one lifetime. The explicit consideration of phenomena or experiments, a switch from pure rationalism to at least a partial empiricism, is thus necessary to account for the details of the natural world.[3] We are able to know by pure reason neither the size of the parts into which matter has been divided, the velocity of these parts, nor their paths. These things could have been ordained by God in an infinite number of different ways—the system of a priori principles is noncategorical. Only through experience, through empirical investigation of the world, can we know them. In order to account for the world as it now appears to us, we are thus free to make hypotheses about how God originally ordered

[2] *Principia*, III, §4. Cf. 'Je pourrois mettre encore ici plusieurs règles . . . De sorte que ceux qui sauront suffisamment examiner les consèquences de ces vérités et de nos règles pourront connaître les effets par leurs causes, et, pour m'expliquer en termes de l'école, pourront avoir des démonstrations a priori de tout ce qui peut être produit en ce nouveau monde.' *Le Monde*, ch. VIII. Cousin edition of *Oeuvres de Descartes*, vol. 4, pp. 262–263. Paris: 1824. 'Démonstrations a priori' is the Scholastic phrase for demonstrations from premises by logical deduction. It was from these Scholastic terms that Kant developed his own ideas of the a priori synthetic.

[3] Cf. next to last paragraph of preface to *Principia*. (This preface was first written by Descartes for the French edition of 1647, but it also appeared in subsequent Latin editions.)

the various parts. We merely require of any such hypothesis that its consequences be in accord with our experience (III, §46). We may in fact know that our hypotheses are false, because, for example, of some revealed truth of religion, but that does not prevent their being useful. They can function as if true to permit the arrangement of natural causes to produce desired effects (III, §44, §47).

Thus the strictest form of completeness, that is, a rationalistic completeness, is certainly not part of Descartes' system of the world. He is explicit on the point that the general a priori principles of part II obtained by consideration of clear and distinct ideas cannot be extended to account for all physical phenomena. Moreover, though he does not discuss explicitly the problem of completeness, it seems fair to infer that he is not advancing any strong thesis of completeness from what he says in article 46 of part III about God's being able to order the arrangements between the elementary parts of the world in an infinity of different ways. It is only by experience that we can determine the actual relation among the parts and it seems correct to claim that instead of finding in Descartes a thesis of completeness, we find only a thesis that certain major principles of physics can be established on a priori grounds. Although Descartes professed to bring to physics a geometric spirit and to emphasize the importance of geometry in physics, he was not so bold as to claim the kind of completeness for physics that was characteristic of geometry. In fact, the first sentence of book I of *La Géométrie* makes an implicit completeness claim for Descartes' analytic geometry. 'Any problem in geometry can easily be reduced to such terms that only knowledge of the lengths of certain straight lines is needed in order to solve it.' Even this restricted completeness of geometry was shown to be wrong by the celebrated theorem (1829) of Abel that a general algebraic equation of the fifth degree is unsolvable.

KANT'S METAPHYSICAL FOUNDATIONS OF PHYSICS

Unlike Descartes, Kant does make an explicit claim for the completeness of his metaphysical foundations of natural science. His views on the subject are probably stated more clearly and succinctly in the preface to the work of this title than in any other

place. It is to be emphasized that his claim is not for the completeness of physics, but for the completeness of the metaphysical
foundations of physics. After giving the reason that it is desirable
to separate heterogeneous principles in order to locate errors and
confusions, he gives as the second reason the argument concerning completeness.

There may serve as a second ground for recommending this
procedure the fact that in all that is called metaphysics the
absolute completeness of the sciences may be hoped for,
which is of such a sort as can be promised in no other kind of
cognitions; and therefore just as in the metaphysics of nature
in general, so here also the completeness of the metaphysics
of corporeal nature may be confidently expected. The reason
for this is that in metaphysics the object is considered merely
as it must be represented in accordance with the universal
laws of thought, while in other sciences, as it must be represented in accordance with data of intuition (pure as well
as empirical). Hence the former, inasmuch as the object
must always be compared with all the necessary laws of
thought, must furnish a definite number of cognitions, which
can be fully exhausted; but the latter, inasmuch as such
sciences offer an infinite manifold of intuitions (pure or empirical), and therefore of objects of thought, can never attain
absolute completeness but can be extended to infinity, as in
pure mathematics and the empirical doctrine of nature.
Moreover, I believe that I have completely exhausted this
metaphysical doctrine of body, as far as such a doctrine ever
extends; but I believe that I have accomplished thereby no
very great work.

The schema for the completeness of a metaphysical system, whether of nature in general or of corporeal nature in
particular, is the table of the categories. For there are no
more pure concepts of the understanding, which can concern
the nature of things. Under the four classes of quantity,
quality, relation, and finally modality, all determinations of
the universal concept of a matter in general and, therefore,
everything that can be thought a priori respecting it, that can
be presented in mathematical construction, or that can be
given in experience as a determinate object of experience,
must be capable of being brought. There is no more to do in

the way of discovery or addition; but improvement can be made where anything might be lacking in clearness or thoroughness. (Ellington translation, 1970, pp. 10–13)

It is not pertinent to examine in depth the Kantian argument for completeness, based as it is upon the transcendental deduction of the categories. I do emphasize the explicitness with which Kant brings the problem of completeness to the surface in this passage and in a number of passages in the *Critique of Pure Reason,* especially the second edition.

In comparison with Descartes, two aspects of Kant's views are especially interesting with regard to the problem of completeness. First, he restricts much more the range of the a priori in physics. On the other hand, he makes a much sharper claim of completeness for the a priori part than does Descartes. As should be apparent from the quotation given, the primary task of Kant's *Metaphysical Foundations of Natural Science* is to carry the concept of matter through the table of the categories, thereby providing the elements of construction necessary to build a mathematical physics that both conforms to experience and has a proper metaphysical basis.

Without entering into all details of Kant's execution of this program it may be of some interest from the standpoint of the history of philosophy of physics to review the four divisions of the theory of motion or matter that are brought under the table of the categories. In the first division, matter is considered purely according to its *quantity* of motion, abstracted from all its qualities. This gives us the theory of *Phoronomy* or Kinematics. In the second division, motion is considered as belonging to the *quality* of matter, and the basic proposition is that matter fills a space not by its mere existence, as Descartes thought, but by virtue of a special moving force of repulsion. This yields *Dynamics,* which has this special sense for Kant. The third division is called *Mechanics*; here motion as quality is considered in relation to other reciprocal motions, or, more exactly, matter with this dynamical quality of possessing an original moving force is considered in reciprocal motion. In the fourth division, entitled *Phenomenology,* matter in motion or at rest is regarded according to its modality; that is, whether in its determination as a phenomenon of the external sense, it is determined as possible, real, or necessary.

The propositions that Kant asserts under these four divisions are meant to provide a complete metaphysical foundation of physics. In working out the details of the program, Kant's development of his concept of the original forces of matter and his views on motion and space are original and sophisticated contributions to the philosophy of science, but what is disturbing from our standpoint is the certainty, as indicated in the open letter of 1799 mentioned earlier, with which Kant holds to the completeness claims he makes for his metaphysical foundations. In many respects, his completeness claims about the metaphysical foundations of physics represent the apex of the historical development of such doctrines, and there has generally been a retreat from the high ground he tried to occupy.

LAPLACE

It might be thought that Laplace's thesis of strict determinism represents an extension of completeness to the whole of physics and thus stretches beyond the metaphysical completeness claimed by Kant. However, it is important to emphasize that Laplace, unlike Kant, is mainly concerned with the detailed working out of examples in which causes are identified and in which phenomena are subsumed under known laws. He recognizes in these detailed investigations the difficulties of reaching complete results, or of extending the methods of analysis without difficulty, not merely to all cases but even to many cases of great interest. In many instances in which Laplace discusses the uses of probability theory to identify constant causes, he is justly proud of some of the triumphs he has achieved, especially in dealing with motions of the planetary system.

As Laplace emphasizes at one point in his philosophical *Essay on Probabilities* (1951 edn, pp. 88–89), the introduction to his treatise on probability, in most cases the analysis of a question does not convert the probability of causes into certainty, but only augments the probabilities, making the attribution of causes more probable. The point is that in practice Laplace has quite a different attitude toward completeness than does Kant, for Kant is mainly concerned to establish the metaphysical completeness of the table of the categories for deriving the fundamental laws of matter. Laplace, on the other hand, is concerned mainly to apply the laws of probability to fallible empirical data in order to determine whether constant causes are operating to produce the disturbances of measurement or whether they are arising simply from observational error.

After Kant, there was important system building in physics during the nineteenth century, and there were attempts by Kelvin, Maxwell, and others to reduce all known physical phenomena to mechanical models, but the philosophical sweep of these investigations was not so imperialistic and forthright in spirit as Kant's, even though the mechanical theory of heat turned out to be one of the most important scientific achievements of the nineteenth century. A case can be made, I think, for taking Einstein's general theory of relativity, especially the attempt at a unified field theory, as the real successor to Kant in the attempt to obtain completeness. However, I do not want to make the parallel between Kant and Einstein too close, for Einstein does not hold an a priori metaphysical view of the foundations of physics. What they do share is a strong search for completeness of theory. In Einstein's case the goal was to find a unified field theory from which all forces of nature could be derived from one common structure. In the grand version of the scheme, for given boundary conditions the differential equations would have a unique solution for the entire universe, and all physical phenomena would be encompassed within the theory. The geometrodynamics of John Wheeler and his collaborators is a recent version of the Einstein vision. Wheeler (1962, p. 361) formulates the problem in a way that is reminiscent of Descartes. 'Are fields and particles foreign entities immersed *in* geometry, or are they nothing but geometry?'

If the program of Einstein and the later program of Wheeler had been carried to completion, then the attitude I am advocating for a proper empiricism toward the problem of completeness in empirical science would have to retreat from bold assertion of inevitable incompleteness. However, it seems to me that there is, at least in the current scientific temperament, total support for the thesis of incompleteness. Grand building of theories has currently gone out of fashion in fields as far apart as physics and sociology, and there seems to be a deeper appreciation of the problems of ever settling in any definitive way the fundamental laws of complex phenomena. Wheeler himself has now asserted that he recognizes the need for a quantum mechanics of particles preceding geometrodynamics of macroscopic space. The efforts to obtain a fundamental theory at the other end of the scale, that is, at the microscopic level or the subatomic level, are also currently in disarray, and in view of the overwhelming complexity of the experimental evidence of the past several decades it is doubtful that we shall ever return to the simple hopes of Laplace or Kant that a completely adequate fundamental theory of physical phenomena can be found.

EINSTEIN–PODOLSKY–ROSEN PARADOX

Einstein's unique feelings about the completeness of physical theories led to the formulation of what is sometimes regarded as a paradox of quantum mechanics and, in terms of the paradox, an argument has traditionally been mounted for the introduction of hidden variables to give a proper account of local causal effects. Using an example suggested by Bohm and Aharonov (1957), let me try to give a qualitative account of the argument meant to lead to the EPR paradox.

For this purpose we need to consider the intrinsic angular momentum or spin of particles. One of the fundamental results of quantum mechanics is that spin can achieve only a discrete set of values. Particles that are said to have spin one-half can have only two values for their intrinsic angular momentum. Consider now two spin one-half particles originally in a singlet spin state moving freely in opposite directions, say along the x-axis. Measurements can be made of the two particles, for example, by Stern-Gerlach magnets, on selected components of the spins of the two particles, that is, selected components oriented in space in any direction we please. Now according to quantum mechanics, if measurement of the component of spin in the direction a yields the value $+1$ for the first particle, then measurement of the spin along this same direction for the second particle must yield the value -1, and vice versa—if the first particle yields a spin of -1, then the second must yield $+1$. What is paradoxical about this result is that the two particles can be separated as far as we want, and in principle the decision of which direction to take the measurement can be made after the particles leave their common source in a singlet spin state. The basic EPR assumption is that if the two measurements are made in this fashion at places remote from one another, then the result obtained for measuring with a magnet on one should not influence the result obtained with the other. However, since we can predict such a result of measurement in advance, there must be hidden variables determining the measurement in advance, and because the quantum-mechanical wave function does not determine the result of an individual measurement but merely a probability distribution, that is, the probability of obtaining the measurement +1 with orientation vector a for the magnet, etc., the predetermination implies that a more complete specification of the state of the system of the two particles can be given. The locality assumption enters, because the value of the measurement taken on each particle is causally determined by the hidden-variable parameters, and we do not have the apparent paradox of a measurement at one place in space seemingly influencing deterministically the measurement in another place without causal transmission on an effect.

The formulation of this paradox has persuaded many people that Einstein was right and quantum mechanics is incomplete. However, the developments described in chapter 2, beginning with Bell's theorem and continuing with a test of hidden-variable theorems with locality assumption by Freedman and Clauser, have led to predictions that verify those of quantum mechanics and that are inconsistent with the locality assumptions of the Einstein–Podolsky–Rosen paradox. As Bell (1966) puts the matter, the paradox is resolved in a way which Einstein would have liked the least. Hidden-variable theories that remedy the incompleteness of quantum mechanics that disturbed Einstein are inconsistent with quantum mechanics and relevant experiments.

I have only sketched the EPR paradox and the way in which it has currently been analyzed by work on hidden variables, especially via Bell's theorem. The qualitative outcome, however, should be clear even if the treatment of the details is sketchy, namely, support for completeness has not been forthcoming, and we are left once again with another argument for incompleteness of fundamental theory.

INCOMPLETENESS OF PROBABILITY SPACES

A variety of stochastic processes now are widely used not only in the natural sciences, but also in the behavioral and social sciences. An interesting aspect of incompleteness about such spaces is worth considering as a further example of retreat from a goal of absolute completeness of scientific analysis. Although a general description of the situation can be given, it will probably be more vivid to consider a particular example. The generalization of that example to other cases will be apparent.

We make take as a simple example the theory of linear learning models set forth in Estes and Suppes (1959), which need be only sketched informally for our present purposes. The theory rests on two axioms. The first says that when a response is reinforced, the probability of making that response on the next trial is increased by a simple linear transformation. The second says that if some other response is reinforced, the probability of making the response is decreased by a second linear transformation. In spite of the simplicity of this theory, it gives a reasonably good account of a number of experiments, and from a mathematical standpoint it is nontrivial to characterize asymptotic properties of its models.

The critical point for the present discussion of incompleteness is the characterization of the probability measure P as being defined on the σ-algebra of cylinder sets of the sample space X representing infinite sequences of possible responses and reinforcements.[4] It would be natural for someone who is not familiar with the situation to ask, Why bother with the σ-algebra of cylinder sets? Why not simply define the probability measure P on the family of all subsets of X? There are several arguments for restricting the measure to being defined on the σ-algebra of cylinder sets. From the standpoint of incompleteness, however, there is a decisive argument, and it is the following.

It is easy to show that three conceptual ingredients enter into determining uniquely the probability of any event happening, for example, any response or response sequence. The first ingredient is the initial probability of response at the beginning of the experiment before any reinforcements have been delivered; the second

[4] Cylinder sets of a sequence space like X are sets that are defined by reference to a *finite* number of trials (or dimensions, in another terminology). The σ-algebra of cylinder sets is the smallest algebra of sets containing all the cylinder sets and closed under union of a countable number of sets. Using the axiom of choice it is easy to show that not all subsets of X are members of the σ-algebra of cylinder sets.

ingredient is the learning parameter that determines how fast change in behavior takes place under various reinforcement schedules; and the third ingredient is the schedule of reinforcement, which in general will be probabilistic in character and contingent upon previous reinforcements or responses. Given these three ingredients, we would expect the probability measure to be uniquely determined for all trials. However, an analysis of the proof of this uniqueness shows that the measure will be uniquely determined provided it is defined only on the σ-algebra of cylinder sets of X, and not on all subsets of X. (For details of the proof, see Suppes, 1981b.) This kind of incompleteness is standard in any theory formulated within the framework of complex spaces and represents an important retreat from a naive attitude toward completeness. In connection with the example from learning theory or others like it, the axiom of choice may be used to construct a variety of events or sets outside of the σ-algebra, whose probabilities are not determined by the theory.

WHAT TO EXPECT

As the several examples considered show, in most areas of knowledge it is too much to expect theories to have a strong form of completeness. What we have learned to live with in practice is an appropriate form of incompleteness, but we have not built this working practice explicitly into our philosophy as thoroughly as we might. It is apparent from various examples that weak forms of completeness may be expected for theories about restricted areas of experience. It seems wholly inappropriate, unlikely, and, in many ways, absurd to expect theories that cover large areas of experience or, in the most grandiose cases, *all* of experience, to have a strong degree of completeness.

The application of working scientific theories to particular areas of experience is almost always schematic and highly approximate in character. Whether we are predicting the behavior of elementary particles, the weather, or international trade— indeed, any phenomenon that has a reasonable degree of complexity—we can hope only to encompass a restricted part of the phenomena.

It is sometimes said that it is exactly the role of experimentation to isolate particular fragments of experience that can be dealt with in relatively complete fashion. This is, I think, a dogma more of philosophers who have not engaged in much experimentation than of practicing experimental scientists. When I have been involved in experimentation myself I have been struck by how much my schematic views of theories applied to observational rather than experimental data also apply to experimental work. First one concrete thing and then another is abstracted and simplified to make the data fit within the limited set of concepts of the theory being tested.

Let me put the matter another way. A common philosophical conception of science is that it is an even closer approximation to a set of eternal truths that hold always and everywhere. Such a conception of science can be traced from Plato through Aristotle and onward to Descartes, Kant, and more recent philosphers, and this account has no doubt been accepted by many scientists as well. It is my own view that a much better case can be made for the kind of instrumental conception of science set forth in general terms by Peirce, Dewey, and their successors. In this view, scientific activity is a kind of perpetual problem solving. No area of experience is totally and completely settled by providing a set of basic truths, but rather we are continually confronted with new situations and new problems, and we bring to these problems and situations a collection of scientific methods, techniques, and concepts, which in many cases we have learned to use with great facility.

The concept of objective truth does not directly disappear in such a view of science, but what we might call the cosmological or global view of truth is looked at with skepticism just as is a global or cosmological view of completeness. Like our own lives and endeavors, scientific theories are local and are designed to meet a given set of problems. As new problems arise new theories are needed, and in almost all cases the theories used for the old set of problems have not been tested to the fullest extent feasible nor been confirmed as broadly or as deeply as possible, but the time is ripe for something new, and we move on to something else. Again, this conception of science does not mean that there cannot be some approximate convergence in a sequence of theories dealing with a particular sequence of problems; but it does urge that the sequence does not necessarily converge. In fact, to express the kind of incompleteness I am after, we can even make the strong assumption that in many domains of experience the scientific theory that replaces the best old theory is always an improvement, and therefore we have a kind of monotone increasing sequence. Nonetheless, as in the case of a strictly monotone increasing sequence of integers, there is no convergence to a finite value —the sequence is never completed—and so it is with scientific theories. *There is no bounded fixed scientific theory toward which we are in general converging.*

6

The Plurality of Science

To answer this initial question, I turned to the introductory essay by Otto Neurath for the *International Encyclopedia of Unified Science* (Neurath, Carnap, and Morris, 1938). He begins this way:

> Unified science became historically the subject of this *Encyclopedia* as a result of the efforts of the unity of science movement, which includes scientists and persons interested in science who are conscious of the importance of a universal scientific attitude.
>
> The new version of the idea of unified science is created by the confluence of divergent intellectual currents. Empirical work of scientists was often antagonistic to the logical constructions of a priori rationalism bred by philosophico-religious systems; therefore, 'empiricalization' and 'logicalization' were considered mostly to be in opposition—the two have now become synthesized for the first time in history. (p. 1)

Later he continues:

> All-embracing vision and thought is an old desire of humanity . . . This interest in combining concepts and statements without empirical testing prepared a certain attitude which appeared in the following ages as metaphysical construction. The neglect of testing facts and using observation statements in connection with all systematized ideas is especially found in the different idealistic systems. (pp. 5–6)

Later he says:

> A universal application of logical analysis and construction
> to science in general was prepared not only by the systemati-
> zation of empirical procedure and the systematization of
> logico-empirical analysis of scientific statements, but also by
> the analysis of language from different points of view. (pp.
> 16–17)

In the same volume of the *Encyclopedia*, the thesis about the
unity of the language of science is taken up in considerably more
detail in Carnap's analysis of the logical foundations of the unity
of science. He states his well-known views about physicalism and,
concerning the terms or predicates of the language, concludes:

> The result of our analysis is that the class of observable
> thing-predicates is a sufficient reduction basis for the whole
> of the language of science, including the cognitive part of the
> everyday language.(p. 60)

Concerning the unity of laws, Carnap reaches a negative but
optimistic conclusion—optimistic in the sense that the reducibility
of the laws of one science to another has not been shown to be impossible. Here is what he has to say on the reduction of biological
to physical laws:

> There is a common language to which both the biological
> and the physical laws belong so that they can be logically
> compared and connected. We can ask whether or not a cer-
> tain biological law is compatible with the system of physical
> laws, and whether or not it is derivable from them. But the
> answer to these questions cannot be inferred from the re-
> ducibility of the terms. At the present state of the develop-
> ment of science, it is certainly not possible to derive the
> biological laws from the physical ones. Some philosophers
> believe that such a derivation is forever impossible because
> of the very nature of the two fields. But the proofs attempted
> so far for this thesis are certainly insufficient. (p. 60)

Later he has the same sort of thing to say about the reduction of
phychology or other social sciences to biology.

A different and less linguistic approach is to contrast the unity of scientific subject matter with the unity of scientific method. Many would agree that different sciences have different subject matters; for example, in no real sense is the subject matter of astronomy the same as that of psychopharmacology. But many would affirm that in spite of the radically different subject matters of science there are important ways in which the methods of science are the same in every domain of investigation. The most obvious and simple examples immediately come to mind. There is not one arithmetic for psychological theories of motivation and another for cosmological theories of the universe. More generally, there are not different theories of the differential and integral calculus or of partial differential equations or of probability theory. There is a great mass of mathematical methods and results that are available for use in all domains of science and that are, in fact, quite widely used in very different parts of science. There is a plausible prima facie case for the unity of science in terms of unity of scientific method. This may be one of the most reasonable meanings to be attached to any central thesis about the unity of science. However, I shall be negative even about this thesis in the sequel.

UNITY AND REDUCTIONISM

What I have said earlier about different sciences having obviously different subject matters was said too hastily because there is a historically important sense of unity. One form or another of reductionism has been central to the discussion of unity of science for a very long time. I concentrate on three such forms: reduction of language, reduction of subject matter, and reduction of method.

Reduction of language. Carnap's views about the reduction of the language of science to commonsense language about physical objects remain appealing. He states his general thesis in such a way that no strong claims about the reduction of psychology to physics, for example, are implied, and I am sure much is correct about what he has had to say. On the other hand, it seems appropriate to emphasize the very clear senses in which there is no reduction of language. The reduction certainly does not take place in practice, and it may be rightly claimed that the reduction in theory remains in a hopelessly vague state.

There are many ways to illustrate the basis for my skepticism about any serious reduction of language. Part of my thesis about the plurality of science is that the languages of the different branches of science are diverging rather than converging as they become increasingly technical. Let me begin with a personal example. My daughter Patricia has a PhD in neurophysiology, and to improve my understanding of what she does she gave me a subscription to what is supposed to be an expository journal, entitled *Neurosciences: Research Program Bulletin*. After several efforts at reading this journal, I have reached the conclusion that the exposition is only for those in nearby disciplines. I quote one passage from an issue (Smith and Kreutzberg, 1976) dealing with neuron-target cell interactions.

> The above studies define the anterograde transsynaptic regulation of adrenergic ontogeny. Black and co- workers . . . have also demonstrated that postsynaptic neurons regulate presynaptic development through a retrograde process. During the course of maturation, presynaptic ChAc activity increased 30- to 40-fold . . . , and this rise paralleled the formation of ganglionic synapses . . . If postsynaptic adrenergic neurons in neonatal rats were chemically destroyed with 6-hydroxydopamine . . . or immunologically destroyed with antiserum to NGF . . . the normal development of presynaptic ChAc activity was prevented. These data, viewed in conjunction with the anterograde regulation studies, lead to the conclusion that there is a bidirectional flow of regulatory information at the synapse during development. (p. 253)

This is by no means the least intelligible passage. It seems to me that it illustrates the cognitive facts of life. The sciences are diverging and there is no reason to think that any kind of convergence will ever occur. Moreover, this divergence is not something of recent origin. It has been present for a long time in that oldest of quantitative sciences, astronomy, and it is now increasingly present throughout all branches of science.

There is another point I want to raise in opposition to a claim made by some philosophers and philosophically minded physicists. Some persons have held that in the physical sciences at least, substantial theoretical unification can be expected in the future and, with this unification, a unification of the theoretical language of the physical sciences, thereby simplifying the cognitive problem of understanding various domains. I have skepticism about this thesis that I shall explain later, but at this point I wish to emphasize that it takes care of only a small part of the difficulties. It is the experimental language of the physical sciences as well as of the other sciences that is difficult to understand, much more so for the outsider than the theoretical language. There is, I believe, no comparison between a philosopher's cognitive difficulty in reading theoretical articles in quantum mechanics and his difficulty in reading current experimental articles in any developed branch of physics. The experimental literature is simply impossible to penetrate without a major learning effort.

Personally I applaud the divergence of language in science and find in it no grounds for skepticism or pessimism about the continued growth of science. The irreducible pluralism of languages of science is as desirable a feature as is the irreducible plurality of political views in a democracy.

Reduction of subject matter. At least since the time of Democritus in the fifth century B.C., strong and attractive theses about the reduction of all phenomena to atoms in motion have been set forth. Because of the striking scientific successes of the atomic theory of matter since the beginning of the nineteenth century, this theory has dominated the views of plain men and philosophers alike. In one sense, it is difficult to deny that everything in the universe is nothing but some particular swarm of particles. Of course, as we move into the latter part of the twentieth century, we recognize this fantasy for what it is. We are no longer clear about what we mean by particles or even if the concept as originally stated is anywhere near the mark. The universe is indeed made of something, but we are vastly ignorant of what that something is. The more we probe, the more it seems that the kind of simple and orderly view advanced as part of ancient atomism, which appeared so near realization toward the end of the nineteenth century, is ever further from being a true description. To reverse the phrase used earlier, it is not swarms of particles that things are made of, but particles that are made of swarms. There are still physicists about who hold that we will one day find the ultimate simples out of which all other things are made, but as such claims have been continually revised and as the complexity of high-energy physics and elementary particle theory has increased, there seems little reason that we shall ever again be able to seriously believe in the strong sense of reduction that Democritus so attractively formulated.

To put the matter in a skeptical fashion, we cannot have a reduction of subject matter to the ultimate physical entities because we do not know what those entities are. I have on another occasion (1974a) expressed my reasons for holding that Aristotle's theory of matter may be sounder and more sensible than the kind of simpleminded atomistic reductionist views dominating our thinking about the physical world for 200 years.

Arguments against reductionism of subject matter can be found even within physics. A familiar example is the currently accepted view that it is hopeless to try to solve the problems of quantum chemistry by applying the fundamental laws of quantum mechanics. It is hopeless in the same way that it is hopeless to program a computer to play the perfect chess game by always looking ahead to all possible future moves. The combinatorial explosion is so drastic and so overwhelming that theoretical arguments can be given that, not only now but also in the future, it will be impossible by direct computation to reduce the problems of quantum chemistry to problems of ordinary quantum mechanics. Quantum chemistry, in spite of its proximity to quantum mechanics, is and will remain an essentially autonomous discipline. At the level of computability, reduction is not only practically impossible but theoretically so as well.

An impressive substantive example of reduction is the reduction of large parts of mathematics to set theory. But even here, the reduction to a single subject matter of different parts of mathematics has a kind of barren formality about it. It is not that the fact of the reduction is conceptually uninteresting, but rather that it has limited interest and does not say much about many aspects of mathematics. Mathematics, like science, is made up of many different subdisciplines, each going its own way and each primarily sensitive to the nuances of its own subject matter. Moreover, as we have reached for a deeper understanding of the foundations of mathematics, we have come to realize that the foundations are not to be built on a bedrock of certainty but that, in many ways, developed parts of mathematics are much better understood than the foundations themselves. As in the case of physics, an effort of reduction is now an effort of reduction to we know not what.

In many ways a more significant mathematical example is the reduction of computational mathematics to computability by Turing machines, but as in the case of set theory, the reduction is irrelevant to most computational problems of theoretical or practical interest.

Reduction of method. As I remarked earlier, many philosophers and scientists would claim that there is an important sense in which the methods of science are the same in every domain of investigation. Some aspects of this sense of unity, as I also noted, are well recognized and indisputable. The common use of elementary mathematics and the common teaching of elementary mathematical methods for application in all domains of science can scarcely be denied. But it seems to me it is now important to emphasize the plurality of methods and the vast difference in methodology of different parts of science. The use of elementary mathematics—and I emphasize *elementary* because almost all applications of mathematics in science are elementary from a mathematical standpoint—as well as the use of certain elementary statistical methods does not go very far toward characterizing the methodology of any particular branch of science. As I have emphasized earlier, it is especially the experimental methods of different branches of science that have radically different form. It is no exaggeration to say that the handbooks of experimental method for one discipline are generally unreadable by experts in another discipline (the definition of 'discipline' can here by quite narrow). Physicists working in solid-state physics cannot intelligibly read the detailed accounts of method in other parts of physics. This is true even of less developed sciences like psychology. Physiological psychologists use a set of experimental methods that are foreign to psychologists specializing, for example, in educational test theory, and correspondingly the intricate details of the methodology of test construction will be unknown to almost any physiological psychologist.

Even within the narrow domain of statistical methods, different disciplines have different statistical approaches to their particular subject matters. The statistical tools of psychologists are in general quite different from those of economists. Moreover, within a single broad discipline like physics, there are in different areas great variations in the use of statistical methods, a fact that has been well documented by Paul Humphreys (1976).

The unity of science arose to a fair degree as a rallying cry of philosophers trying to overcome the heavy weight of nineteenth-century German idealism. A half century later the picture looks very different. The period since the *Encyclopedia of Unified Science* first appeared has been the era of greatest development and expansion of science in the history of thought. The massive enterprise of science no longer needs any philosophical shoring up to protect it from errant philosophical views. The rallying cry of unity followed by three cheers for reductionism should now be replaced by a patient examination of the many ways in which different sciences differ in language, subject matter, and method, as well as by synoptic views of the ways in which they are alike.

I consider now several examples in more detail to illustrate the general points I have been making.

N-BODY PROBLEM

From the time of the ancient atomists the wistful hope has been expressed that all properties of matter could be reduced to the characteristics of atoms in motion. Newton's precise formulation of the axioms of mechanics and his solution of the two-body problem in classical mechanics set the stage for renewed interest in this reductionistic view of the world. The importance of Newton's solution of the two-body problem was to show that simply from knowledge of the gravitational force of interaction between two bodies and their positions and velocities at some instant of time the future and past courses of the system could be predicted, granted of course that the system was isolated from all other influences.

In many respects the philosophical zenith of mechanistic reduction of physical phenomena is reached in the work of the eighteenth-century Jesuit physicist Roger Joseph Boscovich. Historically, his theory has not been of major importance, and he himself does not rank with Lagrange, Euler, and Laplace, but he had considerable impact in the eighteenth century and a much stronger interest in philosophy than most physicists and mathematicians of that century. His philosophical ideas were put in most systematic form in his *Theoria Philosophiae Naturalis*, which was first published in Vienna in 1758 and then in a revised form in Venice in 1763. (References here are to the Venetian edition of 1763, which was printed in a Latin–English edition in Chicago in 1922; references are to articles rather than pages.)

Boscovich compares himself in numerous passages to Descartes, Newton, and Leibniz. He was much opposed to Cartesianism, but in many ways his theory is more similar to Descartes' *Principia* than to Newton's. This similarity in aim and method arises from Boscovich's belief that he has derived *all* physical phenomena from the position, forces, and motions of points of matter. Like Descartes, Boscovich's explanations of most particular phenomena are qualitative rather than quantitative, and they have the same perfunctory air: a host of ad hoc unverifiable hypotheses are introduced in order to subsume well-known empirical phenomena under a general theory. On the other hand, there are many differences from Descartes, in part certainly a reflection of the enormous progress in physics in the hundred years that separate the two. Boscovich's treatise is considerably more mathematical and exact than Descartes', and generally less speculative. Boscovich does not believe it is possible to use the attributes of God to derive any a priori truths about the world, as Descartes does in the first two parts of his treatise.[1] Boscovich has a sharper sense than Descartes of what constitutes the difference between scientific knowledge and ignorance. He holds that Descartes' conception of a plenum is a mental fiction (note to §210) and that the Cartesian conception of material mechanisms makes not only animals but men as well mere automata (§386). (In his own system he gets around this difficulty by introducing the "free motions" of bodies which arise from the mind (§387). At the beginning of the treatise, Boscovich states what he has in common with Newton and Leibniz and how his own theory differs from theirs and is superior. His nonextended points are similar to Leibniz's monads, and the mutual forces acting between them are extensions of Newton's ideas about forces. He differs from Leibniz in making his points homogeneous and he differs from Newton by using repulsive forces as well as attractive

---

[1] '. . . we are absolutely ignorant of the nature of the presence of God; and in no wise do we say that He is really extended throughout divisible space; nor from those modes, surpassing all human intelligence, by which He exists, thinks, wills and acts, can any analogy or deduction be made which will apply to human or material modes of existence and action.' (*Theoria*, §85).

ones. Boscovich acknowledges repeatedly his intellectual debt to Leibniz and Newton, but what is marvelous is the intellectual purity and sweep of his theory. According to Boscovich's ideas, the matter of the universe is composed of a finite number of nonextended points. Attractive and repulsive forces, which are a function of distance only, act between these points according to a single law of forces. The forces are a function pairwise of the distance between the particles. All the observed phenomena of nature are to be explained solely in terms of the distribution and motion of these points and the forces acting between them. In Boscovich's picturesque words 'Matter is interspersed in a vacuum and floats in it' (§7).

Boscovich's metaphysical view of matter reflects the simplicity of his theory. Matter is nonextended, the parts of matter are not contiguous. The primary elements of matter, i.e., the point particles, must be simple, for if they were composite, the indefinitely large repulsive forces would drive the pieces asunder (§81). The radical simplicity of Boscovich's view that matter is nonextended is the especially striking feature of his theory, a view not set forward, as far as I know, with any clarity and explicitness by any of his atomistic predecessors. I shall not review here Boscovich's extended argument for this original and unique claim.

It does form the natural philosophical backdrop for the mathematical work of the nineteenth century on the N-body problem. Mathematicians and physicists who struggled with this problem throughout the century did not hold with Boscovich that matter is nonextended, but the problem, natural in the framework of Newtonian physics, and in many ways the central problem mathematically for Boscovich's theory, was to derive from the pairwise forces of interaction as a function of distance only—in fact the inverse square of the distance—the trajectories of individual particles. The trajectories also depend, of course, on the particles' positions and velocities at a given instant. From a general conceptual and philosophical standpoint, nothing could seem easier as a first step to the extension of Newtonian mechanics, or in the most elementary realization of Boscovich's program, to go beyond Newton's two-body problem to at least the three-body problem, and from there to the N-body problem. Any program that made serious claims about the reduction of the observable properties of matter to the elementary parts must deal with the N-body problem in mathematical and quantitative detail.

Furthermore, it seems clear that detailed reductionist programs aimed at the unification of science must in practice be able to solve such elementary problems in order to get the program off the ground from any serious scientific standpoint.

What is surprising and in a certain sense, especially from the standpoint of such philosophical physicists as Boscovich, wholly unexpected is the enormous mathematical difficulty of solving the N-body problem.

An equally intricate problem closely associated with that of determining the trajectories is the question of the stability of a system of N particles. The problem of stability arose in the eighteenth century in connection with the problem of the stability of the solar system. In the mathematical idealization of the solar system considered in celestial mechanics, can we prove that the periodic motions of the system will continue for the rest of time? Clearly this is a problem of great intellectual and conceptual interest. Proofs of stability were purported to be given by a long series of distinguished mathematicians starting with Laplace. Only in recent years have really satisfactory proofs been given (for details of the recent work see Moser, 1973, and Abraham and Marsden, 1978). Without going into mathematical details I want to consider how finding the trajectories and stability of the system are closely related and counterpoised to random behavior on the part of dynamical systems, a matter already discussed at the end of chapter 2.

First, some historical remarks about the problem of stability. As already mentioned, a first proof was proposed by Laplace in 1773, another proof by Lagrange in 1776, and another by Poisson in 1809. All these proofs depended upon what are known as series expansion techniques. The well-known nineteenth-century mathematician Dirichlet in 1858, not long before his death, claimed to have a solution and because he was known for the rigor and carefulness of his work, King Oscar of Sweden offered a prize for discovery of the proof or the finding of a new proof that the solar system is stable. King Oscar's prize was given to Poincaré in 1889. However, Poincaré (1890) did not really settle the problem in the way desired. Already in 1887 Bruns had shown that no quantitative methods other than series expansions could settle the N-body problem, and Poincaré showed that the series expansions referred to earlier of Laplace, Lagrange, etc., diverged rather than converged as required in order to have a proper solution.

Poincaré was given the prize not because he solved the problem of stability but because of the wealth of new ideas that resulted from prolonged study of the problem.

There are two aspects of unstable systems that make prediction of their behavior difficult and in many cases impossible in practical terms. This is true in spite of the fact that the dynamical systems are deterministic in character. One source of difficulty for unstable systems is that the initial conditions can be measured only approximately. If the systems are not stable in the appropriate sense, it will be impossible to predict their behavior for any but very short intervals of time with any accuracy, because of the errors in measurement of initial conditions. The matter is sometimes discussed as if the whole problem resides in the initial conditions, but this is not the case. Even when the initial conditions are assumed to be known precisely, there are still problems of prediction for unstable systems. The solutions have the problems mentioned for the three-body problem. There is no closed analytical solution. Methods of numerical approximation thus must be used. When the solution function, which may in principle be proved to exist, is sufficiently pathological in character, no extrapolations based on various methods of series expansion will give accurate predictions. Typical examples in which this is the case are predictions of weather, of economic trends, of the stopping point of a turning roulette wheel, or the breakup of a large piece of ice. In other words, for fundamental mathematical reasons accurate and extended predictability of even relatively simple physical systems may turn out to be an impossibility. The linkage in the discussion of many philosophical texts of prediction and determinism is in fact very wide of the mark. (For a good technical but not too difficult exposition of these matters, see the expository article of Gumowski, 1982.)

What these results about prediction and instability that I have sketched lead to is the failure of the naive model of Boscovich to reduce the behavior of physical phenomena to one set of natural laws. Even if we have in some conceptual sense a claim to understand the fundamental forces between particles, a claim that is now being reinstituted in the fashion of Boscovich by recent particle physics, there is no hope of having a buildup from parts to an understanding of the whole. We shall not be able to understand any of the phenomena mentioned above by a microscopic theory of parts, at least on present evidence and in terms of present theoretical ideas. There is reason to think too that these ideas reach down to a fundamental level and will be very difficult to dislodge. The outcome for ideas about unity of science is that, even if we have the pious hope that we understand the fundamental forces of the smallest parts of matter and should be able to constitute by principles of composition the forces between all larger parts of matter, we shall not in actual fact be able to carry through such a program. Many parts of science that deal with macroscopic phenomena must go their own way in an appropriate form of independent pluralism.

INFORMATION AND COMPUTATION

My second example is the basis of an argument against the unity of science that has a different flavor from any of those yet presented. It is an argument that in one sense runs along familiar ground. It is the argument that psychology cannot be reduced to physiology, nor physiology and biology to physics, but the argument can be put in proper terms because of our ability to formulate the concepts of interest in completely explicit terms. I refer to the argument that the most important features of a computer program, namely, its correctness and the characterization of the mathematical function computed, are independent of any particular realization of the program in hardware. It seems appropriate to say that from the standpoint of these main characteristics the particular physical hardware is irrelevant. This does not mean the hardware is irrelevant to all aspects of a program, for example, the particular features of the hardware will have an important effect on running time and in other respects on the possibility of computational error. On the other hand, the important central features of meaning and correctness of a program are in a strong sense irrelevant to the particular physical realization in which the program is embodied. What I am saying is true of any standard computer language. Pick your favorite to have a vivid example in mind. Whether my computer is made up of vacuum tubes, old-fashioned transistors, densely packed silicon chips, Josethson junctions, or optical devices makes no real difference as far as essential features of a program are concerned. The physical realizations could not be more different. There seems absolutely no unifying idea back of their physical realization. Description in purely physical terms of a program embodied in a computer of 1955 and a computer of 1985 have little in common. What they do have in common is purely from the standpoint of information and computation. There is no practical and interesting sense of reduction of the theory of information or the theory of computation to purely physical concepts.

I have concentrated here on computation, but storage of information has exactly the same character. Even in one computer there is a great physical difference between storage in core memory and storage on disks and storage on tape, but we have no problems of talking about the same information being in any one of three places. But it would be regarded as mistaken by almost all knowledgeable persons to try to give a unified *physical* theory of the representation of the information. What is important is to give a representation at a more abstract level, removed from the detailed physics of the different media of storage. Reduction and unification are not hopeless but, even more important, totally irrelevant and uninteresting from either a theoretical or practical standpoint. Here is still another example. It is impossible to imagine the complex operating system for a modern computer of any size being characterized in purely physical terms.

Engineers designing informational and computational storage devices must relate the physical properties of the media and materials they plan to use in an intricate and intimate way with the desired informational or computational structures that are to be implemented. But this intimate linkage from the standpoint of engineering design has little impact in the theory of information or computation, and has even less impact on the programmer or other practictioner hard at work in the real world applying implicitly or explicitly ideas of the theory of information or computation. There is one point that needs to be mentioned so as to avoid any misunderstanding. Modern-day computers are based upon the von Neumann architecture, which is essentially a serial architecture. A single instruction is processed at any single instant of time. In all likelihood we shall see in the future powerful parallel processors and it may turn out to be that in fifty years parallel processors will be the dominant design of current computers. But this does not affect what I have to say. The theory of computation will change to make proper accommodation for the theory of parallel processing. This is a concept of the theory of computation, not a physical concept. It will of course be realized in different ways physically just as current von Neumann architecture is realized in various ways, but it will no more mean that there is a physical reduction of the theory of computation because we move to the theory of parallel computation in physical terms than there was in the cases just mentioned.

MENTAL SOFTWARE AND PHYSIOLOGICAL HARDWARE

Another example, related to the one just discussed but with a different flavor, concerns the relation between mind and brain. It is not my purpose here to review the large philosophical literature on these matters, but to make a certain point related to the earlier point about software and hardware for computers. It is not possible to separate the software from its hardware realization, but the absence of this separation does not imply some strong sense of unity. So it is in the case of our mental life. Most of us accept the thesis that our mental life is totally contingent upon our brains being in good working order, but this does not mean that any strong theses about reducing mental events to brain events can be carried out. There is a particular point about this related to discussion of software and hardware that I want to make.

When computer programs are made adaptive and machines are asked to learn, one feature of the programs is that we cannot predict their exact sequence of lines. Random events intervene, particular questions of timing, exact occurrence of external events, etc. affect what takes place and thereby have an impact on the programs that are written without external intervention. It seems to me that the case is very persuasive for the same thing happening in human beings. Our brains have many common physiological characteristics, but the way in which the software of mental events is written in that hardware varies enormously from individual to individual. There is, I conjecture, no serious exact physical similarity between the way I store the word *computer* and the way any other person stores it. Just by looking at the physical structure of the brain we shall not be able to identify any particular storage of any particular memory, for example, just as we cannot do that in the much simpler and much better understood case of computers. We cannot even decide by physical examination very gross questions such as whether a person whose memories we are supposedly looking at physically spoke English or Chinese. We cannot tell from physical examination whether the person was a poet or an engineer and had the different kinds of memories that we might associate with two such different professions. It is not appropriate to make here the strongest possible argument, but it seems to me that from many different kinds of considerations it is reasonable to believe that the mental software of each individual is idiosyncratically imbedded in the physiological hardware of that individual. There are methods of storing information in computers that lead to similar apparently chaotic results. A good example would be hash coding, where what is stored is spread around in ways I shall not try to describe in detail here but lead to the effect that it would be extraordinarily difficult, if not impossible, by physical examination of the storage media to determine what in the world has been stored there in terms of programs and information.

And so I would claim there will be no unity of science at the level of brain and mind. There will of course be connections just as there are connections between physics and the hydrodynamics of cells. Those connections will not be anything like a vigorous reducing connection. The vivid and intriguing mental history of an individual can only be known by mental means, never in any serious detail by physiological ones.

It is this line of argument that makes psychology as fundamental a science as physics. On various occasions mistaken views have been held about the reduction of psychology to physiology or, in even more bold terms, the reduction of psychology to physics. Nothing, it seems to me, is further from being the case, and it is because of this absence of any evidence that reduction can take place that theses about behaviorism remain important. Psychological concepts, complex skills, and, in a still more traditional terminology, mental events as occurring at least in other persons and other animals can be known only from behavioristic evidence. We will not obtain that evidence by chemical or physical examinations of the cells of the body. Behaviorism as a fundamental methodology of psychology is here to stay. This does not mean that a reductionist thesis of behaviorism either should be accepted. We will not reduce mental events to characterization in purely behavioristic terms. We depend on behavioristic evidence about mental events, but this evidence does not provide adequate defining conditions.

There is one comparative point about these three examples that stands a classical argument about the relation between physics and psychology on its head. It is common on the part of many philosophers to claim that psychology is a very different subject from physics and the theory of individual prediction is not possible in psychology in the way that it is in physics. The kinds of examples I have just been discussing argue strongly against any simple defense of this argument. Classical and especially recent work on simple physical systems shows that individual prediction for many physical systems is out of the question for the fundamental reasons of instability mentioned earlier. On the other hand, the possibility of predicting individual behavior is one of the most important features of human interaction. Without such an ability to predict human behavior, social interaction in most of what we think of as planning and the exercise of prudence would not be possible. The reason back of this is a fundamental one. For many different kinds of reasons there is a stability in biological systems that is often missing from simple physical systems. This presence of structural stability makes prediction possible and is one of the most striking features of biological systems. Perhaps in the next century we will come to think of psychology as being a better predictive science than physics. At the moment, one can only say this with a certain sense of irony, but the examples I have discussed suggest the reasons why this might change.

7

Language

There is a substantial history of applied statistical methodology in linguistics, but for a variety of reasons the use of such methodology has been out of favor among linguists since about 1960. It never had any serious following among philosophers of language. It is not my purpose here to examine the ins and outs of this history, the details of which are rather far removed from my main themes. The conceptual issues raised by this literature are sufficiently subtle and in their own way technical that it would take all the space available to examine them in some detail. Moreover, I am sympathetic with some of the criticisms of the earlier statistical methodology in linguistics and in no sense want to rest the case for the central character of probabilistic aspects of language on this work.

My main thesis about language will be regarded as radical and unacceptable by many. It is that probabilistic features are central to all major aspects of language: phonology, syntax, meaning, and prosody. From a philosophical standpoint the claims about meaning are the most deviant from dominant views in the philosophy of language over the past several decades. I begin with the phonological aspects of speech production and reception, then go to grammar, and devote the last half of the chapter to semantics and meaning. Issues about prosody arise throughout the chapter.

SPEECH PRODUCTION AND RECEPTION

There are at least four levels of units that have been extensively discussed both theoretically and experimentally in attempting to understand the processes of speech production and recognition.

Each of these levels is characterizable in a discrete way, but as I shall argue, this discreteness is only a crude approximation of the complicated continuous data. The four levels, from bottom to top so to speak, are: distinctive features, phonemes, syllables, and words. There is, of course, nothing metaphysically or conceptually privileged about these four levels. Some variants have been proposed and it would be easy to think up new ones, but the points to be considered here can be illustrated by restriction to these four levels, which have the virtue of having been extensively discussed in the linguistic, psychological, and engineering literature on speech production and reception.

At whatever level of unit we focus our analysis, the basic data are about as complicated as one can find in any domain of science. The human vocal tract, which produces desired sounds under the control of the central nervous system, has a shape that is a nightmare from the standpoint of any obvious or simple physical theory of sound production. The subtle contortions produced dynamically are even worse. There is litle hope of having a completely detailed deterministic theory of the action of the muscular system producing the sound-pressure waves that constitute speech. The apparatus of reception proceeding from the pinna, through the middle ear to the cochlea, is just as much a physical nightmare from the standpoint of any thorough understanding of how the sound-pressure wave embodying speech is processed.

Of equal complexity and subtlety are the interactions between the four levels among themselves and with the "higher" levels of grammar and semantics. Factual or speculative details about these interactions cannot be gone into, but there is one conceptual point to be emphasized. Language systems develop as a piece. One level is not set, then the next, etc. There is no rock-bottom ontology of distinctive features or phonemes. But describing the joint development and the inter-action of the various levels identified for purposes of analysis is something that has as yet barely begun in a detailed scientific fashion.

Distinctive features.   As originally formulated by Fant (1960), the principal distinctive features of phonemes are the following contrasting pairs: vocalic or nonvocalic, consonantal or nonconsonantal, compact or diffuse, grave or acute, flat or plane, or sharp or plane, tense or lax, or finally, strident or mellow. Two salient problems seem to beset any feature analysis of the acoustical sound-pressure wave reaching the ear of the receiver. For simplicity in this discussion I shall forgo further detailed remarks about the production of speech in the vocal tract. One problem is that of establishing that distinctive features can be objectively characterized as invariants of the acoustic signal. From an acoustical standpoint, what is the invariant feature of the sound-pressure wave that leads me to say that a vocalic feature, for instance, is present? The second problem concerns showing that the continuous pressure-wave over a short time-interval can be adequately analyzed by a small finite number of distinctive features. It is easy to see how the first problem could be solved by a proof of invariance of a given list of features, but then the list might not be adequate to solve the second problem.

Phonemes. Distinctive features are supposed to provide a discrete analysis of phonemes, which are themselves "units" of sound over a short time interval. In a similar way, phonemes are supposed to provide a discrete temporal analysis of the sound-pressure way of an entire utterance. Distinctive features of a given phoneme occur essentially simultaneously; the phonemes of a given utterance occur in temporal succession. In principle, phonemic sound should be able to reduce the continuous sound wave to a finite linear sequence of phonemes. That such a drastic reduction can be made is an idea much cherished by many linguists. But problems similar to those besetting the claims for distinctive features are now well recognized. They are the problems of invariance and segmentation. Spectographic and other physical analysis of speech sounds shows that there is no straightforward identification of the invariants for a given short time interval that correspond to a given phoneme, and similarly there is no obvious, or even subtle, marking of the segmentation into distinct phonemic units (for a good discussion of the issues, see Pisoni and Sawusch, 1975).

The complexity of the phenomena of speech perception suggests at once that probabilistic considerations will be essential to any adequate theory. It is not appropriate to advance a detailed argument here, but because so much linguistic theory is implicitly deterministic and discrete, it is important to say why such views seem incorrect and, above all, unpromising for future developments.[1] One argument for what I am saying rests on the many experiments showing the significant effects of social context, speaker rate, speaker idiolect, and the like on speech perception. These many contextual effects suggest that any simple deterministic template model of either distinctive features or phonemes is bound to fail. A second argument that is certainly not decisive but carries some weight is this. In the extensive mathematical and quantitative literature on the digital analysis and synthesis of speech, distinctive features and phonemes are scarcely mentioned. The basic parameters that are estimated and theorized about are those of formant and fundamental frequency. A formant is essentially a sinusoidal component of the sound-pressure wave produced by the vocal tract. For an average vocal tract there will be three or four formants identifiable within frequencies up to 3,000 hertzs—the cutoff of most current telephone transmission, and four or five up to 5,000 hertzs. The fundamental frequency is the reciprocal of the pitch period, which is the time-interval between the opening and closing of the vocal folds at the bottom of the vocal tract. Formants and fundamental frequencies are estimated in speech data by sampling methods. Probabilistic considerations are implicit in the entire process. (For a clear technical presentation of methods of analysis, see Markel and Gray, 1976.)

Syllables and words. The same problems of invariance and segmentation beset any simple deterministic theories for identifying syllables or words in the sound-pressure wave. It is especially important to note that word boundaries are not at all well marked in continuous speech. Indeed, the very concept of an exact boundary seems inapplicable.

The arguments I have given do not prove in a decisive way that deterministic theories of the production and recognition of distinctive features, phonemes, syllables, or words are impossible. But the arguments about continuity and complexity are of great practical importance in the actual construction of theories. It will,

[1] In a different spirit but with a clear analogy, the same move to the discrete is made in quantum mechanics. In Mackey's well-known axiomatization (1963), the operators considered are reduced to those corresponding to events, i.e., to yes–no questions. Imagine from a physical standpoint studying the continuous trajectory of a particle with such an apparatus. It is fine for foundations, but not for attack on complex problems. The same move is made in probability theory in complex applications from algebras of events to continuous, or at least piecewise continuous, distributions.

I claim, be very surprising if anything but probabilistic theories do in fact turn out to work.

Although a fully adequate grammar for a substantial portion of any natural language does not exist, a vigorous and controversial discussion of how to choose among competing grammars has developed. On occasion, criteria of simplicity have been suggested as systematic scientific criteria for selection. The absence of such systematic criteria of simplicity in other domains of science inevitably raises doubts about the feasibility of such criteria for the selection of a grammar. Although some informal and intuitive discussion of simplicity is often included in the selection of theories or models in physics or in other branches of science, there is no serious systematic literature on the problems of measuring the simplicity of theories. Nor is there any systematic literature on which criteria of simplicity are used in a substantive fashion to select from among several theories. There are many reasons for this, but perhaps the most pressing one is that the use of more obviously objective criteria leaves little room for the addition of further criteria of simplicity. The central thesis of this section is that objective probabilistic criteria of a standard scientific sort may be used to select a grammar. (The ideas set forth were originally proposed in Suppes, 1970a.)

Certainly the general idea of looking at the distribution of linguistic types in a given corpus is not new. Everyone is familiar with the remarkable agreement of Zipf's law with the distribution of word frequencies in almost any substantial sample of a natural language. The empirical agreement of these distributions with Zipf's law is not in dispute, although a large and controversy-filled literature is concerned with the most appropriate assumptions of a qualitative and elementary kind from which to derive the law. While there is, I believe, general agreement about the approximate empirical adequacy of Zipf's law, no one claims that a probabilistic account of the frequency distribution of words in a corpus is anything like an ultimate account of how the words are used or why they are used when they are. In the same sense, in the discussion here of probabilistic grammars, I do not claim that the frequency distribution of grammatical types provides an ultimate account of how the language is used or for what purpose a given utterance is made. Yet, it does seem correct to claim that the generation of the relative frequencies of utterances is a proper requirement to place on a generative grammar for a corpus.

Because of the importance of this last point, let me expand it. It might be claimed that the relative frequencies of grammatical utterances are no more pertinent to grammar than the relative frequency of shapes to geometry. No doubt, in one sense such a claim is correct. If we are concerned, on the one hand, simply with the mathematical relation between formal languages and the types of automata that can generate these languages, then there is a full set of mathematical questions for which relative frequencies are irrelevant. In the same way, in standard axiomatizations of geometry, we are concerned only with the representations of the geometry and its invariants, not with questions of actual frequency of distribution of figures in nature. In fact, we all recognize that such questions are foreign to the spirit of either classical or modern geometry. On the other hand, when we deal with the physics of objects in nature there are many aspects of shapes and their frequencies that are of fundamental importance, ranging from the discussion of the shapes of clouds and the reasons for their shapes to the spatial configuration of large and complex organic molecules like proteins.

From the standpoint of empirical application, one of the more dissatisfying aspects of the purely formal theory of grammars is that no distinction is made between utterances of ordinary length and utterances that are arbitrarily long, for example, of more than 10^{50} words. One of the most obvious and fundamental features of actual spoken speech or written text is the distribution of length of utterance, and the relatively sharp bounds on the complexity of utterances, because of the highly restricted use of embedding or other recursive devices. Not to take account of these facts of utterance length and the limitations on complexity is to ignore two major aspects of actual speech and writing. As we shall see, one of the virtues of a probabilistic grammar is that it can deal directly with these central features of language.

Still another way of putting the matter is this. In any application of concepts to a complex empirical domain, there is always a degree of uncertainty as to what level of abstraction we should reach for. In mechanics, for example, we do not take account of the color of objects, and it is not taken as a responsibility of mechanics to predict the color of objects. (I refer here to classical mechanics—it could be taken as a responsibility of quantum mechanics.) But ignoring major features of empirical phenomena is in all cases surely a defect and not a virtue. We ignore major features because it is difficult to account for them, not because they are uninteresting or improper subjects for investigation. In the case of grammars, the features of utterance length and utterance complexity seem central; the distribution of these features is of primary importance in understanding the character of actual language use.

A different kind of objection to considering probabilistic grammars at the present stage of inquiry might be the following. It is agreed on all sides that an adequate grammar, in the sense of simply accounting for the grammatical structure of sentences, does not exist for any substantial portion of any natural language. Extravagant claims are sometimes made to the contrary by a fervent advocate of this or that school of grammatical thought, but the many problems still to be solved are recognized by thoughtful people of every theoretical persuasion. In view of the absence of even one adequate grammar, what is the point of imposing a stricter criterion to account also for the relative frequency of utterances? It might be asserted that until at least one adequate grammar exists, there is no need to be concerned with a probabilistic criterion of choice. My answer to such a claim is this. The probabilistic approach is meant to supplement rather than to be competitive with traditional investigations of grammatical structures. The large and subtle linguistic literature on important features of natural language syntax constitutes an important and permanent body of material. To draw an analogy from meteorology, a probabilistic measure of a grammar's adequacy stands to ordinary linguistic analysis of particular features, such as verb nominalization or negative constructions, in the same relation that dynamical meteorology stands to classical observation of the clouds. While dynamical meteorology can predict the macroscopic movement of fronts, it cannot predict the exact shape of fair-weather cumulus or storm-generated cumulonimbus. Put differently, one objective of a probabilistic grammar is to account for a high percentage of a corpus with a relatively simple grammar and to isolate the deviant cases that need additional analysis and explanation. At the present time, the main tendency in linguistics is to look at the deviant cases and to ignore trying to give a quantitative account of that part of a corpus that can be analyzed in relatively simple terms.

Another feature of probabilistic grammars worth noting is that such a grammar can permit the generation of grammatical types that do not occur in a given corpus. It is possible to take a tolerant attitude toward utterances that are on the borderline of grammatical acceptability, as long as the relative frequency of such utterances is low. The point is that the objective of the probabilistic model is not just to give an account of the finite corpus of spoken speech or written text used as a basis for estimating the parameters of the model, but to use the finite corpus as a sample to infer parameter values for a larger, potentially infinite "population" in the standard probabilistic fashion. On occasion, there seems to have been some confusion on this point. It has been seriously suggested more than once that for a finite corpus one could write a grammar by simply having a separate rewrite rule for each terminal sentence. Once a probabilistic grammar is sought, such a proposal is easily ruled out as acceptable. One method of so doing is to apply a standard probabilistic test as to whether genuine probabilities have been observed in a sample. We run a split-half analysis, and it is required that within sampling variation the same estimates be obtained from two randomly selected halves of the corpus.

Another point of confusion among some linguists and philosophers with whom I have discussed the methodology of fitting probabilistic grammars to data is this. It is felt that some sort of legerdemain is involved in estimating the parameters of a probabilistic grammar from the data which it is supposed to predict. At a casual glance, it may seem that the predictions should always be good and not too interesting because the parameters are estimated from the very data they are used to predict. But this is to misunderstand the many different ways the game of prediction may be played. Certainly, if the number of parameters equals the number of predictions the results are not very interesting. On the other hand, the more the number of predictions exceeds the number of parameters, the greater the interest in the predictions of the theory. To convince one linguist of the wide applicability of techniques of estimating parameters from data they predict and also to persuade him that such estimation is not an intellectually dishonest form of science, I pointed out that in studying the motion of the simple mechanical system consisting of the Earth, Moon and Sun, at least nine position parameters and nine velocity or momentum parameters as well as mass parameters must be estimated from the data (the actual situation is much more complicated), and everyone agrees that this is "honest" science.

A third confusion of some linguists needs to be mentioned in this connection. The use of a probabilistic grammar in no way entails a commitment to finite Markovian dependencies in the temporal sequence of spoken speech. Two aspects of such grammars make this clear. First, in general such grammars generate a stochastic process that is a chain of infinite order in the terminal vocabulary, not a finite Markov process. Second, the probabilistic parameters are attached directly to the generation of nonterminal strings of syntactic categories. The process is Markovian only at the level of theoretical structure.

The purpose here is to define the framework within which empirical investigations of probabilistic grammars can take place and to sketch how this attack can be made. In the next section I give a simple example, indeed, a simple-minded example, of a probabilistic grammar, to illustrate the methodology without complications. Technical details of parameter estimation and a more realistic example are given in the appendix to this chapter.

Competence versus performance. An important feature of the linguistic literature on syntax is the preeminent role assigned to the theory of competence. Roughly speaking, this theory is defined to be the theory of the language itself, apart from consideration of precisely how it is acquired and used by speakers and listeners. Presumably the major goal of the theory of competence is to develop a theory of syntax, semantics, and phonology for a spoken natural language or class of languages. Being more amenable to attack, the problems of developing a theory of syntax have received the most attention. I want to express by several different arguments my skepticism about the need for such a theory in dealing with actual language use.

I make my first point by analogy to the study and use of mathematics. The formalization of mathematics within well-defined artificial languages has been for several decades an important part of investigations into the foundations of mathematics. In particular, once a given body of mathematics is formalized in such a language (that is, the formal language is stated, together with rules of inference and axioms of a nonlogical sort, for the mathematics) then a large number of general questions about the body of mathematics in question can be precisely discussed. There are three examples that suggest analogies to problems of language learning. The first is that it is a simple matter in the case of a formalized language to give a recursive definition of the well formed formulas. As everyone recognizes, such definitions are much simpler than the generative grammars that seem to be required for natural languages. But it still also seems true that for purposes of recognizing whether or not a particular expression is well formed, the formal recursive definition itself is seldom used by individuals who work with such a logical language. In difficult or doubtful cases, appeal to the formal definition may take place; typically it will not. Instead, individuals seem to use certain explicitly organized heuristics as cues of recognition.

A simple instance of this is the following. Consider the recursive definition of a well-formed formula in sentential logic. Now consider the expression

$$(((p) \rightarrow (q))($$

Even the novice does not have to apply the formal definition of a formula, working from the inside out and checking each step. Rather, he can instantly recognize that the expression is not a formula. Why? Because he will notice at once the left parenthesis at the right-hand end of the expression, and he need investigate no further. If people resort to heuristics even where the formal characterization is relatively simple, then *a fortiori* we would expect them to adopt such strategies when confronted with a language having a complex generative grammar.

The second example is well corroborated by general experience and is perhaps more appropriate. It concerns the matter of discovering formal proofs of theorems. In principle, it is quite straightforward to give an algorithm for all proofs. One simply begins by enumerating the proofs and eventually any proof will turn up in this list after only a finite number of predecessors. Thus, if a certain conjecture is proposed as a theorem one can begin to enumerate proofs, and if the conjecture is indeed a theorem at some point it will be produced as a proof. If the conjecture is not a proof, then this procedure will not establish this conclusion. The point is, however, that any proof will be produced by this simple algorithmic procedure. But no one would seriously suggest this algorithm as a feasible method of proving theorems. The analogy to learning a language should not be pressed too far, but the basic point is valid; namely, that the existence of algorithms for finding proofs or of formal grammars for characterizing a natural-language grammar hardly guarantees that subjects do in fact employ these particular algorithms or generative rules, or that the rules even have substantial relevance to the actual methods of learning and use.

A third example may be cited to amplify this last remark. It concerns the relation between the theory of games and actually playing a game skillfully. For a game of perfect information (for example, chess) it can be proved that there is a pure strategy such that if a player adopts it, he is ensured of at least a certain outcome in every game. And for a game of imperfect information (for example, bridge) optimal random strategies exist for each player. Moreover, the games mentioned are wholly finitistic, and in the case of bridge the total number of bids and plays is not in-ordinately large. But the complete enumeration of strategies for chess or bridge is far beyond the capabilities of even the best computers, and the analytical computation of optimal strategies is similarly impractical. How, then, do people actually learn to play chess or bridge? It is a question we cannot answer in detail, but there do seem to be cogent reasons for thinking that the mathematical theory of games has little relevance to actual behavior in these more complicated games. Game theory and a theory of competence are analogous in the following sense: neither intends to consider limitations of human information-processing capacities, and neither intends to consider the mnemonics and strategies which people invent to utilize their capacities more effectively.

In this connection I offer two subsidiary remarks about the concept of infinity in a theory of competence. The first is to record the impression that linguists concerned with the theory of competence and with the fact that a generative grammar will generate an infinity of sentences are rather too impressed with this infinity of possibilities. From the standpoint of language learning and use there is certainly no sharp distinction to be made between a collection of 10^{100} sentences and an infinite collection of sentences. A finite language of the size indicated could not be learned by any enumeration routine. If one is going to object to a language that is finite but still quite large, the meaningful objection is not that phrase-structure rules are unnecessary. Rather, it is that the imposition of finite bounds creates mathematical difficulties in the recursive system.

I want to cite another analogy to express my skepticism that the theory of competence as now formulated will be of serious systematic help in developing an adequate theory of performance. This analogy derives from computer science. A decade or so ago many people fondly hoped that the theory of recursive functions as developed extensively in mathematic logic would be of major use in the foundations of computer theory. It is fair to say that this has turned out not to be so, and for reasons that seem obvious. The classical theory of recursive functions involves infinite domains and unbounded operations, whereas the theory of actual computers is necessarily restricted to bounded finite systems. There is good reason to believe that it is precisely the finitistic limitation of actual computers that is responsible for the lack of deeper application of the theory of recursive functions in computer science. Admittedly, we have a relatively clear understanding of the finitistic limitations of the computers now constructed, and we have a much less refined understanding of the finitistic limitations of human powers of learning and memory. Nonetheless, the existence of finite limitations to human capabilities is a fact too obvious to require demonstration. The importance of these finitistic restrictions is sufficient to provoke suspicion that the theory of competence may be irrelevant, just insofar as it does deal with an infinite collection of objects.

A general reason for neglecting the theory of competence is the absence of any probabilistic element in currently formulated theories of competence. I have already mentioned one simplifying abstraction of the theory of competence—that it admits sentences of arbitrary length. A case might be made for the admission of such sentences if, at the same time, the theory of competence were rich enough to derive the probability distribution of sentences. The simplest kind of marginal distribution might well be in terms of sentence length, and here it is apparent that as the length of a sentence became arbitrarily large the probability measure assigned to sentences of this class would become arbitrarily small, for any reasonable theory. In order that this point not be misunderstood I emphasize the word *marginal* in the characterization of the distributions. We would hardly expect that an adequate theory of competence that took into account the distributional character of sentences, phrases, morphemes, phonemes, etc. would regard sentence length as being fundamental. Certainly the assigned probability measure would be a function of sentence structure. Nevertheless, the marginal distribution of sentence lengths should be essentially unimodal in character, with sentences of longer and longer length being assigned smaller and smaller probabilities. In no general sense are probability concepts in conflict with ideas about competence, but it is unlikely that current theories of competence will become probabilistic in character. This, and the other reasons given, make it unlikely that theories of competence will, in the near term at least, be highly relevant to actual language use.

A simple grammar. A simple example that illustrates the methodology of constructing and testing probabilistic grammars is described in detail in this section. It is not meant to be complex enough to fit any actual corpus.

The example is a context-free grammar that can easily be re-written as a regular grammar. The five syntactic or semantic categories are just V_1, V_2, Adj, PN, and N, where V_1 is the class of intransitive verbs, V_2 the class of transitive verbs or two-place predicates, Adj the class of adjectives, PN the class of proper nouns, and N the class of common nouns. Additional nonterminal vocabulary consists of the symbols S, NP, VP, and AdjP. The set of production rules consists of the following seven rules, plus the rewrite rules for terminal vocabulary that belong to one of the five categories. The probability of using one of the rules is shown on the right. Thus, since rule 1 is obligatory, the probability of using it is 1. In the generation of any sentence, either rule 2 or rule 3 must be used. Thus the probabilities α and $1-\alpha$, which sum to 1, and so forth for the other rules.

Production rule	*Probability*
1. S→NP+VP	1
2. VP→V_1	$1-\alpha$
3. VP→V_2+NP	α
4. NP→PN	$1-\beta$
5. NP→AdjP+N	β
6. AdjP→AdjP+Adj	$1-\gamma$
7. AdjP→Adj	γ

This probabilistic grammar has three parameters, α, β, and γ, and the probability of each grammatical type of sentence can be expressed as a monomial function of the parameters. The possible grammatical types (infinite in number) all fall under one of six schemes, which are enumerated in the appendix.

Applications of probabilistic grammars.   Although the concept of a grammar's being enhanced by adding probabilistic parameters can be defended on general theoretical grounds as I have already argued, it is also natural to inquire about the usefulness of this additional structure in dealing with specific issues. I consider two such applications which also strengthen the case for the use of language being a deeply probabilistic phenomenon.

The first application is that of disambiguation. When as listeners we parse utterances as part of understanding their meaning, we are often faced with ambiguity. The surface structure of an utterance can have more than one grammatical interpretation and consequently more than one meaning. There is a well-known example of Chomsky's that illustrates the point. The sentence *Flying planes can be dangerous* can obviously be interpreted as meaning that the act of flying planes can be dangerous or that the objects that are flying planes can be dangerous. It seems plausible and natural that when faced with such grammatical ambiguity listeners pick the most likely parse as determined by the context in which an utterance is heard. In a large number of practical cases, what seems likely cannot be converted to certainty by the evidence available, especially in the short time span that can be devoted to understanding any one utterance as it occurs in a continuous stream of speech. As rough and ready computations of likelihood are quickly made—computations that include the identification of individual words as well—mistakes are made, but it is a function of such probabilistic computations to keep errors to a manageable level.

It could be claimed that I have not presented very much evidence for the inferences I am drawing about the essential role of probability in our practical disambiguation of utterances we hear or read. The general line of argument I have stated, however, seems almost necessarily correct. It is not easy to think of an alternative to the approximate maximization of likelihood, relative to the context, when ambiguity arises and a choice must be made.[2]

---

[2] To give a sense of quantitative results from a straightforward application of the ideas just discussed, I cite the data on probabilistic disambiguation from Suppes, Léveillé, and Smith (1974). Relative to the constructed grammar there were 660 ambiguous types,

The second application concerns the acquisition of language by young children. That children's spoken utterances become more complex between the ages of 2 and 4 years—the period of most significant language development—is undeniable. But there can be significantly different ways of conceiving how this development takes place. Moreover, the data that can be collected are so rich and complex that no current theory can account in any detail for very many aspects of the easily observed linguistic behavior. In fact, there is good reason for skepticism that an adequate deterministic theory will ever be formulated.

A typical and important issue about language learning is whether new rules of grammar come to be acquired and used by the child in a sudden, insightful all-or-none fashion or in a gradual incremental way. Psycholinguists who have been strongly influenced by the approach to cognitive development associated with Jean Piaget naturally tend to favor distinct stages of acquisition, which constitute a form of all-or-none learning. Those like myself who believe that essentially all complex skills are acquired incrementally favor the alternative hypothesis.

By adding alternative probabilistic learning models to probabilistic grammars a theoretical framework is easily set up for testing these two approaches to the development of a child's grammar. A detailed example of such a test is given in the appendix on grammars, but the general point is the direct and natural application of probabilistic concepts to the study of yet another complex linguistic phenomenon.

MEANING AND PROCEDURES

The great successes of set-theoretical semantics in mathematical logic, and the strong tradition, at least since Frege, against psychologism in logic, have been the basis of arguments for a similar approach to the syntax and semantics of natural language. If appropriate limits are clearly recognized, much can be and has been accomplished by set-theoretical methods. Some of the

corresponding to 938 tokens, in the corpus of the French child Philippe discussed in the appendix on grammar. When the simple rule of selecting the most probable of the parses was used, 88 types (133 tokens) were resolved in an intuitively unsatisfactory manner. Considering that the model made no use of semantical or context case, which we all do in practice, the results are reasonably good—over 85 percent of the types or tokens correctly classified.

notable successes are the restricted use of Tarski's definition of truth and the semantic analysis of modal and temporal concepts.

As a final account of meaning or reference, however, set-theoretical semantics in its standard form is clearly inadequate. There are several different ways of making the inadequacy explicit. On this point I agree with Chomsky. Linguistics broadly conceived is a part of cognitive psychology. It is a surprising and important fact that so much of the language of mathematics and science can be analyzed at a nearly satisfactory formal level by set-theoretical semantics, but the psychology of users is barely touched by this analysis. Not only logic, set theory, and modern abstract branches of mathematics but also such physically and perceptually intuitive disciplines as Euclidean or projective geometry can be given a formally very satisfactory set-theoretical semantics. Such easily visualized geometric relations as incidence of point and line, intersection of lines, betweenness of points, and congruence of triangles have natural and simple set-theoretical representations. Ordinary verbs of perception or motion do not. Nor do the many nouns and phrases describing emotional states or propositional attitudes. An excellent detailed case for a procedural approach to meaning, especially from the standpoint of a psychological theory of language acquisition and use, is that set forth by Miller and Johnson-Laird (1976). They emphasize the many different kinds of procedures any adequate theory must embody.

If we were able to give adequate set-theoretical representations of these and similar common words and phrases, we might, as in the case of geometry, be at least partially content with an austere, vegetarian-like, set-theoreltical diet in spite of our knowledge that "real" geometry and the discovery of nontrivial geometrical facts depend not at all on set theory.

But in the case of ordinary language the set-theoretical fare does not offer minimal nutritional content. True, we can have a certain amount of logic, but the gruel of quantifiers and connectives is too thin. Not only, in the case of English, are the four-letter words missing, but also the much more important high-frequency two-letter words: *to, in, of, on, at, by*, and *as*. The set-theoretical semantics of any of these seven two-letter words—or their functional analogues in other languages—is far from having been satisfactorily characterized.

At this point it would be reasonable for an advocate of set-theoretical semantics to respond that set-theoretical requirements of analysis are much weaker than procedural ones—for example, a computable function or relation with a given set-theoretical representation as a set of ordered pairs has ordinarily an unbounded set of procedural representations relative to a given fixed set of primitive procedures. (Anyone who has ever examined student computer programs written to solve a problem of moderate difficulty will recognize the reasonableness of this claim.) So if we cannot solve the weaker set-theoretical problem, why tackle the much harder procedural one?

At a general level, the answer is familiar. It is time for a fresh start. Moreover, the formal nonprobabilistic guidelines for a fresh start are already well laid down by two important lines of research that have been pursued for some time. The earlier line is the identification and definition of the set of computable functions and their representation in terms of Turing machines. The general set-theoretical representation of computable functions is trivial and uninteresting, but their equivalent representations as partial recursive, Turing-machine computable, etc., is one of the most important results of twentieth-century research in the foundations of mathematics.

The second line of research, that on computer programming, depends to a certain limited extent on the first, but the problems of greatest conceptual interest, for example, the efficiency of compilers or the correctness of operating systems, seem to require new and specialized concepts not found in the general theory of recursion. Above all, set-theoretical semantics seems to have been of little serious use in either practical or theoretical problems of programming.[3] What has been important, indeed fundamental, is the concept of procedure or subroutine, which has been central almost from the beginning to the recent theory of structural programming. Some cognitive psychologists, but perhaps no philosophers, talk about human procedures as if humans were a current computer model nearly ready for the marketplace. As will become clear in what follows, I think there are similarities between human procedures and computer subroutines, but there are also many essential differences (see proposition 6 below). Moreover, it should be clear that starting over with a computer analogy will not in itself solve many of the prob-

---

[3] The model theory of the lambda calculus developed especially by Dana Scott may have important applications in programming in the future.

lems left open in the set-theoretical semantics of natural language, for example, that of providing a proper analysis of the seven two-letter words mentioned earlier. But it does provide a more powerful framework for generating and testing hypotheses about the mechanisms of communication previously referred to.

An essential ingredient that is missing, however, is the probabilistic component. Systematic talk about recursion or structural programs is not enough. Communication is a probabilistic act. It is also a psychological act. The prima facie point of communication is to communicate meaning in order to give information, ask a question, issue an instruction, etc. Whether an attempt at communication is successful is ordinarily not certain. It is a probabilistic question whether a speaker expresses what he intended, and it is equally a matter of probability how what is expressed is received by a listener. I want to amplify several aspects of this claim for the central conceptual role of probabilistic processes in language understanding and communication.

First, what I am saying about communication is not inconsistent with set-theoretical semantics. It is rather that new concepts and propositions need to be appended to set-theoretical semantics to make it even a schematic theory of communication. To draw an analogy, statistical mechanics is not inconsistent with classical mechanics. The particles of statistical mechanics have position and velocity and forces acting on them, but the full theory requires something more, namely, probabilistic assumptions about the distributions of velocity and position, and there is no way to derive these distributions from classical mechanics itself. In the same sense there is no possibility of deriving the probability distributions relevant to use of language from Fregean truth values of sentences.

Second, the mere addition of probability in the form, for example, of some general randomness assumption does not yield a serious theory of communication. What is required is a set of assumptions about the process of communication that make at least schematic sense psychologically and define a structural stochastic process whose probabilistic aspects flow in a natural way from the assumptions about the process of communicating. The more secure we are about the details of this theory the firmer will be the metaphysical foundations of meaning we can construct. It is of course easy in the classical philosophical tradition critically discussed in earlier chapters to lay down the foundations in the absence of a satisfactory theory. The general theory I desire is not yet properly worked out, and so what I have to say about the metaphysics of meaning must be taken as tentative and undoubtedly wrong in several essential respects. But I consider it important to criticize certain standard theories of meaning and to indicate what I think is the right direction to go in searching for their replacement.

The key idea, already hinted at, is to adopt a procedural view of semantics. In order to get a more concrete sense of what procedural semantics is intended to be like, I turn now to a number of propositions I am prepared to defend.

Some general propositions about procedures. I begin with the relation between properties and procedures.

Proposition 1. *Properties are abstractions of procedures, just as extensions are abstractions of properties.*

Two different procedures may test for the same property. For example, we may easily have two different methods for deciding whether or not a certain flower has the property of being hybrid. We do not have a precise constructive theory for abstracting properties from procedures, but we do have a great deal of experience in ordinary contexts in making such abstractions. I will discuss this in greater detail later.

Proposition 2. *In finest detail, the meaning of a word, phrase, or utterance is a procedure, or collection of procedures.*

Thus, for me the meaning of the word *red* is the procedure I use in a given context for applying the term. I said *the meaning* and *the procedure*, but this is because I include contextual parameters in the procedure and thus in the meaning. In many ways it is more suggestive to speak of different procedures for applying, using, or understanding a given word or phrase, with the choice appropriate—in most cases at least—to the context, and this is the use I shall favor hereafter.

There is, of course, a tendency both in philosophy and in ordinary talk to use a concept of sameness of meaning that is much coarser than the one I am insisting on. Thus, someone asks: 'What does it mean to say that a triangle is isosceles?' The answer comes back: 'That just means the same as saying that two interior angles of the triangle are equal.' But as the endless literature on synonymy and propositional attitudes has repeatedly brought out, the concept of sameness at work in the above example is really that of semantic paraphrase, which is a quite loose sense of sameness. It is my argument that between semantic paraphrase and the very highly individuated sense of meaning given in proposition 2 there is no natural firm ground on which to stand. It certainly is the case that the definition I advocate will run contrary to much ordinary usage of the sort indicated, but I think the theoretical grounds are extremely good for starting with a highly detailed and private sense of meaning and then abstracting, by appropriate congruence relations, coarser senses. Such a "geometrical" theory of meaning that recognizes no single preferred congruence relation—just as there is none in geometry—is discussed in some detail below, especially in connection with the puzzle about responses.

Proposition 3.   *In finest detail, the meaning of a word, phrase, or utterance is private and probabilistic for each individual.*

The force of this proposition is not to deny the important public aspects of language, but to require an explicit theory of communication of how listeners understand speakers and how speakers test for this understanding. The probabilistic aspect of the privacy of meaning needs to be stressed. The particular procedure called on a given occasion when a word is spoken or heard is not uniquely determined by the context, but often results from current accidental associations that strongly influence the selection. The meaning in this sense is not a matter under conscious control or an object of purely intentional selection.

Because of their obvious inadequacies, earlier psychological theories of meaning built entirely on principles of association have been responsible for the downgrading of the importance of probabilistic processes of association in the mental life of all of us. We need not hold a purely associative theory of meaning in order to recognize the central place of association in our thinking. This point requires amplification. First, our production and reception of spoken utterances, like most of our thought processes, are not under conscious control. Only momentarily and by great efforts of concentration can they be consciously managed. Indeed, not only can thought processes not be controlled in any detail, they cannot even be consciously observed. I cannot observe myself in the process of recognizing a familiar face, a perfume I know, or the voice of a person I cherish. The same is true of what are thought of as purely intellectual processes like that of finding a mathematical proof. There is a considerable body of psychological evidence showing that what are accessible to consciousness are the results of thinking, seldom the processes (for a good review of the literature, see Nisbett and Wilson, 1977). Second, there is a considerable body of evidence demonstrating that the unconscious control mechanisms that guide our thinking processes use in an essential way principles of association, which are intrinsically probabilistic in character (for a wide-ranging discussion, see Anderson, 1976).

To avoid misunderstanding I want to reiterate the importance of having a proper place for a concept of public or linguistic meaning in a theory that takes as primitive private procedures. In principle, public meaning can be defined by abstraction from private procedures, but the converse is not possible. Quite simple models that catch certain essential features of private procedures can be constructed to show the impossibility of defining private procedures in terms of public meaning. It also is impossible to give an account of individual idiosyncratic features of language usage, as reflected, e.g., in the puzzle about responses discussed below, in terms of public meaning. There is an obvious analogy to thermodynamics and statistical mechanics. The macroscopic thermodynamic temperature of a gas, for example, corresponds to the public meaning of a word, the motions of individual particles to the private procedures of individual persons. An important feature of this analogy is that thermodynamics can be constructed from statistical mechanics, but not conversely.

Proposition 4. *High probability of successful communication depends, among other things, on the following factors:*

4.1. *Spoken words, phrases, and utterances are identified as "being the same", that is, being appropriately congruent, by speaker and listener.*

4.2. *The procedures called by words or phrases yield for the given context congruent computational results for speaker and listener.*

4.3.   *The speaker uses nonverbal as well as verbal cues from the listener to determine if the words he uses are calling result-congruent procedures in him and the listener.*

4.4.   *When the speaker judges his words are not calling result-congruent procedures, he uses paraphrases in terms of words he believes will call result-congruent procedures.*

The search for result-congruent procedures must ordinarily terminate successfully for a successful communication to occur.

What I have sketched in proposition 4 is a theory of communication. It is meant to outline how we are to move from private meaning to public communication. Although I am certainly not able to formulate the theory in anything close to a scientifically satisfactory form, there are some clarifying remarks about the various parts of proposition 4 that I want to make. First, as to words being perceived as the same by speaker and listener, this is a necessary nontrivial condition of communication and, in the central case of spoken language, requires an elaborate theory of how sameness of utterance is perceived. Even several occurrences of the same word in a given utterance can have very different acoustical properties, and it is not easy to identify those invariant features necessary for identification of sameness. In fact, it is fair to say that at a fundamental level the theory of such matters is far from being well worked out, as was already discussed earlier in this chapter.

The focus of 4.2 is the calling of result-congruent procedures by speaker and listener. What I mean by *result-congruent* procedures can be made more explicit by a simple example of a sort already alluded to. Consider two programs written to compute a certain function for a given range of input data. The two programs are clearly not identical; one has 500 lines and the other 550. What is more important, the run time (on a given computer) is 95 milliseconds for one and 135 milliseconds for the other. But for any given input selected from the range of input data, the two programs always compute the same result and thus are result-congruent.

Consider now a speaker talking to a listener, say, a pupil he is teaching arithmetic. The speaker says 'Look at this number', and simultaneously points his finger at the number which is at the top of a column of numbers. The procedure called up by these words of the speaker is not the same for the listener—or at least would have a low probability of being the same—but the two procedures in this simple case are result-congruent. Cases of this sort are an important aspect of good teaching of skills such as those of elementary mathematics or reading. Just as important, the good teacher uses 4.3 and 4.4 when 4.2 fails. That written texts cannot offer the devices of 4.3 to aid communication is perhaps their major restriction.

My continued focus is 4.2, and I want now to examine cases of casual conversation where the cognitive fit between speaker and listener is less tight. When this occurs, the sense of result congruence is coarse and loose, in line with the "geometrical" theory of meaning referred to earlier, for which there is no single sense of synonymy or congruence.

Smith says to Jones 'My wife came home from the hospital yesterday', and Jones responds 'I'm glad to hear it'. The sense of result congruence in this exchange is not easy to specify. Jones's response, keyed to his processing of Smith's statement, reflects his feelings as he imagines—visually or possibly propositionally—Smith's wife coming home. Smith's procedures are full of details that are missing in Jones's. In the case of Smith's processing of Jones's response, an even looser match of procedures is required to catch the sense of gladness. Smith will in fact probably depend as much on the prosodic features of Jones's utterance, and perhaps on his facial expression, as he will on any procedures directly called by *glad*. And this will be almost equally true for Jones's production procedures. The appropriateness of the loose sense of congruence is reinforced by our inability at present to say anything interesting about the semantics of *glad* at the more abstract set-theoretical level.

Suppose, on another occasion, Smith asks Jones 'Why does water almost always run out of basins in a counterclockwise direction?' (Smith lives in the northern hemisphere.) Smith is really puzzled by this phenomenon and he is not clear how to look upon the answer in a book on meteorology. All the same, his question evokes a procedure for answering it in his own mind. It is a pictorial matter of the water being twisted around, always in a certain way. He imagines water running out, and an obscure cause is applied to it. He is then satisfied with, and at a qualitative level understands, Jones's explanation of the rotation in terms of the Coriolis force generated by the earth's rotation, because it fits into his own qualitative, pictorial procedure.

I do not want to push these examples too far. There is a variety of psychological evidence that what is evoked by a complicated question can vary enormously from person to person. Some individuals seem to have almost no visual memory and little tendency to visual imagination. In any case, in my casual sketch of Smith's and Jones's internal processing, I have ignored most of what I consider methodologically and theoretically important, namely, the detailed synthesis of complex procedures from simple ones, as reflected either in the processing of complex sentences or in the building up of complex skills from simpler ones. I do want to emphasize that almost always this synthesis is made unconsciously, just as procedures as meanings are ordinarily called up automatically without any deliberate or conscious effort.

The difficulty and elusiveness of some of the examples I have discussed of result congruence may suggest that I think a theory of these matters is not possible at the present time. This is not what I believe about the matter and I want to make clear that I have some optimism about the theoretical possibilities. As I have insisted not only in this chapter but in other places in this book, it is hopeless to think of the theory of any complex phenomena as being complete in a serious sense. Because we cannot give a satisfactory theoretical account of something so elusive as Jones's response to Smith in the above example, it does not follow that a substantial theory cannot be developed for many other kinds of cases. It is obvious how one can proceed with scientific language and especially with programming languages. A more important kind of example to extend the range of the discussion of result congruence is to consider the great variety of social situations in which there is much subtle behavioral evidence that result congruence has been achieved. When a lecturer in a classroom, for example, says 'Look at this diagram', the prima facie evidence of result congruence is provided by the persons who are focused on the diagram only after he makes the request. Individuals will have processed the request in different ways and it will stir minor eddies of different feelings in different persons, but compliance with the request is indicated by the observable focus of attention. Naturally, somebody bent upon deception can satisfy this prima facie criterion and not satisfy a deeper criterion, but this is the kind of problem that arises at a very general scientific level and is not peculiar in investigations of result congruence. Whenever we have one person satisfying the request of another in a way that seems appropriate to the requestor, we have clear prima facie evidence of result congruence, often in cases in which the complete details of the request may not have been thoroughly understood, and certainly in many cases some of the prosodic nuances of the request will not have been grasped.

Thus, a psychological theory of result congruence can, it seems to me, be developed in ways that do not conflict but complement a standard result-congruence theory for such strictly scientific examples as computer programs. The contentious point to what I am saying about the development of such a psychological theory is that it does once again offer a reason to view questions of meaning as strongly psychological in character. I am claiming that many of the public aspects of meaning as reflected in result congruence are to be characterized in terms of psychological, and especially behavioral variables.

Proposition 5. *Classical set-theoretical referential semantics can be obtained, where appropriate, by abstraction from procedural semantics.*

This proposition, a special case of proposition 1, applies particularly to the language of mathematics and theoretical science. There is much that is satisfying and correct about standard model theory. Although it has not been completely and adequately developed for the natural and informal mathematical language of even elementary textbooks, the task does not seem impossible to accomplish. Again, the most obvious and direct examples are constructed by considering sets of computer programs all of which compute the same mathematical function. The possible variety in the programs is easy to demonstrate. The drastic abstraction reflected in saying only what mathematical function is being computed is apparent.

By keeping in mind that procedures are meant to apply to a range of possible input data, we can also easily see how to derive a set-theoretical possible-worlds semantics for propositional attitudes, intentional verbs, words that designate properties, etc. But the procedural approach, when it is specific, provides at once the opportunity of going beyond the general logic of propositional attitudes and the like to much more specific theories that restrict the possible worlds severely, just as in the classical case of geometry, by using the specific content of the procedures and their restricted ranges of applicable data.

As proposition 5 indicates, procedural and set-theoretical semantics are not inconsistent with each other. The procedural approach is meant to be almost infinitely more detailed and to ground the theory of meaning in the privacy of each individual's inaccessible mental procedures. To those in search of a bedrock of certainty as a foundation for fundamental concepts, the ground I have selected for meaning seems soft and unstable. But assigning a serious role to the psychology of language forces such a view to the fore.

To avoid any suggestion that I think procedural semantics leads to a view of persons as being anything like current computers, I end my list of general propositions with the following.

Proposition 6. *Human procedures are similar to computer subroutines, but there are notable differences*:

6.1 *What corresponds to the underlying machine language of human procedures is radically different from any current computer language; moreover, this underlying language is probably unknowable in complete detail.*

6.2 *Human procedures are subject to continual modification and are much affected by use; computer subroutines are not—they can stay the same for a thousand years.*

6.3 *Human procedures are intrinsically connected to perceptual and motor activities; for computer subroutines these connections are still artificial, awkward, and difficult.*

6.4 *Human procedures are intrinsically continuous rather than discrete or digital in character; prosodic features of speech are a prime example.*

6.5 *Human procedures are inextricably linked to human emotion and motivation, which have in turn a subtle physiological base; comparable characteristics of computers have as yet not even been conceptualized in any detail, let alone realized.*

6.6 *Plasticity and power of learning are central aspects of human behavior; computers as yet have little capacity for learning.*

I stressed at the beginning the usefulness of the computer analogy for thinking about human procedures, but a deeper and more detailed theoretical view of the differences is also needed. What I have formulated in proposition 6 is general and can be of use only in a preliminary way.

A puzzle about responses. Even when details about procedures are ignored, by bringing in other psychological variables it is easy to formulate a test for sameness of meaning that is stronger than traditional ones. I have already given examples in which observable psychological features are used to draw conclusions about result congruence or other important aspects of communication. Just because individual procedures are private and in full detail unknowable, it is fundamental to have some intermediate and coarser ground on which to stand in discussing varieties of congruence of meaning. Psychological variables of various sorts provide a natural source, neither too coarse nor too refined and inaccessible. However, in what follows it is important to keep in mind that I am not changing at all my view about procedures, but using some of the psychological ideas already developed to extend some traditional puzzles about sameness of meaning. The extension consists of introducing more psychological response variables than are ordinarily considered. These observable variables I regard as surrogates for individual procedures that cannot be directly observed or identified.

The kind of context I have in mind depends upon statements about the responses of an individual to individual propositions. As would be expected, the examples use indirect discourse.

(1) Jones responds more quickly in judging the truth of the proposition that Cicero was bald than he does in responding to the proposition that Tully was bald.

Ordinarily permutation of the words 'Cicero' and 'Tully' will change the truth value of this sentence and only one will make it true. The truth of (1) depends upon the detailed, highly idiosyncratic behavior of an individual. There is a great deal of data showing that fine distinctions will exist between any two words, no matter how frequent they both are in the individual's vocabulary and how frequently they serve as approximate synonyms. The point of this kind of example is that there is no fixed relation of synonymy that will patch it up—my proposed solution in terms of a hierarchy of congruences is set forth in the next section. I label the puzzle generated by (1) *a puzzle about responses* to distinguish it from puzzles about beliefs (e.g., Kripke, 1979), although the affinity is close.

We can ignore the complicated comparative structure of (1) and consider sentences like the following.

(2) Jones responds affirmatively in less than 200 milliseconds to the assertion that Cicero was bald, and in more than 200 milliseconds to the assertion that Tully was bald.

A possible objection is that indirect discourse is inappropriate, but this objection as far as I can see would apply equally well to the belief cases. The inability to go directly from indirect discourse to direct quotation in the belief cases has been well accepted since Church's discussion (1950). The same thing can be said about (1) and (2) above. These are propositions that are not committed at all to the language in which the propositions are formulated for the given individual who is responding.

There is a tension between philosophical and psychological methodologies that needs explicit attention. Whether in the case of beliefs or of responses, psychologists describing detailed data about beliefs or responses would feel called upon to record the actual sentence types that were used as tokens in eliciting responses from individuals. The form of indirect discourse used in the paradox about belief or the paradox about responses would not be regarded as methodologically acceptable. On the other hand, all speakers of English recognize the indirect discourse idiom, understand its meaning in an intuitive way, and have little difficulty with it. Also, ordinary speakers of English understand Church's point that the indirect discourse does not contain information about which language was used in expressing the proposition, either in the case of responses or beliefs. I am lingering over this point because it is possible someone would try to drive a wedge between the belief case and the response case by saying that only in the latter case are the actual sentences used critical.

It is also worth noting that statements about both beliefs and responses are easily constructed. For example:

(3) Jones responded immediately when asked whether he believes that Cicero was bald, but did not respond immediately when asked whether he believes that Tully was bald.

Or the more explicit sort of formulation used above:

(4) Jones responded affirmatively in less than 150 milliseconds when asked whether he believes that Cicero was bald, but in more than 150 milliseconds when asked whether he believes that Tully was bald.

Given differences in response time, one way of putting the matter is that Jones's beliefs about Cicero are more accessible than his beliefs about Tully, but of course this sounds paradoxical when put in this fashion. We might put it still another way, but this would involve an explicit commitment to the names.

(5) Jones responds to beliefs about Cicero more quickly when Cicero is denoted by 'Cicero' than when Cicero is denoted by 'Tully'.

The examples given have involved proper names, but the puzzle about responses is not so restricted as the following example similar to (1) shows:

(6) Jones responds more quickly when asked whether he believes that Newton was a bachelor than he does when asked whether he believes that Newton was an unmarried man.

The response examples I have given are obviously meant to call for a more complicated concept of assent than is ordinarily used in discussions only of beliefs. From a psychological standpoint, it seems apparent that assent is a complex phenomenon of many dimensions. Here I have only mentioned one new psychological variable, that of latency of response, but there are a host of others, ranging from heartbeat to galvanic skin reaction. I see no principled argument for drawing a line in any definite and final way so as to exclude any of the great variety of psychological variables that indicate the differential status of words, expressions, ideas, or emotions in the mind of a given individual. These many different variables define what I call a *profile of assent*.

Let me put the puzzle in an explicit conceptual fashion. The premises are these:

(7) There is a single fixed concept M of sameness of meaning for expressions.

(8) This concept *M* of sameness of meaning holds between expression tokens that are not identical, i.e., sameness of meaning is not just the trivial relation of identity.

(9) Expression tokens that stand in the relation *M* generate the same profile of assent.

(10) But for any individual there are expression tokens that stand in the relation *M* and yet have distinct profiles of assent.

Premises (7) and (8) are familiar claims about sameness of meaning. Premise (9) corresponds to the claim that expressions that stand in the relation *M* of sameness of meaning have identical cognitive significance. Premise (10) rests on elementary and widespread psychological evidence. It is obvious that these four premises are mutually inconsistent.

Various moves can be made formally to resolve the inconsistency. One is to deny that the profile of assent should include a variety of psychological variables. But this move would seem to emasculate the concept of assent and make it a highly abstract philosophical concept. The response variable of latency, for example, is widely used as a sensitive measure of degree of mastery of a concept or skill. Cognitive studies using this measure are legion. The commonsense basis of its relevance to cognition is also evident.

A variety of other variables that would naturally be included in a psychologically rich profile of assent can also be defended. There is one variable, however, that has not yet been mentioned but that should be accepted as relevant by everyone for testing sameness of meaning. The variable is that of *strength of belief*, which can be measured behaviorally in different ways, the most popular being by means of real or hypothetical bets at different odds. (It is important to emphasize that numerical bets are not required to infer a very good quantitative estimate of strength of belief, which is often also called degree of belief or subjective probability. Purely qualitative methods can be used. For reviews of the extensive theoretical and experimental literature, see Luce and Suppes, 1965; Krantz *et al.*, 1971).

Relevant examples are easy to construct. Because Jones is not quite sure that Tully is Cicero, the following is true:

(11) Jones's strength of belief in the assertion that Cicero was bald is greater than his strength of belief in the assertion that Tully was bald.

This kind of example can also be applied to the paradox of analysis. Given the usual view that strength of belief is a continuous variable, we might want to claim that most if not all cases of the paradox can be explained away by it. Smith is as certain as he can be that Cicero = Cicero, but just slightly less so that Tully = Cicero. The same analysis applies to the familiar example about female foxes and vixens.

In my own view, the argument for the cognitive significance of a rich profile of assent is substantial, and I would not want to reduce the profile just to being strength of belief. If that were insisted on, I would argue that the other behavioral measures mentioned not only define a profile of assent but are highly correlated with strength of belief. As is evident, I have not tried to set forth here a detailed conception of the relation between the psychological variables mentioned or alluded to. Some are more theoretical than others, and strong correlations between them would be expected.

The second and more promising move in dealing with the contradiction that follows from premises (7)–(10) is to deny there is any fixed, context-independent concept of sameness of meaning that must be held through the thick and thin of all possible puzzles or situations. The next section is focused on this approach.

As we go beyond simple ideas of assent to the full range of psychological response variables, it is clear that the assigned differentiations we can make strain the line between direct and indirect discourse. But pursuit of this point is not possible here.

CONGRUENCE OF MEANING

For a number of years I have been advocating a geometrical approach to the theory of meaning (Suppes, 1973a). The geometrical idea is to use various strong and weak concepts of congruence to get varying degrees of closeness of meaning. The idea is not to be caught in the search for a single concept of synonymy, just as in modern geometry we are not caught in a single concept of congruence as were the geometers of ancient Greece and Alexandria. We have in affine geometry, for example, a weaker sense of congruence than in Euclidean geometry, but it is also easy to get a commonsense notion of congruence that is stronger than the Euclidean one, namely, congruence that also requires sameness of orientation.

To continue this analogy with geometry, we would anticipate that extensional uses of language would require a relatively coarse congruence, whereas the expression of propositional attitudes, as exemplified in Mates's puzzle, or in the even stronger puzzle about responses, would require very strong congruence relations. In fact, due to the continuous character of the response data we would ordinarily think of the probability as being zero, that response times or, as psychologists would put it, the latencies of responses, would be the same for two distinct lexical items. Insofar as we want to account for the puzzle about responses, the data would suggest that only the trivial congruence relation of identity, the strongest one possible, will suffice. But I hasten to add that it is not really identity here, but only abstraction at a certain level. For example, if we treat in the ordinary sense two printed tokens of the same type as identical, we are making a certain kind of abstraction. If we look at the ordinary continuous production by sound-pressure waves of two tokens of the same spoken word-type, then the sense of identity in the sense of linguistic identity commonly used is a very gross abstraction from the detailed acoustical facts. The two sound-pressure waves will not be physically the same for the two tokens and in fact it is an intellectual problem of considerable magnitude to identify what are the invariant features in the two tokens that make possible the abstraction leading to their being regarded as two occurrences of the same type, a problem discussed earlier. Moreover, it is not just the sound-pressure wave but the context, including the prosodic features, the nonverbal features of the speaker and listener, etc., which also influence the richness of congruence we consider. It is only in an abstract axiomatic system that congruence can be brought down to the level of identity in any simple way. It would be part of my claim that there is no final or ultimate level of congruence. In actual language we have ever stronger concepts of congruence and there is no realistic bound to the number of levels.

Almog (1984) gives an excellent analysis of the three levels of what I shall call public meaning: namely, extensions, intensions, and characters in the sense of David Kaplan (1977). What I am urging is that above these three levels is an infinite hierarchy of stronger congruence relations. Mates's puzzle (1950) can be solved at the level of congruence corresponding to our conventional talk about identity for two tokens of the same type, but it is the point of my puzzle about responses to emphasize that it is easy to generate stronger puzzles that require us to go beyond this conventional identity of two printed tokens of the same type. Beyond the examples considered in the preceding section, we could easily generate two tokens of the same word which have slightly different stress. We would find it easy to create circumstances in which we could differentiate the responses to these two tokens. A similar exercise could be engaged in by considering for spoken words the familiar parameters of duration and intensity. The possibilities of variation here are properly infinite because of the naturally continuous character of the phenomena. I am not suggesting, of course, that there are conceptually interesting congruence relations for every possible continuous variation, but rather emphasizing that in principle there is a continuum of possibilities open to us.

The main point really is that there is no natural cutoff point in the concept of congruence of meaning at which we have no finer possibilities of congruence available to us. This is a point that I have not sufficiently emphasized in previous discussions, although I have made the point that we need to include congruence relations for speech acts (Suppes, 1980b).

A familiar example that directly involves the intensity of a spoken utterance is repeatedly seen in a parent's instructions to a child. There are many circumstances in which a child does not respond until the intensity of the request from the parent reaches a certain decibel level. A representation of what is taking place here by simple written transcription of what has been said orally would be utterly unfaithful to the facts, and thus not have the appropriate congruence relation. It is in fact surprising that the intricate and subtle aspects of spoken speech have entered so little into the large literature on sameness of meaning. I hope that my point about the infinite hierarchy of congruence of meaning is clearly understood to refer to and to provide an apparatus for dealing with the significant continuous variations of spoken speech.

Let me put the matter another way. Each token at whatever level we define it—sound-pressure wave, speech act with physical expression, etc.—is identical to itself, but the theory is not really interesting at this level of identity. For all purposes we want to abstract so that types contain more than single tokens. There is an infinite hierarchy of types between the public types of extension, intension, and character, on the one hand, and identity at the level of tokens on the other. This is a familiar problem of scientific theories, but not one that is dealt with in detail in ordinary model theory. The concept of individual in standard model theory is unanalyzed. There is no fixed concept of individual in the sense of model theory that is usable in the conceptual analysis of natural language. We should not be discontented with this state of affairs but should simply put it on the table as a fact of life. Depending upon the purposes at hand, we will abstract to relatively finer or relatively more coarse degrees of congruence. For printed scientific and philosophical texts the requirements of congruence are ordinarily relatively coarse. Analysis of the speech interaction between mother and child is quite another story. Prosodic nuances and shifts in stress may initially be more important than the extensional abstraction in ordinary printed language of what has been said. In principle, for each of the continuous points at which we can fix a level of congruence, a puzzle focused on identification of type at a lower level in the hierarchy is always possible. In practice, only certain points in the hierarchy will be of interest. I believe that the puzzle about responses shows that the consideration of such additional psychological variables does provide a natural way of identifying more refined congruences of interest than are reflected in propositional attitudes about beliefs alone.

Indirect discourse.   In considering the puzzle about responses or others of a similar sort, it is always natural to try to eliminate the idiom of indirect discourse, especially as a direct method of solving the puzzles. In my view, Church's arguments of many years ago (e.g., 1950 and 1954), mentioned earlier, remain valid. No simple scheme for replacing indirect discourse by direct discourse is going to work. Rather than review his arguments, I want to make some related points that reinforce the case for indirect discourse.

The first is this. When we examine individual sentences like any of (1)–(4) or (6) (pp. 161–163), there is an almost irresistible tendency for many to seek a direct-discourse replacement. But this move focused on individual sentences misses an important point. Deep uses of language are totally dependent on indirect discourse. Any adequate conceptual analysis of natural language must be able to deal correctly and in detail with indirect discourse. Examples of this essential dependence on indirect discourse lie immediately at hand. Any report of a long conversation depends on indirect discourse: she said that so and so, but I said that what really mattered was the following . . . In a conversation of two hours or so, easily 10,000 words can be spoken, and nobody can remember exactly even a small percentage of the sentences spoken—even those spoken by oneself.

Exacting and detailed as legal standards of evidence are, reports by witnesses of conversations must depend on indirect discourse. In all these cases the reason is obvious. Human memory and cognition function beautifully at paraphrasing, but are exceedingly limited in the exact and explicit recall of sequences of words spoken. It is essential to understand the semantics of indirect discourse because its continual use is an essential feature of the human mind.

My second point constitutes a move away from Church insofar as he argues for a single concept of synonymy (see especially Church, 1954), for then the concept of proposition is not really explained. The introduction of an infinite hierarchy of congruences permits the concept of proposition to be relativized and, correspondingly, appropriately fine distinctions to be introduced into the theory and practice of paraphrase. The formal theory cannot be worked out here, but it will be useful to sketch some of the main ideas. On the view of congruence I am advocating there is no single fixed proposition that a sentence-token expresses. Rather, a proposition is expressed by a sentence modulo a given congruence relation. Any other sentence standing in the given congruence relation to the given sentence expresses the same proposition—again, modulo the congruence relation. Given an infinite heirarchy of congruence relations, a given sentence-token expresses a potentially infinite number of different propositions.

In accepting a report in indirect discourse, we naturally make use without explicit acknowledgment of a principle of trust in partial truths. The congruences imposed by the paraphrasing reporter do not distort or leave out facts or nuances essential to the main thrust of the conversation being reported. Contrary to the oath administered to witnesses, we never really expect to hear the whole truth, and in most cases it would be intolerable if we had to. What we hope for is the right set of partial truths with the choice of the level of congruence left to the wisdom and good taste of our reporters, sensitive to how much we really want to know.

Grody to the max.   The title of this section is one of the more colorful phrases of what is called in California 'the Valley Girls'. Their idiomatic language and other habits have recently become a matter of some publicity. Their colorful language exemplifies a final point I want to make about the narrow conception of modern theories of reference and meaning.

My central point is that the readings given in simple ordinary sentences in English are fine for philosophical seminars and scientific textbooks. They are often far removed from much ordinary talk. It is important to be clear on my claim. I am not against the scientific or philosophical use of language. Much of it is good and it is an important part of our culture. It is just that it is a limited part of our use of language. Overemphasis on sentences that have a clear and definite literal meaning can lead to a mistaken view of reference and meaning for what may be the dominant use of ordinary language.

When one Valley Girl says to another 'Grody to the max' as they contemplate some drab, fat, and serious citizen walking toward them, how are we to think of the extension of their gleefully used phrase? By looking at an example or two we might begin to think we are making headway, but as we follow the Valley Girls around for an afternoon or two we find that *grody to the max* is a byword of conversation and any well-focused sense of its extension begins to fade away.

Let me examine the problem from another viewpoint, more systematically metaphysical. It seems to me there is much to be said for the view that contemporary theories of reference and extension follow hot on the trial of atomic theories of matter and the great success of such theories in the nineteenth century. If we have, on the other hand, a holistic view of the world, with context all-important, it is harder to see how a systematic concept of reference and extension can be made to work for individual terms and phrases. If the meaning of *red* or the meaning of *snowflake* or *headache* is, intuitively speaking, changing from context to context, there is little possibility of talking seriously about the reference or extension of such terms.

Let us consider a more scientific example that brings the point home in a stronger fashion. We can ask ourselves what are the *real* properties of hydrogen. It is easy enough to get a list from a chemistry book which talks about hydrogen in its free state or as a gas. We can also get a highly theoretical description in terms of its atomic structure, but if we ask for its phenomenological properties we do not get anything like a serious answer. There is an excellent discussion of this problem in the nineteenth-century literature of controversy on atomic theories of matter. It was pointed out by some acute commentators how absurd it was to think that hydrogen had real properties in any ordinary sense of property that it kept invariant in its different states. So hydrogen as a part of water has very different properties from hydrogen as a gas or hydrogen as a part of dry hydrochloric acid. We feel comfortable talking about the real properties of hydrogen only because we have an atomic theory that we rely on as our dominant way of thinking about hydrogen, even if we do not understand that theory very well or have much of a feeling for its formulation or what the limitations of the theory are. Apart from the atomic theory of matter we find it hard to sustain a serious discussion of the real properties of hydrogen. What is sometimes said of weak personalities can be said of certain elements: the influence of context is everything. Hydrogen taken in and of itself is but a mere shadow.

Let me take another kind of example that is rather like *grody to the max*. I have in mind the use by ordinary folk of what appear to be ordinary sentences that would, if formulated in a philosophical seminar, seem to have definite reference and sharp truth value. The key idea is the use of terms in a way that is not meant in any sense to be taken seriously or literally. Here are some instances.

One young man, wanting to impress his friends, says: 'I have been having trouble with my car—something wrong with the carburetor'. In fact, he does not have the vaguest idea that it is the carburetor, but he heard somebody use this phrase and it seems a happy one for him to use to sound impressive and specific.

One pensioner says to another: 'I have been having trouble with my liver lately'. And the immediate competitive response is 'So have I'. Neither pensioner has the vaguest idea that his complaint is really due to his liver, but the phrase is common, conventional in many ways, and so it is easy to use for a generally identified but vaguely identified sort of complaint.

In each of these sentences if the literal and exact meaning is followed through, the sentences uttered are false. But this would be the wrong way to take the sentence. It would be like asking, is a *grody to the max* expression appropriate or a sentence in which it occurs true? A more delicate and subtle approach to this kind of usage is needed.

Still another kind of example is provided by the familiar tale of romance. The young woman says 'no' to the young man, though he knows and she knows that she really means 'yes'. This is a different sort of example, but still an important one for which to provide an appropriate interpretation.

There is another way of making the essential point about *grody to the max*. The point comes out in responding to the claim that the reference or meaning of a word or phrase can always be determined by a disjunction of simpler references or meanings, each of which is appropriate in a certain set of circumstances. The response to this claim is that no proper conceptual formulation of such sets of circumstances can be given, and for fundamental reasons. Occasions of use of phrases like *grody to the max* represent volatile and unstable choices that can no better be accounted for than can an actual sequence of red and black in roulette. Retrospective study of various instances of use is not successful, for the flickers of feeling that pass from one Valley Girl to another as they look about them and pass their special phrases back and forth have, in my view, an irreducible random component. I await with skepticism serious deterministic proposals to explain their linguistic behavior.

The case is rather different in the nonstandard use of standard terms like *carburetor* and *liver*. The occasions of nonstandard use are very likely not so quicksilverish and unpredictable as the ones I have just been discussing. A theory of reference and meaning of nonstandard uses of standard words along familiar lines does not seem unfeasible. Saying 'no' when 'yes' is meant is a more difficult kind of case, but not one so hard as *grody to the max*.

My general point is that we use sentences for many purposes. There is not just one literal use of sentences that requires a theory of fixed reference and definite truth. Rather, there are uses that are not straightforward and that require considerable circumspection to interpret. Moreover, as I have already emphasized repeatedly, it is hopeless to strive for an analysis that catches all nuances of spoken utterances.

APPENDIX ON
PROBABILISTIC GRAMMARS

From what has already been said it should be clear enough that the imposition of a probabilistic generative structure is an additional constraint on a grammar. It is natural to ask if a probabilistic grammar can always be found for a language known merely to have a grammar. Put in this intuitive fashion, it is not clear exactly what question is being asked.

As a preliminary to a precise formulation of the question, an explicit formal characterization of probabilistic grammars is needed. In a fashion familiar from the literature we may define a (context-free) grammar as a quadruple (V_N, V_T, R, S), where V_N, V_T, and R are finite sets, S is a member of V_N, V_N and V_T are disjoint, and R is a set of ordered pairs, whose first members are in V^+, and whose second members are in V^*, where $V = V_N \cup V_T$, V^* is the set of all finite sequences whose terms are elements of V, and V^+ is V^* minus the empty sequence. As usual, it is intended that V_N be the nonterminal and V_T the terminal vocabulary, R the set of productions, and S the start symbol. The language L generated by G is defined in the standard manner and will be omitted here. A probabilistic grammar is obtained by adding a conditional probability distribution on the set R of productions. Formally we have:

Definition: *A quintuple* $G = (V_N, V_T, R, S, p)$ *is a probabilistic grammar if and only if* $G = (V_N, V_T, R, S)$ *is a grammar, and* p *is a real-valued function defined on* R *such that*

(1) *for each* (σ_i, σ_j) *in* R, $p(\sigma_i, \sigma_j) \geq 0$,
(2) *for each* σ_i *in the domain of* R, $\sum_{\sigma_j} p(\sigma_i, \sigma_j) = 1$

where the summation is over the range of R.

Various generalizations of this definition are easily given; for example, it is natural in some contexts to replace the fixed start symbol S by a probability distribution over V_N. But such generalizations will not really affect the essential character of the representation problem as formulated here.

For explicitness, we also need the concept of a probabilistic language, which is just a pair (L, p), where L is a language and p is a probability density defined on L, i.e., for each x in L, $p(x) \geq 0$ and

$$\sum_{x \in L} p(x) = 1.$$

The first formulation of the representation problem is then this.

Let L *be a (context-free) language, with probability density* p. *Does there always exist a probabilistic grammar* G *that generates* (L, p)?

What is meant by generation is apparent. If $x \in L$, $p(x)$ must be the sum of the probabilities of all the derivations of x in G. Ellis (1969) answered this formulation of the representation problem in the negative. His example is easy to describe. Let $V_T = \{a\}$, and let $L = \{a^n | n \geq 1\}$. Let $p(a^{n+1}) = 1/\sqrt{t_n}$, $n > 0$, where $t_1 = 4$, and $t_i =$ smallest prime such that $t_i > \max(t_{i-1}, 2^{2i})$ for $i > 1$. In addition, set

$$p(a) = 1 \sum_{n=1}^{\infty} p(a^{n+1})$$

The argument depends upon showing that the probabilities assigned to the strings of L by the above characterization cannot all lie in the extensions of the field of rational numbers generated by the finite set of conditional probabilities attached to the finite set of production rules of any context-free grammar.

From the empirically-oriented standpoint of this paper, Ellis's example, while perfectly correct mathematically, is conceptually unsatisfactory, because any finite sample of L drawn according to the density p could be described also by a density taking only rational values. Put another way, algebraic examples of Ellis's sort do not settle the representation problem when it is given a clearly statistical formulation.

LIKELIHOOD ESTIMATION

To give an example of how one goes about in a straightforward fashion giving a maximum-likelihood estimate of the probabilistic parameters in grammar, consider the simple grammar with seven rules introduced in the main text. Recall that this grammar was introduced with three probabilistic parameters, α, β, and γ. The six grammatical types and their associated probabilities are as follows.

Grammatical type	*Probability*
1. $PN+V_1$	$(1-\alpha)(1-\beta)$
2. $PN+V_2+PN$	$\alpha(1-\beta)^2$
3. Adj^n+N+V_1	$(1-\alpha)\,\beta(1-\gamma)^{n-1}\gamma$
4. $PN+V_2+Adj^n+N$	$\alpha\beta(1-\beta)(1-\gamma)^{n-1}\gamma$
5. Adj^n+N+V_2+PN	$\alpha\beta(1-\beta)(1-\gamma)^{n-1}\gamma$
6. $Adj^m+N+V_2+Adj^n+N$	$\alpha\beta^2(1-\gamma)^{m+n-2}\gamma^2$

On the hypothesis that this grammar is adequate for the corpus we are studying, each utterance will exemplify one of the grammatical types falling under the six schemes. The empirical relative frequency of each type in the corpus can be used to find a maximum-likelihood estimate of each of the three parameters. Let $x_1, \ldots, x_n$ be the finite sequence of actual utterances. The likelihood function $L(x_1, \ldots, x_n ; \alpha, \beta, \gamma)$ is the function that has as its value the probability of obtaining or generating sequence $x_1, \ldots, x_n$ of utterances given parameters α, β, γ. The computation of L assumes the correctness of the probabilistic grammar, and this implies among other things the statistical independence of the grammatical type of utterances, an assumption that is violated in any actual corpus, but probably not too excessively. The maximum-likelihood estimates of α, β, and γ are just those values α, β, and γ that maximize the probability of the observed or generated sequence $x_1, \ldots, x_n$. Let y_1 be the number of occurrences of grammatical type 1, i.e., $PN+V_1$ (as given above), let y_2 be the number of occurrences of type 2, i.e., $PN+V_2+PN$, let $y_{3,n}$ be the number of occurrences of type 3 with a string of n adjectives, and let similar definitions apply for $y_{4,n}$, $y_{5,n}$, and $y_{6,m,n}$. Then on the assumption of statistical independence the likelihood function can be expressed as:

(1) $L(x_1,\ldots,x_n;\alpha,\beta,\gamma)=[(1-\alpha)(1-\beta)]^{y_1}[\alpha(1-\beta)^2]^{y_2}$

$$\prod_{n=1}^{\infty}[(1-\alpha)\beta(1-\gamma)^{n-1}\gamma]^{y_{3,n}}\cdots\prod_{n=1}^{\infty}\prod_{m=1}^{\infty}[\alpha\beta^2(1-\gamma)^{m+n-2}\gamma^2]^{y_{6,m,n}}$$

Of course, in any finite corpus the infinite products will always have only a finite number of terms not equal to one. To find $\hat{\alpha}$, $\hat{\beta}$, and $\hat{\gamma}$ as functions of the observed frequencies $y_1,\ldots,y_{6,m,n}$, the standard approach is to take the logarithm of both sides of (1), in order to convert products into sums, and then to take partial derivatives with respect to α, β, and γ to find the values that maximize L. The maximum is not changed by taking the log of L, because log is a strictly monotonic increasing function. Letting $\mathcal{L}=\log L$, $y_3=\Sigma y_{3,n}$, $y_4=\Sigma y_{4,n}$, $y_5=\Sigma y_{5,n}$, and $y_6=\Sigma\Sigma y_{6,m,n}$, we have:

$$\frac{\partial\mathcal{L}}{\partial\alpha}=-\frac{y_1+y_3}{1-\alpha}+\frac{y_2+y_4+y_5+y_6}{\alpha}=0$$

$$\frac{\partial\mathcal{L}}{\partial\beta}=-\frac{y_1}{1-\beta}-\frac{2y_2}{1-\beta}+\frac{y_3}{\beta}+\frac{y_4+y_5}{\beta}-\frac{y_4+y_5}{1-\beta}+\frac{2y_6}{\beta}=0$$

$$\frac{\partial\mathcal{L}}{\partial\gamma}=\frac{y_3+y_4+y_5+y_6}{\gamma}-\left[\frac{y_{3,2}+y_{4,2}+y_{5,2}}{1-\gamma}\right.$$

$$+\ldots+\frac{(n-1)(y_{3,n}+y_{4,n}+y_{5,n})}{1-\gamma}+\cdots\Big]$$

$$-\left[\frac{y_{6,1,1}}{1-\gamma}+\ldots+\frac{(m-n-2)y_{6,m,n}}{1-\gamma}+\cdots\right]=0$$

If we let:

$$z_{6,n}=\sum_{m'+n'=n+1}\sum y_{6,m',n'}$$

then after solving the above three equations we have as maximum-likelihood estimates:

$$\hat{\alpha} = \frac{y_2 + y_4 + y_5 + y_6}{y_1 + y_2 + y_3 + y_4 + y_5 + y_6}$$

$$\hat{\beta} = \frac{y_3 + y_4 + y_5 + 2y_6}{y_1 + 2y_2 + y_3 + 2y_4 + 2y_5 + 2y_6}$$

$$\hat{\gamma} = \frac{y_3 + y_4 + y_5 + z_6}{\Sigma n(y_{3,n} + y_{4,n} + y_{5,n} + z_{6,n})}$$

As would be expected from the role of γ as a stopping parameter for the addition of adjectives, the maximum-likelihood estimate of γ is just the standard one for the mean of a geometrical distribution.

Having estimated α, β, and γ from utterance frequency data, we can then test the goodness of fit of the probabilistic grammar in some standard statistical fashion, using a chi-square or some comparable statistical test. Some numerical results of such tests are reported below. The criterion for acceptance of the grammar is then just a standard statistical one. To say this is not to imply that standard statistical methods or criteria of testing are without their own conceptual problems. Rather, the intention is to emphasize that the selection of a grammar can follow a standard scientific methodology of great power and wide applicability, and methodological arguments meant to be special to linguistics—like the discussions of simplicity—can be dispensed with.

FRENCH EXAMPLE

I give now an example of probabilistic analysis of the grammar of the noun phrases only of the spoken French of a young Parisian child, Philippe. The details of the collection of the corpus, the recording conditions, and the procedures for transcribing and editing are all described in Suppes, Smith, and Léveillé (1973). I mention here just that the corpus consisted of 56,982 tokens recorded in 33 one-hour sessions of spontaneous speech from the time that Philippe was 25 months old to 38 months old.

A fragment of a noun-phrase grammar for Philippe is taken from Suppes, Smith, and Léveillé (1973). Only enough will be said here to illustrate how once the probabilistic parameters are estimated by the maximum-likelihood method discussed earlier, a direct comparison can be made between theoretical predictions and observed data. Standard chi-square computations or goodness-of-fit tests can then be made. Table 2 gives high frequency noun-phrase types for the second grammar in that paper. The various noun-phrase types are generated by the grammar, which will not be described here. The types referred to in table 2 have the following intuitive meaning: PE is the abbreviation for personal pronoun, PD for demonstrative pronoun, PR for interrogative and relative pronouns, PI for indefinite pronoun, DN for definite article, IN for indefinite article, NC for common noun, NP for proper noun, EP for prepositions, AO for possessive adjective, AQ for qualitative adjective, AD for demonstrative adjective, AC for cardinal adjective, and DT for certain of the words which were placed in what was called a denotative category. (Examples are *outre*, *là* (when it follows a noun) and *même*.) As can be seen from the data, the fit is pretty good but far

Table 2   Noun-phrase types for grammar II

Noun-phrase	Observed	Expected	Chi-square
PE	1,436	1,331.9	8.1
PD	835	796.7	1.8
DN NC	792	817.7	0.8
NP	324	357.1	3.0
IN NC	284	335.8	7.8
EP NC	245	245.0	0.0
PR	171	160.6	0.6
NC	167	167.0	0.0
PI	152	139.5	1.0
AO NC	107	101.3	0.3
EP DN NC	60	18.6	90.3
IN AQ NC	52	27.7	20.4
AQ NC	43	53.4	1.8
DN AQ NC	40	67.5	10.8
AD NC	37	66.3	12.5
AC NC	18	11.4	3.2
DN NC AQ	16	19.6	0.5
DN DT NC	15	8.6	4.1

from perfect. Only one category has a really outlandish chi-square value, although others are larger than one would like in a grammar that fits extremely well.

One of the most significant and important topics in developmental psychology is that of the language development of the child. There exists a large literature on the subject, and many interesting examples of the acquisition of particular language skills, either of comprehension or of production, have been given. On the other hand, because of what appears to be the bewildering complexity of the language usage taken as a whole, even of a fairly young child, there have been few if any attempts to test systematic models of language development. The kind of probabilistic grammar advocated here provides the sort of quantitative framework within which it is possible to conceive and test specific mathematical or probabilistic models of language development. Prior work in learning theory and cognitive psychology generates immediate conceptual interest in differentiating between language development occurring incrementally or in discrete stages.

Before entering into any details, it is important to recognize that in either a discrete stage approach or a continuous, incremental one we must take account of the obvious fact that all normal children develop new language capacities and new skills as they get older, in an especially striking way in the period running from approximately 24 months to 48 months. The intellectually interesting task is not to affirm this obvious fact, but rather to distinguish whether the concept of stages or the equally intuitive concept of continuous development provides a better account.

The all-or-none stage model. The basic assumptions of the all-or-none stage model are two. First, development is discontinuous and may be represented by a relatively small number of stages. Secondly, within each stage, there is a constant probability P_r of grammatical rule r being used. The technical assumption is that these probabilities within a given stage for a given group of rules constitute a multinomial distribution, and thus satisfy assumptions of independence and stationarity. But it should be emphasized that we shall not test the assumption of a multinomial distribution with fixed parameters for each rule during a given stage by testing, for example, for independence or stationarity. The only detailed test we shall consider here is the identification of stages and the comparison of the fit of the stage model to the incremental model described below.

It also should be clear that if we do not limit the number of stages, then for each group of rules the data can be fit exactly by an n-stage model, namely, we just assign a stage for each of the n time sections of the data and fit each probability without error. Such a model, of course, is not interesting and does not give us any insight into the comparison between stage and incremental models. What we have done is impose the requirement that for each group of rules only two stages of development are to be looked for within the period covered by our data. Thus, for example, if a given group of rules is n in number, then we want to fit $2n-2$ parameters. We subtract two parameters because at each stage for a given group the sum of the probabilities assigned to each rule or subgroup of rules must sum to 1. If we have n rules or n subgroups of rules and six stages (the actual number we consider) we have in general $6n-n$ degrees of freedom and with $2n-n$ parameters we have left a net of $4n-(n+2)$ degrees of freedom that provide a test for the 2-stage model. However, we shall not really make use from a statistical standpoint of this number of degrees of freedom; that is, we shall not really be interested in assigning a significance level to the goodness of fit of the models, because the data are in too crude a form and the fit of the models not sufficiently good to warrant a detailed goodness-of-fit investigation.

Incremental model. A qualitative formulation of the discrete stage model is relatively straightforward and has been outlined above. Matters are more complicated in the case of the incremental model. The most desirable approach is to derive a stochastic differential equation from qualitative considerations, and then to solve this differential equation to obtain the predicted developmental curve for a given group of grammatical rules.

Without claiming that we are yet in a position to give a definitive qualitative theory of the incremental model, we do believe we can offer postulates that are intuitively sensible at a relatively gross level of approximation. As in the case of many attempts to model a highly complex situation, we introduce probabilistic assumptions that we test only in their mean validity, without any claim to being able to extend the theory to examine in detail individual sample paths.

In the five assumptions that follow, a central concept is that of a *conducive occasion* for a given group of rules to be used. Some such notion is needed because the developmental probabilities for use of a rule are conditional probabilities—conditional on the use of some one rule of the group to which it belongs. It is apparent from the formulation of the five assumptions that this concept of conducive occasion is taken as primitive, and the fifth assumption makes explicit our probabilistic postulate about the occurrence of such occasions. In our judgment it is a central task of a deeper developmental theory that includes the semantics of context to account for the specific character and occurrence of such occasions. It is not within the power of a purely syntactic developmental theory.

Assumption 1. On the occasion of an utterance the probability is one that the child will try a grammatical rule from a group that is conducive to the occasion.

Assumption 2. Immediately after a rule r is used, from his more developed model of comprehension the child will judge the appropriateness of the best choice of a rule from the given group. This appropriateness is represented in the mean by a constant probability π_r.

Assumption 3. For each rule r of a group there is a linear incremental change in the probability of use on a conducive occasion as a function of the constant probability π_r of its appropriateness. Thus on conducive occasions

$$p(t+h,r) = (1-\theta)p(t,r)+\theta\pi_r$$

Assumption 4. The probability of using a rule r is changed only on occasions conducive to use of the group of grammatical rules to which r belongs.

Assumption 5. The occurrence of occasions that are conducive to the child's use of any given group of grammatical rules follows a Poisson law, i.e., the intervals between occurrence of these conducive occasions are independently and identically distributed.

From these five assumptions, we can derive a simple mean stochastic differential equation. First, let μ be the parameter of the Poisson process for the occurrence of occasions conducive to the use of a given group of rules. As already indicated, let p (t,r) be the mean probability of using rule r of a given group at time t.

Thus with probability h we have

$$p(t+h,r) = (1-\theta)p(t,r) + \theta\pi_r$$

with probability $o(h)$ more than one conducive occasion occurs in the interval h, and with probability $1-\mu h-o(h)$ no such occasion arises at all, and thus by assumption (4)

$$p(t+h,r) = p(t,r)$$

Combining probabilities and dividing by h, we have:

$$\frac{p(t+h,r)-p(t,r)}{h} = -\theta\mu p(t,r) + \theta\mu\pi_r + \frac{o(h)}{h}$$

Whence as $h \rightarrow o$ we obtain the differential equation:

$$\frac{dp(t,r)}{dt} = -\theta\mu p(t,r) + \theta\mu\pi_r$$

the solution of which for the boundary condition $p(t,r) = p_r$ for $t = t_1$ is:

$$p(t,r) = \pi_r - (\pi_r - p_r)e^{-\alpha(t-t_1)}$$

where $\alpha = \theta\mu$.

Empirical test of the two models.   Detailed data comparing the incremental and stage models is to be found in Suppes, Léveillé, and Smith (1974), and in briefer form by the same authors in 1979. It is not to the point here to enter into the quite detailed picture that may be presented of how the data of the speech of Philippe, the young French child referred to earlier, do or do not fit reasonably well these two models. From a broad conceptual standpoint the important point here is that it is hard to see the use of any but probabilistic methods for a general and systematic consideration of fit.

As might be expected for data of this kind, the fit of neither model is really accurate, but the incremental model is very much superior. Reflection upon other skills makes the superiority of the incremental model hardly surprising. It is almost inconceivable that one would have a theory of a child learning to throw a ball or play a musical instrument of the sort that would give a good account in terms of a small number of stages rather than more or less continuous incremental improvements—of course, use of an incremental model does not commit one to the increments always being uniform. Almost without exception, complex skills show continuous improvements with practice, and in this respect talking is just like walking. The path of improvement is the probabilistic path of practice.

8

Rationality

The concept of rationality has a long and diversified career in philosophy. It will not be my purpose to give a faithful sense of this history, but to focus on a number of central issues that have received a great deal of attention in the last thirty or forty years. Broadly speaking, there seem to be two different but related concepts of rationality, with most analyses clustering around one of the two. To use an analogy from mechanics, the kinematical concept, concerned mainly with the description of action or choice, is the utilitarian view, familiar from at least the time of Bentham and dominant both in economics and in Bayesian conceptions of rationality. The single maxim of rationality of this approach is the rule that the decision maker should always choose so as to maximize his expected utility. The ingredients of this conception of rationality are familiar. The decision maker has a utility or evaluation function on possible consequences and a subjective probability function reflecting his beliefs about the state of nature. The importance of including uncertainty about the true state of nature was not adequately recognized by Bentham or by nineteenth-century utilitarian philosophers and political economists. In this century it has come to be seen as a key aspect of the theory of rationality in this extended utilitarian sense. Thus, a man who is faced with alternative medical treatments cannot simply choose the possible consequence he most desires, but must also evaluate the probability that that consequence or others can be achieved, given at least partial ignorance about the true state of his disease and efficacy of treatment. The generalizability of this medical example supports quite directly my claim in chapter 1 that the theory of rationality is intrinsically probabilistic (proposition 8).

Mainly in deference to the literature, I shall often refer to the conception of rationality that centers on the maximization of expected utility as Bayesian. The usage derives from the eighteenth-century ideas of the Reverend Thomas Bayes (1764) on prior probabilities, although others had similar ideas earlier and Laplace was most responsible for developing in a deep way the use of prior probabilities as in his early memoir on causality (1774). The use of the term *Bayesian* is also strongly associated with the subjective view of probability. The examination of this expected-utility model of rationality is the focus of the last half of the chapter.

The other central tradition goes back to Greek philosophy and was given an articulate formulation by Aristotle. In this alternative view, the rational man is one who acts in accordance with good reasons, and the reasons themselves are for the purpose of achieving an end in view. This Aristotelian view might be characterized as a kind of qualitative dynamics of rationality. The good reasons play the role of causes or of forces in mechanics. The cluster of ideas I consider important here I have called the model of justified procedures. It is developed extensively in the second section, with some attention given to Aristotle but without pretense at a genuinely historical account. There is an ambiguity in the Aristotelian view as to whether good reasons can be given for ultimate ends, but this rather delicate point is not dealt with here. In fact, the many tangled issues involving reasoning about ends that are not instrumental for other ends are ignored; although important, they are not central to the main problems considered in this chapter.

My use of *meanings* of rationality is meant to emphasize the pluralism of my approach. Dominant single concepts or unified theories do not exist for any major scientific discipline, not even for most highly specialized subdisciplines. Physicists forever love to talk of a unified theory, and some biologists write as if the theory of the genetic code is the whole of biology, but the evidential support for such views is thin. Just as pluralism is the order of the day in any developed science, as I argued in chapter 6, so it should be in a topic of such theoretical importance and practical value as rationality. The fact that I have restricted my analysis to the concepts that cluster around two models of rationality does not mean I think there are no more than these two. These are, however, the most important. In what follows I often speak of *the* theory of rationality, but from what I have said it should be clear I do not believe in a single tightly knit theory. The use of the phrase *the theory* is more a matter of custom than intended content.

Other philosophical senses of being rational are set aside as not relevant. For example, rationalism as the view that reason rather than the senses provides the proper foundation of knowledge is not considered. Indeed, historically what has been known as the "rational" school of physicians—being rationalists in the sense just defined—would in the sense of interest here be regarded as irrational because of the refusal to use empirical evidence. In a similar way I am not concerned with the contrast between rational and divine theology. Nor am I concerned with "rational" as a form of abstraction, as in that glorious subject of eighteenth-century natural philosophy, rational mechanics.

I also want to remark in a preliminary way on the primacy of the theory of rational action over the theory of rational talk. In ordinary conversation it is certainly true that we attribute rationality both to talk and to action. We are quite prepared to say 'That sounds very rational', in commenting perhaps on a speech by a politician of our own persuasion. But we are prepared to say of someone that, although his talk is sensible, his actions are not. Both our commonsense psychology of individuals and the general philosophical view that a man's moral principles are best exhibited by his actions rather than by his words support the notion that rationality is to be assessed in terms of actions rather than in terms of talk. This thrust is central to the modern Bayesian theory of decision making.

There is a further point to be made about these matters. There is a natural tendency to think of Bayesian methods as an extension of those of classical logic. But there is a departure from classical logic in the consideration of actions and events rather than sentences or propositions. This sharp dichotomy should be greeted with suspicion, because of the lack of a sharp distinction between deductive and inductive reasoning in ordinary talk. In ordinary argumentation and in the use of words that state evidential grounds, we seldom make a clear and definite distinction between a deductive and an inductive consideration. It seems wrong, therefore, to have the theory of rationality draw a sharp distinction between actions on the one hand and sentences on the other, assigning the one to the theory of rational action and the other to logic.

This sharp dichotomy is more a matter of appearances than of reality. First, there is a classical tradition of ambiguity in probability theory of whether to speak of the probability of events or of propositions, and I do not think it important which one we choose. Second, the assignment of values to consequences—consequences in the sense of the consequences of action, of course, and not logical consequences—is simply the addition of a further feature not considered in classical logical terms. If we restrict Bayesian theory or the general theory of rationality in situations of uncertainty to the theory of partial belief, we can claim that the theory of partial belief or the theory of subjective probability—call it what we will—is a natural and continuous extension of classical deductive canons of inference.

MODEL OF JUSTIFIED PROCEDURES

The Aristotelian model of rationality centers around the giving of good reasons for actions. The main texts about these matters are to be found in the *Nicomachean Ethics*, but important and significant remarks are to be found in *De Motu Animalium* and some other of Aristotle's writings as well. From a formal standpoint, Aristotle's concept of the practical syllogism is meant to provide for reasoning about actions the analogue of the theory of reasoning about knowledge embodied in the concept of the theoretical syllogism developed especially in the *Prior Analytics*. There is rather substantial literature on how the practical syllogism should be thought about in modern terms. For example, should the conclusion be thought of as being an action or a proposition? It is not my purpose here to review the ins and outs of this literature, which, in spite of its subtlety in the treatment of many points, does not get very far from a systematic standpoint.

There is, I think, a richer and better model in Greek thought that does not seem to have been much discussed but that I want to use, properly modernized of course, and that I think still catches much of the general spirit of the Aristotelian model. As already indicated, I have entitled the model that of justified procedures. The idea is that good reasons are given for the procedures we invoke. In the spirit of much recent philosophical literature, I could have used the phrase *model of justified actions*, but as will become clear I have deliberately chosen *procedure* to link the concept I have in mind both to ancient mathematical distinctions and the concept of a procedure in contemporary psychology and computer science.

The relevant Greek mathematical distinction corresponds only roughly to Aristotle's distinction between theoretical and practical syllogisms. It is the distinction in Euclid between problems and theorems. It is a distinction made by many other Greek mathematicians and commented upon extensively by Proclus. Although the Greek term is *problama* and there is therefore little excuse for not translating it as *problem*, the concept of what is intended is more easily understood in our terms if we think of the contrast between theorems and constructions. A theorem asserts something that is true of a given type of figure or combination of figures. A problem of construction, on the other hand, poses something that must be done, for example, to give a procedure 'on a given finite straight line to construct an equilateral triangle', which is proposition 1, book 1, of Euclid. The solution of a problem naturally has two parts. One is to give the construction itself and the second is to prove that the construction is correct. Characteristically in Euclid, the proof that a construction is correct is concluded by saying 'being what it was required to do'. In such a proof the construction and the justification are given hand in hand. On the other hand, in the case of a theorem the characteristic closing of the proof is to say 'being what it was required to prove'.

One of the important features of Euclid's intertwining of problems and theorems as occurs throughout the *Elements* is that, although there is a sharp conceptual distinction between problems and theorems, the justification of each proceeds along very similar lines. There is no general distinction in the methods of proof that constructions are correct and theorems valid. Such a close intertwining of practice and theory, to use the implicit Aristotelian distinction, seems natural and straightforward in the case of a highly focused subject like geometry. The issue is complex and subtle, however, when we turn to more general questions of rational action. In the first place, it is a mistake to contrast the theoretical syllogism as dealing with theoretical scientific knowledge and the practical syllogism as dealing with practical actions, as the proper model, at least from the viewpoint I am advocating. But the question still remains for either facts or procedures in the case of a practical domain of action: can we give a proof of correctness? What is important here is that it is not the distinction between procedures or theoretical knowledge that is critical but whether the domain itself will support justification in the sense of proof for either knowledge or procedures.

On the other hand, the Euclidean example can itself be misleading in talking about most cases of justified procedures because the completeness of proof of correctness from a few basic axioms hardly ever obtains. In one sense, in comparing Aristotle and Euclid we seem to be faced with a dilemma. Aristotle's examples all seem trivial and rather uninteresting in terms of their content. The Euclidean examples, on the other hand, are interesting and nontrivial but far too restricted in character and use a methodology of proof that we scarcely believe possible to emulate in most domains of experience.

For these and other reasons it seems desirable to look at a number of different kinds of examples of procedures with and without intuitively adequate justification. I also want to emphasize that justified procedures are a matter of importance in every substantive area of experience.

Recipes as procedures. One of the places where we can find nontrivial procedures that almost everyone has some experience with is in a subject of universal interest, cooking. It is also possible to accept that we have a good intuitive understanding of the goal of the procedure, namely, the preparation of food of a certain quality and taste, even if the standards of evaluation may not always be completely and explicitly verbalized.

Let us begin with an example drawn from a book that is full of highly codified recipes without any justification of the procedures given at all, *An Encyclopedia of Chinese Food and Cooking*, by Winona W. and Irving B. Chang and Helene W. and Austin H. Kutscher (1970). As a typical recipe, I pick the one for stir-fried beef with broccoli (p. 358):

A. 2 tablespoons peanut oil
B. 2 tablespoons salted black beans
C. $\frac{1}{2}$ clove garlic, minced
D. 1 to 2 slices ginger, minced
E. $\frac{1}{2}$ teaspoon salt
F. 1 lb flank steak
G. 1 teaspoon peanut oil
H. 1 teaspoon cornstarch
I. 1 teaspoon light soy sauce
J. 2 teaspoons sherry
K. $\frac{1}{2}$ teaspoon sugar
L. 1 bunch fresh broccoli
M. 2 teaspoons cornstarch
N. 2 tablespoons heavy soy sauce

Preparation
  I Slice F into $\frac{1}{8}$-inch, bite-size pieces.
 II Mix G, H, I, J, K and marinate F in mixture 15 minutes.
III Mix B, C, D, E. Set aside.
 IV Slice stems of L diagonally into $1\frac{1}{2}$ inch segments, splitting heavier stems. Parboil stems 2 minutes and set aside.
  V Mix M, N. Stir well before using.

Cooking
  1. Put A in very hot skillet and bring to high heat
  2. Add B–E mixture and stir-fry rapidly 15 seconds to brown garlic slightly.
  3. Add F and G–K and stir-fry until F is nearly done but remains rare on inside.
  4. Add L. Stir-fry 15 seconds.
  5. Add M–N mixture slowly. Stir-fry until sauce thickens and coats all ingredients well.

The hundreds of recipes in this book are admirably clear in terms of the procedures to be followed. They are all written in this style, but there is no justification of individual steps or of the choice of ingredients. On the other hand, at the beginning of the volume there are brief sections on Chinese cuisine, utensils for cooking, serving, and eating, a general discussion of cooking preparations and cooking techniques, and a guide to ingredients. What is totally missing is any attempt to justify individual steps in a recipe.

Staying with Chinese cuisine for the moment, a strong contrast is to be found in the book *How to Cook and Eat in Chinese* by Buwei Yang Chao (1963). Let me quote her recipe for red-cooked whole pork shoulder (p. 52):

1 whole shoulder or fresh ham, 6–8 lbs with skin and bone on	1 cup soy sauce
	1 tbsp. sugar
2 cups cold water	2 or 3 slices fresh ginger (if you
$\frac{1}{4}$ cup sherry	can get it)

Leave the whole fresh ham or shoulder with skin and bones on just as it is bought. After washing outside, cut a few long slashes on the sides where there is no skin (so that the sauce will seep in more easily when cooking). Place your shoulder in a heavy pot with the 2 cups water. Turn on big fire and cover pot. When it boils, add the sherry, soy sauce, and maybe ginger. Cover the pot tight again. Change to very low fire and cook for one hour. Then turn skin side down. Still with low fire cook for another hour. After this, add sugar and cook again for another $\frac{1}{2}$ or 1 hour ($2\frac{1}{2}$ or 3 hours altogether, depending on the tenderness of the meat bought).

To test your cooking, stick a fork or chopstick through the meat. It is done when the stick goes through very easily. If not, cook over low fire a little longer. Make allowances of course that the prongs of a fork are sharper than most chopsticks.

On second serving, as must be done in a small family, it can be warmed over or eaten cold. Warm over low fire so you won't burn the bottom. When eating cold, it is stiffer and can be cut into more chewsome slices, with the jelly. (Save the fat on the top for making other dishes.)

Note the tendency to give justifications at various points, for example, in the parenthetical phrase 'so that the sauce will seep in more easily when cooking' or, in the last paragraphs, the reason for warming over a low fire 'so you won't burn the bottom' and in the last phrase one should save the fat 'for making other dishes'.

Note also another feature of this recipe. It is to provide tests that, if satisfied, show that a goal or a subgoal has been accomplished and, if not, how to proceed. The example here is in the passage: 'To test your cooking, stick a fork or chopstick through the meat. It is done when the stick goes through very easily. If not, cook over low fire a little longer.' Here it is understood that one of the goals of the recipe is to make the meat tender.

Finally, as a third example let me quote from an Italian cookbook by Marcella Hazan (1977) that my wife and I particularly like. I want to quote some passages from the recipe for *Ossobuco alla milanese*. Because of the length of the recipe I have only selected certain passages. In the first paragraph she says: 'The hind shanks are better than the front ones for *ossobuco* because they are meatier and more tender.' Notice this justification for selecting the hind shanks. She also suggests tests where appropriate, for example, 'When the oil is quote hot (test it with the corner of one of the pieces of veal; a moderate sizzle means the heat is just right), brown the veal on all sides.' As part of that same instruction about heating the oil, she also has the following, just after the sentence quoted above: '(Brown the veal as soon as it has been dipped in flour, otherwise the flour may dampen and the meat won't brown properly.)' The force of the *otherwise* is to justify the instruction for quickly browning the veal after it has been dipped in flour. A couple of paragraphs later, in talking about herbs and salt she says: 'Hold off on salt until after cooking if you are using canned beef broth. It is sometimes very salty.' The last sentence provides the justification for the holding off. Finally, another implicit test procedure is found in the following two sentences: 'The broth should come up to the top of the veal pieces. If it does not, add more.' In our opinion, one of the great virtues of the Hazan book is the lucid justifications she gives for various recommended procedures.

Even in the cases of such excellent cookbooks as those of Chao and Hazan, we would not expect to find the kind of meticulous justification of each step found in Euclid. This is not a defect of these excellent cookbooks, but is appropriate to the procedures for preparing and cooking food. Of course it is not sufficient just to say that. We can also easily recognize that there is a profound difference in the two cases along the following important dimension. In the case of the geometry, each step is justified in a way that makes no further discussion or analysis of any kind appropriate, at least not within the confines of the subject matter as laid down by the axioms and postulates. (Fundamental investigations of the nature of space do properly challenge the Euclidean foundations, but these are very specialized enterprises that can be set aside in the present context.) In the case of cooking, on the other hand, the whole matter is very much more open-ended. There is not an intellectual regimentation of the subject. We do not have clearcut reasons to justify each step, and there would be a large amount of variation as well as debate about the proper formulation of each procedure. The variation here is not the kind to be found in Euclid. There are different ways of making the same construction, but here there are actually procedures that produce different results to obtain the same goal and there can be argument about the virtues of one procedure over another in terms of the outcome, quite apart from the question of which is more elegant or more efficient, an aspect of the geometrical constructions that could also be considered.

There will be a tendency on the part of many to make a separation between the problems of Euclid and the recipes I have cited along a traditional division between pure mathematics and a practical art. I want to insist on the point that I think such a division is wrong. For purposes of administrative classification, the organization of universities, the awarding of degrees, etc., such divisions play a useful role, but I do not think they have any fundamental intellectual status. I think of the constructions of Euclid as being of the same sort as the recipes of Chao and Hazan. The subject is much better developed. We understand how to axiomatize geometrical constructions in a way that we do not understand how to axiomatize cooking, and it may very well be inappropriate even to seek for an axiomatization of cooking in the sense of axioms that lead to a justification of procedures. But in both cases we are being shown a procedure that we can use in the real world and that will lead to a specific concrete result when applied in a specific case. It is not to the point here to engage in a complicated argument about whether mathematics has a special a priori status. From what I have said in chapter 4 it is obvious that I think it does not. It seems to me especially true of the particular mathematical subject of plane geometry, which has so many practical applications, from carpentry to bridge-building.[1]

Rawls (1971, pp. 85–86) defines three kinds of procedural justice. Perfect procedural justice obtains when there is an independent criterion for judging the result and there is a procedure that in principle guarantees the just result. Imperfect procedural justice obtains when there is an independent criterion, but not necessarily a procedure to guarantee the desired result. Finally, pure procedural justice obtains when there is no independent criterion for judging the result, but there is a criterion for judging the fairness or correctness of the procedure itself.

It may be useful to see how well this tripartite division works with rational procedures as discussed here. Euclidean geometrical constructions exemplify perfect procedural rationality, for the fit between the desired result and the procedures used is exact. Practical geometry, e.g., surveying, cooking, and other practical arts, abound in examples of imperfect procedural rationality, because

---

[1] Practical geometry, closely associated with standard Euclidean geometry as its theoretical counterpart, has a long history going back to ancient times. A good description of medieval treatises on practical geometry, their varying content, and their varying conceptions of rigor is to be found in Victor (1979).

of the inevitable errors of measurement and variations in physical materials used. The Euclidean constructions are perfect only because of the high level of abstraction.

It is perhaps less clear what are the analogs of pure procedural justice. One reasonable candidate are recipes, not just for cooking, but in all the areas of activity for which how-to-do-it books are written. We may judge a recipe pure, but at the same time we can give no principled guarantee of the results obtained by using it. Experience validates the procedure but not the result. How probability comes into this picture is discussed in the next section.

Applications of procedures and probability. When we look at geometry à la Euclid there seems to be no place for probability. There also seems to be no use of probabilistic concepts in the cooking recipes quoted, but there is a difference in the two cases. The recipes implicitly refer to *expected* results. Test procedures are also given for varying cooking times to get the desired tenderness, firmness, etc. The recipes are written at a more detailed level of application than is Euclid or similar geometry texts. Probability enters in terms of expectations when cooking, but where does it enter in geometry? At the level of abstraction of Euclid hardly at all, except in terms of mistakes in proofs as discussed in chapter 4. But when specific methods of application are considered, probabilities and expectations enter in a natural way, because the level of detail can be even more fine-grained than that of the recipes quoted. Here is an example of instructions for using dividers, which are compasses without a pen or pencil at the end of one leg. The passage is taken from a classic text on engineering drawing (French, 1941):

> The dividers are used for transferring measurements and for dividing lines into any number of equal parts. Facility in the use of this instrument is most essential, and quick and absolute control of its manipulation must be gained. It should be opened with one hand by pinching the chamfer with the thumb and second finger. This will throw it into correct position with the thumb and forefinger outside of the legs and the second and third fingers inside, with the head resting just above the second joint of the forefinger . . . It is thus under perfect control, with the thumb and forefinger to close it and the other two to open it. This motion should be practiced until an adjustment to the smallest fraction can be made. In

coming down to small divisions the second and third fingers must be gradually slipped out from between the legs while they are closed down upon them. Notice that the little finger is not used in manipulating the dividers. (p.17)

Comparable detail in recipes would mean that they include directions for how to hold a skillet or a ladle, how to empty a pot, etc.

That the kind of manipulation of dividers described above is in practice never perfect is an obvious consequence of the continuous nature of the geometric quantities measured. In applications where it matters, a complicated and developed probabilistic theory of errors is used, e.g., in surveying. Instructions like those given above are intended to help reduce errors to a manageable level, but there is no illusion that errors can be eliminated.

I also emphasize that there are not two levels of geometry, the abstract and the concrete, or, in other familiar terms, the pure and the applied. There are many levels. An important feature of modern geometry has been to increase the level of abstraction found in Euclid. Perhaps the clearest and philosophically most satisfactory account of this view is the classic article of Tarski (1959). Clarity in the other direction is less standard. Geometrical procedures like other procedures can always be described by ever finer attention to detail. Probabilistic considerations enter more prominently as the level of detail increases. For example, we could expand upon the instruction for manipulating dividers given above by recommending how fast to move the dividers either in adjusting the radius or in moving from one fixed point to another. An actual path of motion that approximates the recommended one is most naturally viewed as a sample path of a certain continuous stochastic process. The refined study of important motor skills is properly conducted within such a stochastic framework.

Someone might claim that the execution of procedures by a computer constitutes an important class of counterexamples to what I am saying about how we execute procedures. The instructions are written, so it would be claimed, in a formal computer language, e.g., BASIC, FORTRAN or LISP, and their digital execution leaves no room for variation and thus no room for probability or error. But this claim is mistaken. As we enter into the details of the hardware, the digital view dissolves into a continuum of electromagnetic waves and pulses. Acceptable tolerance levels of variation are one of the most important features of hardware design, but the nature of the variation is no more described in any ultimate terms than is the variation of human motor skills. Expected hardware behavior is characterized carefully, along with less explicit tolerance bounds. Probabilistic variation within these limits is inevitable and accepted.

What I have said about the bottomless pit of detail raises at once a question about rationality. Is there an appropriate concept of rationality at every level of description and analysis? My answer should be apparent from what I have already said about procedures. In principle, there is a concept of rationality to match each level of detail. The explicit development of the concept, however, depends upon the demand or need for standards at the given level. The use of dividers by ordinary draftsmen is not monitored at a highly detailed level in order to obtain optimal results either in terms of accuracy or efficiency. Time-and-motion studies of assembly lines are often a different matter. Perhaps the best examples are in highly competitive sports where performance is measured on some simple quantitative dimension like time or distance. The best coaches study extraordinarily fine details of behavior in order to improve performance. Their constant recommendations for change always depend on an implicit criterion of rationality.

What I have just said also should make clear how I think the model of justified procedures can be joined without inconsistency to the model of expected utility, which I discuss at some considerable length later. The model of expected utility is formulated and analyzed at a high level of abstraction. The more detailed the level of analysis, the harder it is to apply in a genuine quantitative fashion. Justification of procedures in the sense of Aristotle and Euclid easily takes over. Then at some finer level still, verbal justification itself disappears, even though adjustments and improvements continue unceasingly. Adults, like children, are always in the process of learning and changing without knowing how or why. Verbal schemas of analysis and justification can rationally organize only the tip of the behavioral iceberg.

Rational cooks and carpenters.   By just mentioning carpentry and spending earlier so much time on cooking there is a point about the way we ordinarily discuss rational behavior that needs consideration. In most circumstances it would sound unusual to talk about a rational cook or a rational carpenter. For this reason it would be possible to think that my extended examples of cooking are mistaken, that we really do not ever talk about rational cooking just as we do not talk about rational cooks, and consequently the model of justified procedures I am proposing has a much more limited range than I am claiming. The appropriate response is clear. We tend to use the word *rational* in evaluating practical activities or particular aspects of behavior. Consider, for example, Julia Child's advice that when a finished sauce starts to separate try beating into it a tablespoon of cold water to bring it back. It is easy to imagine somebody watching this procedure and saying 'Well, that was a case of thinking quickly and saving your sauce'. In a more formal and mannered discourse someone might say 'Well, I see you are really a rational problem solver when you run into trouble in the kitchen'. I can also imagine someone saying to a carpenter who has done an excellent job of fitting a new wall to an old one in remodeling a house that the carpenter approached the problem rationally and found the best solution to a messy problem.

There is another more troublesome point. In saying that the carpenter solved a problem rationally or the cook quickly found a rational solution for saving a sauce, we ordinarily are evaluating the character of the procedure itself and not any justification of it. This is in clear violation of the Aristotelian or Euclidean model in the sense that no justification of the procedure has been given, except possibly the pragmatic one of claiming that the results are highly appropriate, especially when it was suspected that no really good solution could be found. These are cases that come under the slogan of 'The result justifies the means'. They reflect an important aspect of rational behavior. The point is that the Euclidean model is deceptive. We ordinarily are not able in any serious way to justify each step of a complicated procedure, and yet we still want to claim we can often judge which complex procedures are rational or sensible and which are not. We make this judgment in an overall intuitive fashion and we consider that evaluation a justification for the procedure as a whole. There is a process of justification involved because we evaluate the results of the procedure or even in some cases its line of attack or intention without attempting to build up the kind of complex justification so splendidly exhibited in Euclid. Although we may wish for better, we often have to be satisfied with holistic judgments that are about as far from Euclid's methodology as we can imagine. I am not saying we should complacently accept such justification, but only that we recognize that in many practical situations of importance there will be no other.

The practical and the theoretical.   Not everyone would agree with what I am claiming about the essentially homogeneous character of justifying arguments in geometry and in practical arts such as cooking. For example, Martha Nussbaum in her book *Aristotle's De Motu Animalium* (1978) argues that those interpreters of Aristotle who want to draw a strong parallel between the theory of the practical syllogism and the theory of the theoretical syllogism are mistaken. Aristotle, she claims, did not really want to have a theory of practical reasoning that would be as close as possible to the foundations of theoretical knowledge laid down in the *Posterior Analytics*. Without going into the details of her argument, what she emphasizes is that there is a good case for claiming that reasoning about practical affairs for Aristotle should be dialectical in character.

In discussing a doctor's deliberation about the health of a patient in Book VII, chapter 7 of the *Metaphysics*, Aristotle says the following (Nussbaum's translation):

> Health comes to be as a result of thinking of the following kind: Since health is *this*, it is necessary, if there is to be health, that *this* be present—for example, balancing of the humors. And if this, then heat. And he goes on thinking in this manner until he arrives at the first thing that he himself is capable of doing. (1032^b6–9)

In giving such examples, Aristotle is reinforcing his familiar views about purpose. When an agent has desires and beliefs of a certain form, he must of necessity act on these beliefs and desires. They constitute in themselves a kind of complete explanation or justification of his action. It is worth noting how close this is in general form to what the utilitarians are saying about maximizing expected utility—no further justification is needed for an action taken.

The basic model of Aristotle's theory of practical reasoning is that we make inferences from a desired goal to the first action necessary to begin the achievement of the goal. Aristotle does not offer anything that is an epistemological parallel for practical action to the kind of demonstrative foundations he proposes for theoretical knowledge in the *Posterior Analytics*. On the other hand, there is no theory of constructions as such in the *Posterior Analytics*. As is evident, I am very much inclined to assimilate our actual reasoning about theoretical matters to Aristotle's model of reasoning about practical matters.

There is another distinction in ancient Greek mathematics to invoke in order to expand upon this point. This is the distinction between analysis and synthesis. Rather obscure definitions of analysis and synthesis are to be found in book 13 of Euclid. There is much discussion of these matters in Proclus and Pappus. Here is what Pappus has to say, quoting from Heath's translation in his introduction to *Euclid's Elements*:

> Analysis then takes that which is sought as if it were admitted and passes from it through its successive consequences to something which is admitted as the result of synthesis: for in analysis we assume that which is sought as if it were (already) done, and we inquire what it is from which this results, and again what is the antecedent cause of the latter, and so, until by so retracing our steps we come upon something already known or belonging to the class of first principles, and such a method we call analysis as being solution backwards.
>
> But in synthesis, reversing the process, we take as already done that which was last arrived at in the analysis and, by arranging in their natural order as consequences what were before antecedents and successively connecting them one with an other, we arrive finally at the construction of what was sought; and this we call synthesis. (p.138)

Thus, in analysis if we want to establish a certain proposition we assume it is a hypothesis and investigate its consequences. This would seem to be the fallacy of affirming the consequent, but of course the Greeks were careful to insist on what they called complete convertibility or, in modern logical terms, equivalences and not simply implications. Ordinarily, analysis was followed by synthesis, which gave the formal proof. (For an excellent detailed exposition of these matters, see Hintikka and Remes, 1974.)

Now the real place that analysis was applied was to problems, i.e., constructions, rather than theorems. As Proclus put it, it was the one general method used for solving all 'the more abstruse problems'. The method was to assume all the conditions required in the problem to be solved, to investigate how those conditions may be transformed and to continue these transformations until we reach conditions that can be satisfied, rather like Aristotle's actions that can be taken as the first step by the physician in treating the health of the patient. But there is also an important difference from Aristotle. The geometrical procedures are required always to be sufficient to make the desired construction, but Aristotle gives only necessary procedures for health. In many practical situations, including much of medical practice, it is easy to see that the procedures adopted for solving the problem at hand are neither necessary nor sufficient. Probabilistic considerations enter. We often feel fortunate to have a reasonable probability that the procedures adopted will produce the desired outcome.

It is an obvious remark that what is missing in the practical cases is the kind of subsequent treatment that puts everything back together again in the form of synthesis to give us two things: first, the construction in the order in which it has to be carried out, and, second, the demonstration of the proof that the construction is in fact correct. I would not want to argue that we can directly or easily extend to other problems the important method of analysis applied to geometrical problems, a vast store of which are to be found in Euclid's *Data*, the medieval Latin translation of which has recently been published (Ito, 1980). From the standpoint of exhibiting the explicit analysis—followed-by-synthesis routine applied to a collection of problems, a better example is Archimedes' *On the Sphere and Cylinder*, Book II. In any case the parallel to Aristotle is surprisingly good, and supports, I believe, my argument for bringing together the methods of theoretical reasoning and those of practical reasoning.

There is still another point I want to make of a different sort to bring even closer together theoretical and practical methods. The example of Greek geometry is misleading in the full context of ancient Greek mathematical sciences. I have argued elsewhere (Suppes, 1980a) that strict use of the axiomatic method is not at all characteristic outside of geometry and I analyze there three important examples, Euclid's *Optics*, Archimedes' *On the Equilibrium of Planes*, and Ptolemy's *Almagest*. Because of its central importance in the history of science, let me restrict my remarks here just to Ptolemy's *Almagest*. Ptolemy uses mathematical argument and mathematical proof with great facility, but he uses the mathematics in an applied way. He does not introduce explicit axioms about the motion of stellar bodies, but reduces the study of their motion to geometrical propositions, much in the spirit of what I have been saying about the Greek method of analysis of problems.[2] But, as in the case of Aristotle's practical reasoning, he does not go on to give a resulting synthesis and is quite content with the analysis. Even in theoretical science the model of axiomatic mathematics is not the one that is followed. Something much more informal and more dialectical in character is typical of real theoretical as well as practical reasoning. I have cited Ptolemy as an example because I have introduced the methodological point I am making in the context of ancient Greek science and philosophy, but it is easy enough to substantiate exactly the same sorts of points about modern physics or any other modern science. If we had to say which Aristotelian model treatises in modern physics followed it seems clear to me what we should answer.

My point is not to try to assimilate in its entirety theoretical science to the model of justified procedures I have been setting forth as a model of rationality, but rather to make clear why it is that we should not be disappointed at the absence of axiomatic analyses of practical action that are nontrivial in character. On the other hand, we should also not be firmly entrenched in the position that there is a radical difference between theoretical reasoning and practical reasoning. The difference is a matter of degree and not of kind. In almost all cases of practical reasoning we are not in a position to proceed axiomatically, but this is also usually so in science. Axiomatic methods are seldom used at the same time that any detailed data or experimental evidence are considered. Those parts of theoretical science that do proceed axiomatically, as for example in parts of modern economics, are usually not set forth in conjunction with any complex and subtle consideration of data.

---

[2] As Jules Vuillemin pointed out to me, it may seem appropriate to regard as an axiom Ptolemy's fundamental hypothesis on the representation of the sun's apparently irregular motion by composition of regular and circular motions, stated in book III of the *Almagest*. It is used later in more general form to study the motion of the moon and the five planets. But what I said about the work not being axiomatic in character stands, and, from a Greek standpoint, the right term is *hypothesis,* not *axiom,* for Ptolemy's general assumption about the motion of the heavens does not have the status of an axiom.

The Russian mathematician Manin (1979/1981) has put the matter very nicely as to how different theoretical physics is from mathematics: 'Modern theoretical physics is a luxuriant, totally Rabelaisian, vigorous world of ideas, and a mathematician can find in it everything to satiate himself except the order to which he is accustomed' (p. x). The modern physicist will be as disdainful of a requirement of mathematical rigor as will a practical man who is going to town to sign a real estate deed and is asked, after he says that that is why he is going to town 'Well, why *are* you doing it?' It is for him a nonsense question, just as it is a nonsense question to ask of the physicist, in most circumstances, 'Can you rigorously justify the answer?'

There is still another way to look at theoretical science from the standpoint of procedures. The *activity* of doing theoretical science falls directly under the model of justified procedures. The results of the activity have a different form from the results of what we ordinarily call practical activities such as cooking or carpentry. In terms of results, I have no quarrel with the traditional distinction between the practical and the theoretical. There are, however, two other distinctions that are sometimes made and that I do not accept. The first is that the epistemological or metaphysical status of the activity of a theoretical scientist is different from that of an artisan. Different particular skills are used, but this is true of scientists working in different disciplines. We can, of course, analyze different activities in terms of their uniqueness, originality, or significance, but these general dimensions certainly do not discriminate the practical from the theoretical.

The second proposed distinction is that it seems ridiculous to talk about having an axiomatic treatment of cooking, dancing, or any other practical art, but that in contrast it is sensible for some branch of physics or psychology, say, even if such an axiomatic analysis has not yet been given. But axiomatic analysis of a practical art like cooking seems feasible. To obtain serious and systematic results it would be necessary to reach for a level of abstraction and generality that is not customary. The resulting axiomatizations might not be very interesting, but I see no obstacle of principle. In fact, the several efforts to develop a proper notation for choreography constitute the beginning of an axiomatic analysis. The many decisions about what to have notation for and what to ignore fix at an early stage the approximate level of abstraction. Such an elementary axiomatization is already realized in musical notation. A musical score stands in about the same degree of abstraction from a musical performance as does one of Euclid's constructions from an engineering drawing.

Where I have meant to come out in this analysis is that the model of justified procedures dominates much of our practical reasoning, and proper use of its leads us to say that a person is acting rationally. I have also tried to make the point that the way in which the model is used in practice varies enormously, but that in most cases some explicit deductive canon of justification will not be satisfied. On the other hand, the denial of the desirability of such a canon seems pointless when it is possible that sharp deductive arguments of justification can be given.

EXPECTED-UTILITY MODEL

Although the idea of maximizing expected utility goes back at least to the eighteenth century, the main stimulus for most of the current research was the axiomatization given in the second and third editions of von Neumann and Morgenstern's classic book, *Theory of Games and Economic Behavior* (1947/1953). These authors did not axiomatize probability in a strict sense but only utility, because they assumed that numerical probabilities were already available. The basic idea was as follows. Let a and b be possible outcomes; they might, for example, be physical objects or amounts of money. We then form a new object $a\alpha b$, which has the following meaning. Outcome a is obtained with probability α and outcome b with probability $1 - \alpha$. We may think of objects such as $a\alpha b$ as gambles. We start with a set of objects and close them under such a gambling operation, that is, if a and b are in the set, then for any numerical probability α, $a\alpha b$ is also in the set. The next step is to pose a relation of preference on such gambles. Other axiomatic treatments along similar lines with various kinds of improvements have been given by Marschak (1950), Herstein and Milnor (1953), Blackwell and Girschick (1954), and Aumann (1962, 1964).

It should be emphasized that even from a modern standpoint von Neumann and Morgenstern's analysis was not the first one. In a certain sense, a more satisfactory theory was already given earlier by Ramsey (1931/1964). Ramsey's central idea was to compare simple gambles based on a partition composed of two equi-probable events. In von Neumann and Morgenstern's terms this was finding an event A whose probability is 1/2. Then under the hypothesis of expected-utility theory the following equivalence holds:

$$a \tfrac{1}{2} b \geq c \tfrac{1}{2} d \text{ iff } u\,(a)+u(b \geq u(c)+u(d)$$

where $u(a)$ is the numerical utility of outcome a, etc. Ramsey sketched this theory, and it has been worked out in detail by various authors, including Suppes and Winet (1955), Davidson and Suppes (1956), Suppes (1956), and Debreu (1959).

The most important work has been Savage's book, *The Foundations of Statistics*, first published in 1954. Because Savage's work has had so much influence, it will be useful to discuss his theory in more detail. His axioms are rather complicated from a formal standpoint, and so I shall not state them explicitly here, but shall try to describe their intuitive content. The axioms are about preference among decisions, and decisions are mappings or functions from the set of states of nature to the set of consequences. The point of Savage's theory is to place axioms on choices or preferences among the decisions in such a way that anyone who satisfies the axioms will be maximizing expected utility. This means that the way in which he satisfies the axioms will generate a subjective probability distribution about his beliefs concerning the true state of nature and a utility function on the set of consequences such that the expectation of a given decision is defined in a straightforward way with respect to the subjective probability distribution on states of nature and the utility function on the set of consequences. As one would expect, Savage demands, in fact in his first axiom, that the preference among decisions be transitive and that given any two decisions one is at least weakly preferred to the other. Axiom 2 extends this ordering assumption to having the same property hold when the domain of definition of decisions is restricted to a given set of states of nature; for example, the decision maker might know that the true state of nature lies in some subset of the whole set— events are just such subsets. Axiom 3 requires that knowledge of an event cannot change preferences among consequences, where preferences among consequences are defined in terms of preferences among decisions. Axiom 4 requires that given any two events, one is at least as probable as the other, that is, the relation of qualitative probability among events is strongly connected. Axiom 5 excludes the trivial case in which all consequences are equivalent in utility and, thus, every decision is equivalent to every other. Axiom 6 says essentially that if event A is less probable than event B (A and B are subsets of the same set of possible states of nature), then there is a partition of the states of nature such that the union of each element of the partition with A is less probable than B. As is well known, this axiom of Savage's is closely related to the axiom of de Finetti and Koopman, which requires the existence of a partition of the states of nature into arbitrarily many events that are equivalent in probability. Finally, his last axiom, axiom 7, is a formulation of the sure-thing principle: one decision is to be weakly preferred to another if, no matter what the state of nature, the consequences of the first decision are at least as good as the second.

Good summaries and elaborations of Savage's work are to be found in Luce and Raiffa (1957) and in the more recent detailed summary of Fishburn (1970). Formulation of a more general theory and an extensive discussion of the previous literature are to be found in Krantz *et al.* (1971).

An interesting variant has been proposed by Jeffrey (1965). Contrary to the Savage approach of ending up with a probability measure on possible states of nature and a utility function on possible consequences with states of nature and consequences thought of as quite different sorts of objects, Jeffrey insists that both probability and utility adhere to the same entities, namely, propositions. To a certain extent, the viewpoint of Jeffrey has a relation to the earlier work of de Finetti, which makes the concept of expectation central, or the still earlier work of Bayes himself, who defined probability in terms of expectation. However, there are a number of peculiar features to Jeffrey's theory that have been extensively criticized; see, for example, Sneed (1966). (The appendix to this chapter has a detailed discussion of the relation between expectation and probability and the question of which is a more appropriate primitive notion. The story is rather tangled because expectation is, of course, central to Savage's theory. It is just that expectation, that is, the expectation of decisions, is decomposed into probability and utility, with the probability and utility functions being over different objects, whereas for Jeffrey they are over the same objects.)

I have discussed the history of what might be called the joint theory of probability and utility since Ramsey, but it is important to recognize that much of the work on either subject has been done independent of the other. Thus, there is an independent history of the qualitative concept of probability as a theory of subjective partial beliefs. As already mentioned in the preceding section, analysis of the concept goes back to the eighteenth century and certainly was given a major impetus by Laplace, who held that in every sense probability was a subjective concept meant to deal with our ignorance of true causes. In this century, the most distinguished and constant proponent of a subjective view of probability has been Bruno de Finetti (in many works, of which I cite only the earliest—1931 and 1937), whose views were already discussed in the final section of chapter 4. Another early contributors to the theory of subjective probability was B. O. Koopman (1940a and 1940b).

The literature on the subject continues to grow, but I shall not try to sketch the more recent history and I certainly have not dealt in detail with the many excellent papers written during the period I have been discussing. It has been my purpose here to provide only a brief historical sketch for the systematic points on which I concentrate.

An explicit concept of utility on which to build a quantitative demand theory of the market came somewhat later in the nineteenth century in the work of Gossen, Jevons, Walras, and others, but they made the overly strong assumption that utility was additive, in the same way that height or weight is. At the next stage this assumption was weakened by Edgeworth, Antonelli, and I. Fisher to the concept of an indifference surface for commodity bundles. Early in this century, Pareto took the step of proposing a theory of demand in terms of the behavioristic concept of purely ordinal preferences for commodity bundles.

Contemporary expected-utility goes beyond the ideas of Pareto in two essential respects. First, preferences are not restricted to commodity bundles, but to any field of choice about which decisions are to be made. And, second, the theory is set up explicitly to deal with uncertainty. Ordinal preferences are sufficient in general only in situations of essentially complete knowledge of the relevant possible states of affairs.

The intuition back of the expected-utility model is one that is widely accepted. When, as individuals, we are forced to make decisions, especially consequential ones, we must deal with two main factors: first, our beliefs about what is going to happen and, second, the value we attach to each of the possible consequences of our possible decisions. It is important to recognize that both beliefs and values are essential ingredients of the expected-utility model. A person with beliefs but no values does not know what to choose, and a person with values or feelings but no beliefs can easily choose foolishly.

Weaknesses of the expected-utility model. I shall now give some of my reasons for thinking that the standard normative model of expected utility is not satisfactory. In the normative applications the intention is to make the computations explicit and with the most self-conscious deliberation possible. In many cases the normative model, at least in my own conception, is a model made for application by a group designed to take a weighty decision and to assess by extensive effort both the beliefs and the consequences relevant to the possible actions. Some, if not many, in the past have talked as if the normative model were made in heaven and would solve in one stroke all the problems of providing a theory of rationality. (Some of the points I discuss here are treated in more detail in Suppes, 1981a.)

There are, it seems to me, two serious limitations to the perfect workings of this normative model. One is that even in the most deliberate circumstances we do not really understand how to make the calculations required by the model. A head of state, assisted by all the technical expertise of a modern bureaucracy, is still faced with a very poor estimate of the consequences of any particular set of economic decisions he may make. It is reasonable to reply that rationality does not require that decisions be good ones, in the sense of having the consequences intended, but rather that the rationality of the decisions be guaranteed by appropriate computation, first of beliefs, then of values. But the difficulty is that both the theory and practice of these computations is far from satisfactory. I shall not enter into details here, but the central difficulty is that of passing from qualitative judgments to quantitative results and though the theory has been much developed in the past several decades it is still deficient.

The second and deeper difficulty of the normative model is that it can be satisfied by cognitive and moral idiots. Put another way, the consistency of computations required by the expected-utility model does not guarantee the exercise of judgment and wisdom in the traditional sense. The Aristotelian view that the rational man acts in accordance with good reasons is not a necessary part of the normative model of expected utility, and it is not clear that these two concepts can always be put together in satisfactory form. In the earlier discussion of the application of procedures I tried to sketch a practical view of their interaction.

Fantasy of intention. In chapter 2 I tried to make a case for the existence of objective probabilistic laws in nature or, as another way of putting it, the ontological character of randomness. Some philosophers who will accept randomness in parts of the physical world, especially in atomic and subatomic phenomena, want to hold on to a determinate theory of human action and intention. It is part of this philosophical conception of rationality that actions are taken to execute conscious intentions and consequently that a rational man is one whose intentions are not so much honorable as systematic and conscious.

I propose to criticize this view and suggest an alternative. There are two distinct aspects to what I believe about intentions. The first concerns the status of simple intentions in their ordinary expression; for instance, I may assert 'I'm going to town to buy a shirt'. Here my view is that intentions and correlated actions cannot be grounded in some bedrock of determinism, but represent gross averages of possible stochastic sample paths. Let me explain what I mean. When I announce my intention to go to town to buy a shirt, I do not spell out how I am going to do it. In probabilistic terms, there is an infinite number of different possible paths I may follow, and neither my statement nor my conscious views about my intention provide many clues about the one I shall actually follow in going from home to store. Intentions and actions are afloat on a sea of random happenings. (A similar point was made about procedures earlier.) This point is not aimed at the elimination of intentions as practically useful, but only at locating them at a rather high level of abstraction.

The deeper aspect of my alternative view is to challenge the central place assigned to intentions in the theory of actions held by many philosophers. Acting is much like talking. Most of the time we do not consciously and reflectively form the sentences we utter. They tumble out, in odd shapes and sizes. Like our listeners, we do not usually know what we are going to say until we also have heard it said. So it goes with actions and decisions. We are driven by our pasts and by our hormones in ways we have no hope of consciously understanding. It is part of a realistic theory of rationality to recognize this fact. Conscious intentions can constitute constraints on what we do, but it is mistaken to think that the bubbling cauldron of our unconscious urgings can be cooled by rational introspection. At the deeper levels we do what we do as an expression of urges that are partly random in character and that we can never fully comprehend in any conscious manner.

In these matters Freud is a better guide than Aristotle, but even Freud's conception of the unconscious is overly intellectual. Moreover, Freud was too impressed by the deterministic theories of nineteenth-century physics and sought a similar determinism for mental events. We do not have for mental events experimental data comparable to those for radioactive decay or a fundamental theory even remotely similar to quantum mechanics. But a proper psychological theory of motivation will, I am sure, have a proper random component, which will not be subsumed under an Aristotelian analysis of incidental causation.

I am skeptical that many common philosophical views about intention are correct. Put another way, I hold a strong thesis of incompleteness about conscious intentions. They have a role to play that is often far from negligible, but they do not have the overriding role often attributed to them in determining how individuals in fact behave. Let us take the classical case of a young man asking his attractive teacher an endless variety of questions, a common phenomenon when the young man is about 12 and the teacher is in her 20s or 30s. On any given occasion, if the young man is asked his intention it will be easy for him to say 'Yes, I want to know about this problem', or 'I want to know about this assignment'. The larger sense of intention, namely, that he is anxious to talk to her and to be physically close to her, is not something he is even conscious of at this stage, but it is something that external observers, probably the teacher herself, would easily infer. My theoretical view would be that random urgings of all kinds reach a threshold level from one occasion to another and drive him to find a suitable pretext to walk up and talk to the teacher. At a deeper conceptual level, it is these random urges that generate his actions and not some process of conscious deliberation.

Such situations have been described repeatedly, often in great detail, by a variety of dramatists and novelists. What we do not seem to have done is to absorb the concept of a random urge into our analysis of intentions. Let me end by amplifying just one final example. As we look at our young man's behavior, where can we look to demonstrate randomness in the drives behind his actions? It seems to me that the time and occasion provide the right focus. He who attempts a deterministic theory of when the student will walk up to his teacher or when another young man in different circumstances will telephone his loved one or be telephoned by her is laboring in vain. These events are beyond any deterministic analysis foreseeable in the future and in my own view will in principle forever retain a strong random component. Our best psychological theory of impulses will surely come to resemble something like the probabilistic theory of particles and waves.

The same skepticism applies to desires and beliefs, concepts central to expected-utility theory, insofar as it is claimed that they are conscious. It is often said that thought is only made explicit by talk. In similar fashion, intentions, desires, and beliefs are often only crystalized and made a matter of conscious awareness after action has been taken. Moreover, there are good grounds for arguing that many of our deepest desires never become conscious, even when there is good external evidence that they play an important role in such significant decisions as the choice of a spouse and the selection of friends.

Intentional randomness. There is another side to intention and randomness that is not easily included in the expected-utility model. This is the intentional use of randomized procedures. The two places where the theory is best developed are in the theory of games and in the theory of sampling. In many games of imperfect information, i.e., games in which a player must make a move without full knowledge of the moves by other players, it may be shown that an optimal strategy is a random strategy. Such a result follows from the famous minimax theorem of von Neumann (see von Neumann and Morgenstern, 1947/1953). The explicit formulation of the theorem or specific consideration of the methods for computing an optimal random strategy need not be considered here to make the central conceptual point. In a competitive en-vironment where we are competing with another intelligent agent, by randomizing and thus making our behavior unpredic-table at the level of explicit choice we can guarantee to ourselves a best possible result in the sense of minimizing our maximum expected loss.

It is difficult for Bayesians to accept such results. For a pure Bayesian, in every situation he has an optimal deterministic strategy that will maximize his expected utility—or minimize his expected loss. The weakness of the Bayesian position is that the probability distribution expressing beliefs about an opponent's expected choice of moves often represents very infirm ideas about what the opponent is going to do. In such situations, prudence should rightly overrule purity, and a random minimax strategy should be adopted.

Similar arguments properly transformed apply to the use of randomization in sampling procedures. Once again, pure Bayesians can find no compelling reasons to randomize when sampling, whether in a scientific experiment, a social survey, or any other kind of systematically designed study for collecting evidence. Randomizing in scientific experimentation is not an old idea. Serious examples or explicit conceptual discussion of randomization can only be found in this century, but since Fisher's strong advocacy in the early 1920s, randomization is a standard procedure in a wide variety of scientific disciplines. There are, I think, three distinct central arguments for randomization which weigh against the view of pure Bayesians (an expanded account of the three arguments is to be found in Suppes, 1983).

First, there is the classic argument of Fisher (1935/1949) that randomizing is the most effective way to eliminate bias, conscious or not. The medical experimenter who selects which patients are to receive a new treatment for a disease and which are to receive the standard treatment or none at all, can unconsciously select for the new treatment patients that are healthier and have therefore a better chance of recovery. Randomization prevents the exercise of such bias.

A second argument is that randomization provides in non-theoretical settings a probabilistic model in terms of which calculations can be made, and in whose absence it would not be possible. The most familiar example of this sort is the use of randomization to provide a proper statistical model for statistical tests of significance. Is there, for instance, a significant difference between the treatment and control group in the kind of medical experiment mentioned above? If there is no intrinsic probabilistic model of the phenomena, as there ordinarily would not be for such medical studies, then explicit justification of tests of significance depends upon creating a probabilistic model by randomization. Bayesian attempts to get around this point are not, in my view, successful. I grant, however, that the matter is controversial and the subject of much discussion in the literature.

A third argument is that randomization facilitates proper identification of causes. Well-designed experiments with appropriate randomization should lead to identification of prima facie or genuine causes. With small sample sizes an experiment might fail to do so, but as the sample size increases the guarantee of identification becomes ever more certain. Systematic designs cannot in general guarantee such results. On the other hand, it is important to note that a good randomized experimental design will not in itself lead us from prima facie to genuine causes. This more depends on generating hypotheses that depend on the conjectured structure of the phenomena being studied, analogy with similar phenomena, and other factors that we only dimly understand.

In a word, intentional randomization is no panacea, but it is an important methodology for the reasons stated.

Fantasy of attention.   Bayesians emphasize the importance of understanding the process of changing beliefs in accordance with information newly received. A problem of equal importance that has not received comparable scrutiny is the process of information selection and the closely correlated process of attention. From a rational standpoint, how do we think about the selection of those slices of experience on any given occasion that should be attended to? There are, of course, obvious and extreme examples. A rational man driving down a highway at a high speed does not attend to an untied shoelace for more than a second or two. Any kind of situation requiring closely coupled perceptual and motor activity almost automatically fixes the main focus of attention. But such cases are limited. A general rational theory of attention does not seem to be available and also has not been widely recognized as a missing ingredient of a fully worked out theory of rationality.

Additional reinforcement for the need for a rational theory of attention is that a variety of psychological studies have established the severe limitations of the amount of information that people can process at any given moment. We might put the matter this way. At any given time, of the information available only some is perceived and less is responded to or remembered.

Within statistical decision theory proper, there have been studies of optimal decision making under conditions of limited memory (e.g., Cover, 1969), but the problems of attention raise different and rather more subtle issues. I have seen no explicit normative analysis, especially of what we might call "on-line" selection mechanisms, that is, mechanisms that operate in real time in situations requiring a fast processing of information and rapid evaluation for purposes of decision. There is a substantial psychological literature on speed-accuracy tradeoffs in performing a variety of tasks. What is pertinent here is how much our conception of optimal behavior is determined by subtle empirical constraints. Our view, for instance, of the best way to type pages of written text, i.e., with a certain speed and error rate, depends almost entirely on empirical performance characteristics. The rational aspects of such matters are swamped by pervasive and subtle facts. We easily lose our way in trying to justify specific normative goals of behavior.

It is not possible here to develop even the outlines of a rational theory of attention, but there is a general philosophical point that I have made before (Suppes, 1966a) and that I would like to amplify. As the Bayesian theory of rationality becomes more realistic and detailed, it should be apparent it must become more psychological. Any permanently interesting concept of rationality for the behavior of men must be keyed to detailed psychological appraisal of the powers and limitations of our perceptual and mental apparatus. Problems of attention and selection do not exist for an omniscient God or even for a computer whose inputs are already schematized in some highly definite way. Failure to attend to these problems of attention and selection are the source, I am sure, of criticisms of decision theories' being applied in too mechanistic and algorithmic fashion.

Matters of context and approximation. Almost everyone who reflects on the problems of measuring beliefs in the tradition of subjective probability feels some uneasiness about asking for arbitrary refinement of the measurement. There is something in fact paradoxical about demanding an exact probability distribution of our beliefs. If we compare this situation with the one that exists in the case of physical measurement, we can see how absurd the thrust for exact results is. We would consider it unthinkable to require of a physical theory that it be based on exact measurements of mass or position. In all cases of continuous quantities, we expect a statement about the nature of errors of measurement, and, in standard practice, we expect some error estimate. The explicit realization that errors can be estimated is one of the main contributions of the theory of probability to general scientific methodology. Without such an explicit theory of error, much of the more exact and sophisticated science of the latter part of the nineteenth century and the twentieth century would have been conceptually difficult, if not impossible, in terms of serious confrontation between theory and data.

On the other hand, if we are asked for our beliefs about the probability of rain tomorrow, the rate of inflation, or the growth of GNP, we find it hard to think through how to assign definite errors of measurement to the process of determining these beliefs. In fact, so far as I know there is no serious literature on the subject of developing anything like a direct analogy with the theory of measurement errors in the experimental sciences. However, another approach that has been discussed much less than one might think seems promising. This is the approach that assigns not exact probabilities, but upper and lower probabilities, to the occurrence of an event. The general idea of such an approach was stated very early by Bayes (1764), but the twentieth-century theory of upper and lower probabilities as upper and lower estimates of the probability of the occurrence of events is quite recent. Let me describe my own approach (Suppes, 1974c). The idea is quite simple and I shall not enter into any technical details. We have available standard events, like standard weights and measures, and we approximate the probability of any complex event by the use of standard events. As a simple example, I might say that in my mind the occurrence of rain tomorrow is less probable than getting a head in one flip of a fair coin and more probable than getting two heads in two flips of the coin. The theory is set up in such a way that a small finite set of rational numbers are all that we need for approximating the probabilities of our beliefs. It might be said that now the problem of exact measurement of probability has been replaced by the exact measurement of upper and lower probabilities, but it is clear there has been a radical reduction in complexity, for only a small number of standard events measured in terms of a small number of rational numbers are needed. It is true that these rational numbers are given exactly, but all measurement estimates about our beliefs are expressed in terms of this selected, fixed, and usually rather small set of rational numbers. As already indicated, it is apparent that there is a close analogy to the one that exists in the use of an equal-arm balance in the measurement of mass or in the use of a measuring rod in the case of distance. For the given scales of measurement, uniqueness is expected for the standard events and, for the equal-arm balance, the standard weights. But precision beyond the selected fixed finite set of standard weights is not expected and cannot be obtained, without changing the framework and introducing a refinement of having more standard events or standard weights as the case may be. I do not think that the kind of theory I am describing meets all the problems about approximation and error in measuring the probabilities we assign to our beliefs, but it does have the virtue of showing how a simple theory, very close to the kind of simple theory used in practice in physics for the measurement of such fundamental quantities as mass and length, can be developed. I am very much persuaded that deeper and more detailed attention to such matters of approximation is essential to developing really usable quantitative theories of rational behavior.

PLACE OF JUDGMENT

Given these limitations of any standard model of rationality, I turn to the essential place of intuitive judgment. There are four things I want to say. The first concerns experimentation and data analysis. Published articles about experiments may make it seem as if the scientist can in a simple, rational way relate data to theory in the finished form commonly found in the scientific literature. In my own experience, nothing can be further from the truth. In the setting up of experiments and in the analysis of the results there are countless informal decisions of a practical and intuitive kind that must be made. There is no serious evidence that this set of decisions can be reduced to an explicit theory of rationality. Many practical and conceptually inexplicit decisions must be made in every area of experimentation, or indeed of empirical inquiry, ranging from high-energy physics to the psychology of auditory judgments.

The second point is that it is relatively straightforward to think about applying a criterion of rationality to decisions formulated in a theoretical framework. This reflects a general scientific fact of life, which I emphasized in chapter 6. In every branch of science, the theoretical language is relatively simple and easy to learn compared with the complex, arcane, and esoteric language used to express the lore of experimental procedures, from the calibration of instruments to the collection of data. I will not here attempt to document this thesis. I, in fact, consider it obvious to anyone acquainted with actual scientific practice in some developed branch of investigation. Decisions taken in the framework of such highly empirical language and thought routinely seem too highly context-dependent to be assessed in terms of any general criterion of rationality.

The third point is that the fantasy of explicit formality, with elimination of all need for intuitive judgment, is recognized as an outmoded concept, even in mathematics. Hilbert's program of formalism was upset years ago by Gödel's incompleteness theorems, and the gap between formal theories of proof, for example, and actual mathematical practice, requiring judgments of all kinds, is now widely acknowledged, a point discussed in detail in chapter 4. I emphasize the essential place of judgment in science and mathematics, because this is the area of thought and experience that seems most amenable to regimentation by simple models of rationality.

The essential place of judgment in decision making has been recognized by various people, including de Finetti, for some time. But there has been a countertendency, generated by the thicket of technical results about decision making in modern mathematical statistics, that tends to suggest that judgment can be eliminated in favor of the application, in a routine, objective, and possibly even algorithmic way, of technical results. There has also been a pernicious trend of long standing in classical philosophy of both ancient and modern times that reinforces this view—perhaps the best example is the foolish attempt to construct our knowledge of the world from indubitable sense data. What I have said about the essential role of intuitive judgment in assessing evidence in scientific experiments extends naturally to less regimented regimes of information processing. To think that evidence is somehow brought to bear in a clear and objective way without continual intuitive decisions about relevance, timeliness, significance, etc., is to be fundamentally mistaken about our actual empirical dealing with the world around us. It is this irreducible component of intuitive judgment, unable to be formulated in a set of rules—above all, to be reduced to algorithms—that argues perhaps most strongly of all for the severe limitation of explicit models of rationality.

If the conclusions I am arguing for about the irreducible and essential nature of intuitive judgments are correct, they constitute a powerful, fundamental argument against overextending the domain of bureaucracy, which always and everywhere aims for, even if it does not achieve, the codification of explicit rules and the implementation of algorithmic procedures.

Positive theory of judgment.   I have emphasized the importance of the role of intuitive judgment in any realistic theory of decision making, and I have stressed the limits of any computational model of rationality. What I have not said much about is the positive theory of intuitive judgment, which is my fourth point. It might seem from some of my earlier remarks that I believe intuitive judgment cannot be made a matter of detailed investigation or subject to explicit analysis.

Because this is not my view, I want to develop at least briefly the outlines of a positive theory. The essence of the theory is easy to state. Intuitive judgment is a skill like jogging, playing tennis, or finding mathematical proofs. Even simpler and more universal examples are walking and talking. Indeed, it is easy to claim that a number of skills are more essential and more characteristic of human activity than any body of explicit knowledge. It is a familiar fact that we learn to walk and talk without much explicit training, but in the case of more specialized skills, competent performance is very much a matter of practice and training. The most familiar examples lie in the area in which the regimes of practice and training are, in many respects, most thoroughly thought out and most carefully developed, namely, the area of physical skills. To become a marathon runner or a first-class tennis player requires continued practice—and in most cases explicit teaching by an experienced coach. We are, for a variety of reasons, more romantic and unsystematic about learning mental skills.

To a considerable extent, however, the area of agreement appears to be greater than that of difference. A more important point is one that cuts across the division between mental and physical skills. This is whether or not there is a simple and agreed-upon objective criterion of performance. If we are training a marathon runner or a competitor for the 1,000-meter race, we can, by measuring his running time each day, have an excellent simple and objective criterion of performance and improvement in performance. In the case of competitive games, the criterion is more complicated but still in the end rather simple because of our ability to tabulate who won and who lost when real play starts. The same can be said for mental skills that involve objective tasks like those of arithmetical computation. In the case of physical skills like that of mountain climbing, or mental skills such as those of judging the qualities of complex objects, for example, paintings, horses, or beautiful people, agreed-upon, simple, and easily applicable criteria of performance are absent. All the same, the absence of such simplicity does not prohibit highly successful training and teaching; this general observation applies whether we are talking about physical skills like mountain climbing or mental skills like judging works of art of a given category.

I emphasize also my optimism about developing a proper psychology of such skills, in particular, a proper educational psychology for teaching such skills. The important reservation to this optimism is that the teaching will not be verbally explicit; it will not be algorithmic in the sense of providing the student with a fixed procedure for reaching the intended result. Rather, it will depend upon the kinds of complicated, indirect, and subtle methods already familiar in the training of many different physical and mental skills. The long tradition of apprenticeship in training craftsmen is one of the finest examples. This tradition, it should be noted, has flourished in modern scientific laboratories.

Because of the overly rationalistic and linguistically oriented approach to intuitive judgment in the past, we have not developed in any adequate way the kinds of effective teaching regimes that are possible. The first step is to understand the nature of intuitive judgment—that it is a skill more like running than the organization of some body of knowledge—and the second, to realize that once we get a conceptual basis for an understanding of intuitive judgment we will be in a position to develop appropriate regimes of instruction.

Linear models for aggregating judgments. Another aspect of the positive theory is the possibility of going beyond purely intuitive judgments to the use of structural models that provide methods of aggregating intuitive judgments. There is a conceptually important literature in psychology dealing with a comparison of clinical intuitive judgment and statistical models. The classical work is Paul Meehl's *Clinical Versus Statistical Prediction: A theoretical analysis and review of the literature*, published in 1954. Meehl analyzes a number of studies showing that the prediction of a numerical criterion of psychological interest is almost always done better by a proper linear regression model using numerical predictor variables than by the intuitive judgment of individuals supposedly skilled in such prediction. Some good recent studies are summarized in Dawes (1971 and 1979).

What is to be made of these results from a broad conceptual standpoint and what is their implication for decision making? Perhaps the most important conclusion is that human judges are comparatively poor at integrating diverse data, especially multidimensional quantitative data, but much better at understanding what variables are liable to be useful predictors and how their direction of variation will relate to direction of variation in the target dependent variable. The importance of essentially universal agreement on how signs of variation in variables should be related is easy to underestimate. A vast fund of qualitative knowledge is represented in such agreements; it would be difficult to replace intuitive judgments by bootstrapping statistical models that did not use preselected variables. (Application of these ideas to problems of rational allocation of resources is to be found in Suppes, 1982.)

I have not tried to present a great many specific details about these linear models, but I believe they represent a robust approach to structuring the way in which intuitive judgments are obtained and how they are analyzed. An excellent reprint collection of articles on biases in judgment as well as heuristics used, including Dawes's 1979 study of linear models, is to be found in Kahneman, Slovic, and Tversky (1982). This volume is suggestive of what new theoretical ideas may eventually subsume the expected-utility model to give a deeper account of both actual and normative behavior, but a full-blown formal theory is as yet far from being developed.

THE BAYESIAN CORE

It should not be inferred from what I have just said that the place of judgment is the only place of honor. Calculations, computations, and estimates within the framework of the Bayasian or expected-utility model have an important role. It has been my point to emphasize the limitation of such models, but I in no sense want to argue for their irrelevancy to practical decision making or the conduct of scientific investigations. When used with a proper appreciation of their limits, such models can play an important role in many domains of experience. One point of realism about the application of the expected-utility model that I would like to focus on concerns the implications of the earlier claim that measurements of subjective probability and utility can only be approximate in character. It is a familiar experience in quantitative parts of science, especially physics, to deal with the implications of errors of measurement. The theory of such matters has been a prominent topic since the latter part of the eighteenth century. With some exceptions, a similar focus on problems of error or approximation has not been of concern in the technical development of models of rational behavior, but as applications become more widespread and more familiar, such problems of measurement are bound to receive attention. As in the early case of celestial mechanics, they will bring an immediate sense of complexity to computations that, looked at purely theoretically, are relatively simple. But this complexity will have a salutary effect. As has already been discussed, one standard weakness of the expected-utility or Bayesian model is the view that new information is processed simply by forming a new probability distribution, conditioned on the new evidence. But when problems of approximation are faced, it is easy to see that it is not simply a matter of conditioning on the new evidence but also of recalibrating and remeasuring the probability distribution and also the quantitative assessment of values. Such recalibration is a familiar part of standard procedures in the physical sciences. Moreover, contrary to what was thought in the days of Laplace, when probability was viewed as purely a subjective matter, it is reasonable to maintain, as I have already argued, that there is not even a theoretical exact value to be measured and thus there is no hope even theoretically of refining the approximations to an exact value, which was one of the mistaken ideals of classical physics.

The utility or loss functions of the statisticians, which are at the heart of the expected-utility model, are designed for the factory and the marketplace. As the demand for greater psychological realism and philosophical subtlety grows, conceptual refinements will be necessary. But with the Aristotelian tradition to draw on, we should be able to follow the proper golden way of calculation and judgment in undogmatic splendor. What we teach our students or ourselves about practical decision making cannot be wholly reduced to algorithms or even to explicit axioms, but we can, on the other hand, improve on Aristotle just because we can apply axioms and procedures as appropriate. The use of modern quantitative methods of decision making is necessarily limited but powerful when properly applied. The role of judgment and practical wisdom in applying these methods will continue to be of central importance. The tension between calculation, qualitatively justified procedures, and judgment will not disappear. Nor will its philosophical analysis.

APPENDIX ON PROBABILITY
AND EXPECTATION

The purpose of this appendix is to develop various qualitative foundations for probability and expectation. In the standard treatment of these matters the introduction of expectation follows the introduction of probability. One begins with the standard Kolmogorov axioms for probability spaces and then defines random variables as real-valued measurable functions on the probability space. Expectation is then the expectation of a random variable. Perhaps the most important novelty in what I have to say here is that I think this familiar current story has the cart before the horse. The proper notion to start with is expectation, for reasons that will become clear, and in terms of expectation to define probability. It is worth noting that this view also has good support from the past. It is to be found both in the early writings of Huygens and of Bayes. Here is the definition that Bayes gives of probability in terms of expectation in his well-known essay of 1764.

> The *probability of any event* is the ratio between the value at which an expectation depending on the happening of the event ought to be computed, and the value of the thing expected upon it's [sic] happening. (p. 376)

Bayes's meaning in this brief statement is not entirely clear, but if we think in terms of gambles it is easy to give examples. Bayes himself, in the first proposition following the definitions, gives a rather clear example that it will be useful to quote.

> When several events are inconsistent the probability of the happening of one or other of them is the sum of the probabilities of each of them.

Suppose there be three such events, and which ever of them happens I am to receive N, and that the probability of the 1st, 2d, and 3d are respectively a/N, b/N, c/N. Then (by the definition of probability) the value of my expectation from the 1st will be a, from the 2d b, and from the 3d c. Wherefore the value of my expectations from all three will be $a+b+c$. But the sum of my expectations from all three is in this case an expectation of receiving N upon the happening of one or other of them. Wherefore (by definition 5) the probability of one or other of them is $(a+b+c)/N$ or $(a/N)+(b/N)+(c/N)$. The sum of the probabilities of each of them. (pp. 376–377)

Finally it is worth quoting proposition 2, which has a very decided modern flavor.

If a person has an expectation depending on the happening of an event, the probability of the event is to the probability of its failure as his loss if it fails to his gain if it happens. (p. 377)

De Finetti as well, in his coherence argument, certainly takes random variables or, as he prefers, random quantities as primitive and as logically prior to events. Thus there is an honorable and important tradition for moving away from events as the proper objects to which probability should be attached.

Before turning to systematic developments about expectation, there are some things I want to say about the qualitative theory of probability treated strictly in terms of events. If events are used as the primitive objects with a binary ordering relation between events having the interpretation that $A \geq B$ if and only if A is at least as probable as B, then axioms that are about as simple as can be achieved for the finite case were given by Scott (1964). (His axioms improve on earlier ones given by Kraft, Pratt, and Seidenberg, 1959.) These axioms are within the de Finetti framework of qualitative subjective probability in which decisions and consequences are not explicitly considered. Scott's axioms are embodied in the following definition, in which the notation A^i is used for the indicator function of a set A, and $\emptyset$ for the empty set. The indicator function A^i for the event A is defined as follows for every x in Ω where Ω is the set of possible outcomes:

$$A^i(x) = \begin{cases} 1 \text{ if } x \in A \\ 0 \text{ if } x \notin A \end{cases}$$

Definition 1.   *Let* Ω *be a nonempty finite set and* $\geq$ *a binary relation on the set of all subsets of* Ω. *Then a structure* $<\Omega,\geq>$ *is a* (finite) qualitative belief *structure if and only if for all subsets* A *and* B *of* Ω:

> **Axiom 1.** $A \geq B$ *or* $B \geq A$;
> **Axiom 2.** $A \geq \emptyset$;
> **Axiom 3.** $X > \emptyset$;
> **Axiom 4.**   *For all subsets* $A_0, \ldots, A_n, B_0, \ldots, B_n$ *of* Ω, *if* $A_i \geq B_i$ *for* $0 \leq i < n$, *and for all* x *in* Ω
>
> $$A_0^i(x) + \ldots + A_n^i(x) = B_0^i(x) + \ldots + B_n^i(x)$$

then $B_n \geq A_n$.

Axiom 4 only requires that any element of Ω belong to exactly the same number of A_i and B_1, for $0 \leq i \leq n$. To illustrate the force of Scott's axiom 4, we may see how it implies transitivity. First, necessarily for any three indicator functions

$$A^i + B^i + C^i = B^i + C^i + A^i$$

i.e. for all elements x of Ω

$$A^i(x) + B^i(x) + C^i(x) = B^i(x) + C^i(x) + A^i(x)$$

By hypothesis, $A \geq B$ and $B \geq C$, whence by virtue of axiom 4,

$$C \leq A$$

and thus, by definition $A \geq C$, as desired. Scott proves that for any finite structure $<\Omega,\geq>$ satisfying the axioms of definition 1 there is a probability measure P such that for A and B subsets of Ω

$$A \geq B \text{ if and only if } P(A) \geq P(B)$$

A first point to note is that the probability measure P is not unique, nor apparently can its uniqueness up to a given set of transformations be characterized in an interesting way, a situation that is true for many finite geometries when the set of transformations is as general as possible, consistent with the finite number of relationships expressed. An even more serious difficulty is that when the probability measure is not unique, then there is no clear way of making unambiguous additional inferences as reflected in conditional probabilites. A second difficulty with Scott's axioms as a theory of belief is that they do not generalize in a natural and simple way to the infinite case.

Other related axiomatizations in terms of the algebra of events have also run into difficulties. For example, Luce's axiomatization (1967), which gives sufficient but not necessary conditions for uniqueness, requires axioms that are strong and rather difficult to understand in literal formulation, as in the case of Savage's axioms. Luce's axiom is the following (Krantz *et al.*, 1971, p 207):

(1) For any events A, B, C, and D such that $A \cap B = \emptyset$, $A > C$, and $B \geq D$, there exist events C', D', and E such that

   (i) $E \approx A \cup B$;
   (ii) $C' \cap D' = \emptyset$;
   (iii) $C' \cup D' \subset E$;
   (iv) $C' \approx C$ and $D' \approx D$.

Here $>$ is the strict ordering relation and $\approx$ the equivalence relation defined in terms of the weak ordering $\geq$. The meaning of this axiom is complex and not easy to state in words. As we search for weaker axioms, closer to being necessary and not merely sufficient, the situation seems likely to get worse. A rather detailed discussion of these matters is to be found in chapters 5 and 9 of Krantz *et al.* (1971).

As I see it, the moral of the story is that events are the wrong objects to consider. Some slightly richer concept that is better behaved from a formal standpoint is needed. A move from one concept to a richer one that is exemplified by a larger and richer set of objects is a characteristic move in mathematics and science. Familiar examples are extension of the rational numbers to the real numbers and extension of the real numbers to the complex numbers. Because of the almost universal acceptance of Kolmogorov's (1933) axioms for probability where events are taken as the appropriate objects to which to attach probability, it is not an easy matter to make a persuasive case for an alternative viewpoint. Prior to Kolmogorov's axiomatization, various somewhat vague alternatives were used. For example, in his influential early book Keynes (1921) took propositions as primitive.

The move that I advocate is rather like the move from a sample space to random variables. There is a positive history already mentioned for taking expectations of random variables as the more fundamental concept. It may be argued that in ordinary experience expectation rather than probability is the more widely used concept. As I have put it elsewhere, the argument for this is evident from a practical standpoint. Once we leave events and talk about what correspond to random variables it is natural in ordinary talk to want to know only the expectation and not the full probability distribution. Thus we talk about the expectation of walking at least ten kilometers in the next three days, the expectation of at least three centimeters of rain in the next eight hours, or the expectation that the rate of inflation in the next year will be about 9 percent. In all of these cases we are dealing in a natural way with a quantitative variable, but we are not prepared to give, and are really not interested in giving, the full probability distribution of that variable—we are quite satisfied with its expectation.

The course that I propose to follow, already described briefly in Suppes and Zanotti (1976a), is a conservative one of making what seems to be a minimal extension of the algebra of events in order to get simple necessary and sufficient conditions for the existence of a probability measure on the algebra and also to get uniqueness of expectation in terms of the restricted random variables considered. It is natural to call the structures introduced 'qualitative expectation structures'.

The extension from events is easy to describe. First, we replace events by their indicator functions. Remember that an indicator function is just a function defined on the set of possible outcomes such that the function has the value 1 for possible outcomes included in the event considered as a set, and has the value 0 for all other possible outcomes. Of course, the move from events to their indicator functions does not change the conceptual situation at all. The move that does create a change, however, is to extend the set of indicator functions by closing them under addition. More explicitly, this closure condition has the following meaning. Let Ω be the set of possible outcomes and let $\mathcal{F}$ be an algebra of events on Ω, that is, $\mathcal{F}$ is a nonempty family of subsets of Ω and is closed under complementation and union. Let, as before, A^i be the indicator function of event A. The algebra $\mathcal{F}^*$ of *extended* indicator functions relative to $\mathcal{F}$ is then just the smallest semigroup (under function addition) containing the indicator functions of all events in $\mathcal{F}$. In other words, $\mathcal{F}^*$ is the intersection of all sets with the property that if A is in $\mathcal{F}$ then A^i is in $\mathcal{F}^*$, and if X and Y are in $\mathcal{F}^*$, then $X+Y$ is in $\mathcal{F}^*$. It is easy to show that any function X in $\mathcal{F}^*$ is an integer-value function defined on Ω. It is the extension from indicator functions to integer-valued functions that justifies calling the elements of $\mathcal{F}^*$ extended indicator functions.

Here are a couple of examples to illustrate the naturalness of such extended indicator functions. These applications arise whenever we have a collection of events that are not mutually exclusive and we are interested in the expectation from the collection and not from the individual events. Jones wants to evaluate two weather forecasters, but he wants to do this only in a general way by examining their ability to predict rain in Ithaca 24 hours in advance. He does this by simply looking at their record for the past year and then making an estimate of the expectation of each for the coming year. In making this judgment of expectation he is making a qualitative judgment about the relative value of two extended indicator functions.

Here is a second example. Consider a particular population of n individuals, numbered $1, \ldots, n$. Let A_i be the event of individual i going to Hawaii for a vacation this year, and let B_i be the event of individual i going to Acapulco. Then define

$$A^* = \sum_{i=1}^{n} A_i^i \text{ and } B^* = \sum_{i=1}^{n} B_i^i$$

Obviously A^* and B^* are extended indicator functions—we have left implicit the underlying set Ω. It is meaningful and quite natural to compare qualitatively the expected values of A^* and B^*. Presumably such comparisons are in fact of definite significance to travel agents, airlines, and the like.

Such qualitative comparisons of expected value are natural and derive from ordinary usage as already discussed. We could, of course, take a more general setting than the very restricted one of extended indicator functions, but such functions are sufficient to give us a nice setting for the qualitative statement of necessary and sufficient conditions. Once a unique expectation for such functions is found, extension to other functions via the probability measure defined on the sample space or set of possible outcomes is straightforward and familiar.

Appendix

FORMAL DEVELOPMENT

The axioms are embodied in the definition of a qualitative algebra
of extended indicator functions. Several points of notation need
attention. First, Ω^i and $\emptyset^i$ are the indicator functions of the set Ω of
possible outcomes and the empty set $\emptyset$, respectively. Second, the
notation nX for a function in $\mathcal{F}^*$ is just the standard notation for the
(functional) sum of X with itself n times. Third, the same notation
is used for the ordering relation on $\mathcal{F}$ and $\mathcal{F}^*$, because the one on
$\mathcal{F}^*$ is an extension of the one on $\mathcal{F}$: for A and B in $\mathcal{F}$,

$$A \geq B \text{ iff } A^i \geq B^i$$

Finally, the strict ordering relation $>$ is defined in the usual way in
terms of the weak ordering $\geq$.

Definition 2. *Let Ω be a nonempty set, let $\mathcal{F}$ be an algebra of sets
on Ω, and let $\geq$ be a binary relation on $\mathcal{F}^*$, the algebra of extended
indicator functions relative to $\mathcal{F}$. Then $<\Omega,\mathcal{F}^*,\geq>$ is a qualitative
expectation structure if and only if the following axioms are
satisfied for every* X, Y, *and* Z *in* $\mathcal{F}^*$:

Axiom 1. *The relation $\geq$ is a weak ordering of $\mathcal{F}^*$;*
Axiom 2. $\Omega^i > \emptyset^i$;
Axiom 3. $X \geq \emptyset^i$;
Axiom 4. $X \geq Y$ *iff* $X+Z \geq Y+Z$;
Axiom 5. *If* $X > Y$, *then for any* Z *there is a positive integer* n
such that

$$nX \geq nY+Z$$

These axioms should seem familiar from the literature on qualitative probability. Note that axiom 4 is the additivity axiom that
closely resembles de Finetti's additivity axiom for events: if
$A \cap C = B \cap C = \emptyset$, *then* $A \geq B$ *iff* $A \cup C \geq B \cup C$. As we move
from events to extended indicator functions, functional addition
replaces union of sets. What is formally of importance about this
move is seen already in the exact formulation of axiom 4. The additivity of the extended indicator functions is unconditional—there is
no restriction corresponding to $A \cap C = B \cap C = \emptyset$. The absence of
this restriction has far-reaching formal consequences in permitting

us to apply without any real modification the general theory of extensive measurement. Axiom 5 is a form of the Archimedean axiom close to that used in the earlier work of Roberts and Luce (1968) and Alimov's (1950) formulation of the Archimedean axiom in terms of the nonexistence of anomalous pairs. Roberts and Luce's axiom has the form:

If $X > Y$ then for every U and V in $\mathscr{F}^*$ there is a positive integer n such that

$$nX + U \geq nY + V$$

But in their general theory of extensive measurement weak positivity is not assumed, which here is expressed by axiom 3 of definition 2. It is easy to show that axiom 5 implies and is implied by Roberts and Luce's Archimedean axiom in the presence of axioms 1–4. First, assume axiom 5. Then for any V there is an n such that

$$nX \geq nY + V$$

but for any U, we have from axioms 3 and 4:

$$nX + U \geq nX + \emptyset^i = nX$$

and thus by transitivity

$$nX + U \geq nY + V$$

as desired. On the other hand, their axiom obviously implies axiom 5, for we may always set $U = \emptyset^i$.

In the statement of the theorem that follows, to say that a probability measure P is strictly agreeing with an ordering on the algebra $\mathscr{F}$ of events is to say that for all events A and B

$$P(A) \geq P(B) \text{ iff } A \geq B$$

To refer to a unique strictly agreeing expectation function on $\mathscr{F}^*$ is to refer to a real-valued function E on $\mathscr{F}^*$ such that for X and Y in $\mathscr{F}^*$

(1) $E(X) \geq E(Y)$ iff $X \geq Y$,
(2) $E(X+Y) = E(X)+E(Y)$,
(3) $E(\emptyset^i) = 0$ and $E(\Omega^i) = 1$.

Theorem 1. *Let Ω be a nonempty set, let $\mathscr{F}$ be an algebra of sub-*
sets of Ω, and let $\geq$ be a binary relation on $\mathscr{F}$. Then a necessary
and sufficient condition that there exist a strictly agreeing proba-
bility measure on $\mathscr{F}$ is that there is an extension of $\geq$ from $\mathscr{F}$ to $\mathscr{F}^*$
such that the structure $<\Omega,\mathscr{F}^*,\geq>$ is a qualitative expectation
structure. Moreover, if $<\Omega,\mathscr{F}^*,\geq^*>$ is a qualitative expectation
structure, then there is a unique strictly agreeing expectation func-
tion on $\mathscr{F}^*$ and this expectation function generates a unique strictly
agreeing probability measure on $\mathscr{F}$.

The main tool in the proof is from the theory of extensive measurement: necessary and sufficient conditions for existence of a numerical representation, as given in Krantz *et al.* (1971, pp. 73–74, theorem 1). The detailed proof of theorem 1 is given in Suppes and Zanotti (1976a).

The procedure has been to axiomatize in qualitative fashion the expectation of the extended indicator functions. There was no need to consider all random variables and, on the other hand, the more restricted set of indicator functions raises the same axiomatic difficulties confronting the algebra of events. The natural sequence of developments is then:

(1) axiomatize qualitatively the expectation of extended indicator functions;
(2) use the unique numerical expectation to determine a unique (finitely additive) probability measure by defining for each event A, $P(A) = E(A^i)$;
(3) use the probability measure P to determine the expectation of any random variable defined on the space.

References

Abraham, R. and Marsden, J. E. (1978), *Foundations of Mechanics* (2nd edn). Reading, Mass.: Benjamin/Cummings Publishing Company.

Alimov, N. G. (1950), On ordered semigroups. *Izvestia Akademia Nauk SSSR, Ser. Mat.*, **14,** 569–576. (in Russian).

Almog, J., (1984), Would you believe that? *Synthese*, **58,** 1–37.

Anderson, J. R. (1976), *Language, Memory, and Thought*. Hillsdale, N. J.: Lawrence Erlbaum Associates.

Anscombe, G. E. M. (1975), Causality and determination. In E. Sosa (ed.), *Causation and Conditionals*. London: Oxford University Press.

Archimedes (1897), *On the Sphere and Cylinder*. Translated by T. L. Heath. Cambridge, England: Cambridge University Press.

Archimedes (1897), *On the Equilibrium of Planes*. Translated by T. L. Heath. Cambridge, England: Cambridge University Press.

Aristotle (1941), *Nicomachean Ethics*. New York: Random House.

Aristotle (1966), *Posterior Analytics*, Loeb edition. Translated by H. Tredennick. Cambridge, Mass.: Harvard University Press.

Aristotle (1967a), *On Interpretation*. Loeb edition. Translated by H. P. Cooke. Cambridge, Mass.: Harvard University Press.

Aristotle (1967b), *Prior Analytics*, Loeb edition. Translated by H. Tredennick. Cambridge, Mass.: Harvard University Press.

Aristotle (1968a), *Metaphysics*, Loeb edition. Translated by H. Tredennick. Cambridge, Mass.: Harvard University Press.

Aristotle (1968b), *Physics*, Loeb edition. Translated by P. H. Wickstead and F. M. Cornford. Cambridge, Mass.: Harvard University Press.

Aristotle (1978), *De Motu Animalium*. Translated by M. C. Nussbaum. Princeton, N. J.: Princeton University Press.

Aumann, R. J. (1962), Utility theory without the completeness of axiom. *Econometrica*, **30,** 445–462.

Aumann, R. J. (1964), Utility theory without the completeness axiom: a correction. *Econometrica*, **32,** 210–212.

Ayer, A. J. (1946), *Language, Truth and Logic* (2nd edn). London: Victor Gollancz.

Bailey, C. (1928), *The Greek Atomists and Epicurus*. London: Oxford University Press.

Barrow, John D. (1982), Chaotic behaviour in general relativity. *Physics Reports* (Review Section of Physics Letters), **85,** 1–49. Amsterdam: North-Holland.

Bayes, T. (1764), An essay toward solving a problem in the doctrine of chance. *Philosophical Transactions of the Royal Society*, **53,** 370–418.

Bell, J. S. (1964), On the Einstein Podolsky Rosen paradox. *Physics*, **1,** 195–200.

Bell, J. S. (1966), On the problem of hidden variables in quantum mechanics. *Reviews of Modern Physics*, **38,** 447–452.

Bentley, R. (1838), *Works* (Vol. III). London.

Bickel, P. J., Hammel, E. A., and O'Connell, J. W. (1975), Sex bias in graduate admissions: Data from Berkeley. *Science*, **187,** 398–404.

Bjelke, E. (1975), Dietary vitamin A and human lung cancer. *International Journal of Cancer*, **15,** 561–565.

Blackwell, D., and Girshick, M. A. (1954), *Theory of Games and Statistical Decisions*. New York: Wiley.

Bohm, D., and Aharonov, Y. (1957), Discussion of experimental proof for the paradox of Einstein, Rosen, and Podolsky. *Physical Review*, **108,** 1070–1076.

Boscovich, J. R. (1763/1922), *Theoria Philosophiae Naturalis* (Venetian edn, 1763; Latin– English edn, 1922. Chicago: Open Court, 1922.)

Cagan, R. H., and Kare, M. R. (eds) (1981), *Biochemistry of Taste and Olfaction*. New York: Academic Press.

Carterette, E. C., and Friedman, M. P. (eds) (1975), *Handbook of Perception* (Vol. V): *Seeing*. New York: Academic Press.

Carterette, E. C., and Friedman, M. P. (eds) (1978), *Handbook of Perception* (Vol. VIA): *Tasting and Smelling*. New York: Academic Press.

Cartwright, N. (1979), Causal laws and effective strategies. *Nous*, **13,** 419–437.

Chaitin, G. (1969), On the length of programs for computing finite binary sequences. *Journal of the Association of Computing Machinery*, **16,** 145–159.

Chang, W. W. and I. B., and Kutscher, H. W. and A. H. (1970), *An Encyclopedia of Chinese Food and Cooking*. New York: Crown Publishers.

Chao, B. Y. (1963), *How to Cook and Eat in Chinese* (3rd edn). New York: Random House.

Church, A. (1950), On Carnap's analysis of statements of assertion and belief. *Analysis*, **10,** 97–99.

Church, A. (1954), Intensional isomorphism and identity of belief. *Philosophical Studies*, **5 (5),** 65–78.

Clauser, J. F., Horne, M. A., Shimony, A., and Holt, R. A. (1969), Proposed experiment to test local hidden-variable theories. *Physical Review Letters*, **23**, 880–884.

Cohen, M. R., and Nagel, E. (1934), *An Introduction to Logic and Scientific Method*. New York: Harcourt, Brace.

Collingwood, R. J. (1939/1972), *Essay on Metaphysics*. Chicago, Ill.: Henry Regnery Company, Gateway Edition, 1972. (First published in 1939.)

Cover, T. M. (1969), Hypothesis testing with finite statistics. *Annals of Mathematical Statistics*, **40**, 828–835.

David, F. N. (1962), *Games, Gods and Gambling: The origins and history of probability and statistical ideas from the earliest times to the Newtonian era*. London: Charles Griffin.

Davidson, D., and Suppes, P. (1956), A finitistic axiomatization of subjective probability and utility. *Econometrica*, **24**, 264–275.

Dawes, R. M. (1971), A case study of graduate admissions: Application of three principles of human decision making. *American Psychologist*, **26**, 180–188.

Dawes, R. M. (1979), The robust beauty of improper linear models in decision making. *American Psychologist*, **34**, 571–582.

Debreu, G. (1959), Cardinal utility for even-chance mixtures of pairs of sure prospects. *Review of Economic Studies*, **71**, 174–177.

de Finetti, B. (1931), Sul significato della probabilità. *Fundamenta Mathematicae*, **17**, 298–329.

de Finetti, B. (1937), La prévision: ses lois logiques, ses sources subjectives. *Annales de l'Institut Henri Poincaré*, **7**, 1–68. English translation in H. E. Kyburg, Jr, and H. E. Smokler (eds), *Studies in Subjective Probability*. New York: Wiley, 1964.

de Finetti, B. (1970/1974), *Theory of Probability* (Vol. 1). Translated by A. Machi and A. Smith. New York: Wiley, 1974. First published 1970.

de Moivre, A. (1718/1756), *The Doctrine of Chances* (3rd edn). London: Chelsea.

Descartes, R. (1647), *Principia Philosophiae*. Translated from Latin into French by L'Abbé Picot. Paris.

Descarttes R. (1824), *Le Monde*. Cousin edition of *Oeuvres de Descartes*, Vol. 4, 262–263. Paris.

Descartes, R. (1931), *The Meditations*. Translated by J. Veitch. Chicago, Ill.: Open Court Publishing Company.

Descartes, R. (1940), *Regulae Directionem Ingenii*. French translation. Librairie Joseph Gibert: Paris.

Descartes, R. (1954), *La Géométrie*. Translated from the French and Latin by D. E. Smith and M. L. Latham.) New York: Dover.

Eddy, J. A. (1976), The Maunder minimum: the reign of Louis XIV appears to have been a time of real anomaly in the behavior of the sun. *Science*, **192**, 1189–1202.

Edmunds, L. (1975), *Chance and Intelligence in Thucydides*. Cambridge, Mass.: Harvard University Press.

Einstein, A., Podolsky, B., and Rosen, N. (1935), Can quantum-mechanical description of physical reality be considered complete? *Physical Review*, **47**, 777–780.

Ellis, C. (1969) 'Probabilistic languages and automata'. Unpublished doctoral dissertation, University of Illinois at Urbana-Champaign.

Estes, W. K., and Suppes, P. (1959), Foundations of linear models. In R. R. Bush and W. K. Estes (eds), *Studies in Mathematical Learning Theory*. Stanford, Calif.: Stanford University Press.

Euclid (1926), *The Thirteen Books of Euclid's Elements*. Translated from the text of Heiberg with introduction and commentary by Sir Thomas L. Heath (2nd edn). Cambridge: Cambridge University Press.

Euclid (1945), Optics. Translated by H. E. Burton. *Journal of the Optical Society of America*, **35**, 357–372.

Evans, J. V. (1982). The sun's influence on the earth's atmosphere and interplanetary space. *Science*, **216**, 467–474.

Fant, G. (1960), *Acoustic Theory of Speech Production, with Calculations based on X-ray Studies of Russian Articulations*. 'S-Gravenhage, Sweden: Mouton.

Fine, T. L. (1973), *Theories of Probability*. New York: Academic Press.

Fishburn, P. C. (1970), *Utility Theory for Decision Making*. New York: Wiley.

Fisher, R. A. (1935/1949), *The Design of Experiments* (5th edn). Edinburgh and London: Oliver and Boyd. Originally published, 1935).

Freedman, S. J., and Clauser, J. F. (1972), Experimental test of local hidden-variable theories. *Physical Review Letters*, **28**, 938–941.

French, T. E. (1941), *A Manual of Engineering Drawing for Students and Draftsmen* (6th edn). New York: McGraw-Hill.

Gleason, A. M. (1957), Measures on the closed subspaces of a Hilbert space. *Journal of Mathematics and Mechanics*, **6**, 885–893.

Greenwood, M., and Yule, G. U. (1915), The statistics of anti-typhoid and anti-cholera inoculations, and the interpretation of such statistics in general. *Proceedings of the Royal Society of Medicine*, **8**, 113–190.

Gumowski, I. (1982), Chaos in dynamics. *Jahrbuch Überblicke Mathematik*, 9–36.

Hazan, M. (1977), *The Classical Italian Cookbook*. New York, Alfred A. Knopf.

Herstein, I. N., and Milnor, J. (1953), An axiomatic approach to measurable utility. *Econometrica*, **21**, 291–297.

Hesslow, G. (1976), Two notes on the probabilistic approach to causality. *Philosophy of Science*, **43**, 290–292.

Hesslow, G. (1981), Causality and determinism. *Philosophy of Science*, **48**, 591–605.

Hintikka, J., and Remes, U. (1974), *The Method of Analysis*: *its geometrical origin and its general significance*. Dordrecht: Reidel.

Hintzman, D. L. (1980), Simpson's paradox and the analysis of memory retrieval. *Psychological Review*, **87**, 398–410.

Horgan, T. (1980), Humean causation and Kim's theory of events. *Canadian Journal of Philosophy*, **10**, 663–679.

Hume, D. 1888), *A Treatise on Human Nature*. Edited by L. A. Selby-Bigge. Oxford University Press.

Hume, D. (1902), *An Enquiry Concerning Human Understanding* (2nd edn). Oxford: University Press.

Humphreys, P. (1976), 'Inquiries in the philosophy of probability: Randomness and independence.' Unpublished doctoral Dissertation, Stanford University.

Ito, S. (1980), *The Medieval Latin Translation of the Data of Euclid*. Boston, Mass.: Birkhäuser, University of Tokyo Press.

Jeffrey, R. C. (1965), *The Logic of Decision*. New York: McGraw-Hill.

Kahneman, D., Slovic, P., and Tversky, A. (eds) (1982), *Judgment under Uncertainty*: *Heuristics and Biases*. Cambridge: Cambridge University Press.

Kant, I. (1883), *Prolegomena to Every Future System of Metaphysics*. Translated by E. B. Bax. London: George Bell and Sons.

Kant, I. (1949), *Critique of Pure Reason*. Translated by F. M. Müller. London: Macmillan and Company.

Kant, I. (1949), *An Inquiry into the Distinctness of the Principles of Natural Theology and Morals*. Translated by L. W. Beck. In *Critique of Practical Reason and Other Writings in Moral Philosophy*. Chicago, Ill.: University of Chicago Press.

Kant, I. (1970), *Metaphysical Foundations of Natural Science*. Translated by J. Ellington. Indianapolis, Indiana: Bobbs-Merrill.

Kaplan, D. (1977), 'Demonstratives', Draft No. 2, UCLA; unpublished.

Kendall, M. G., and Stuart, A. (1961), *The Advanced Theory of Statistics* (Vol. 2). *Inference and Relationship*. London: Griffin.

Keynes, J. M. (1921), *A Treatise on Probability*. London: Macmillan.

Kohlrausch, K. W. F. (1926), Der experimentelle Beweis für den statistischen Charakter des radioaktiven Zerfallsgesetzes. *Ergebnisse der Exakten Naturwissenschaften*, **5**, 192–212.

Kolmogorov, A. N. (1933/1950), *Foundations of the Theory of Probability*. Translated by N. Morrison. New York: Chelsea Publishing Company.

Kolmogorov, A. (1963), On tables of random numbers. *Sankhya Ser. A*, 369–376.

Koopman, B. O. (1940a), The axioms and algebra of intuitive probability. *Annals of Mathematics*, **41**, 260–292.

Koopman, B. O. (1940b), The bases of probability. *Bulletin of the American Mathematical Society*, **46**, 763–774.

Kraft, C. H., Pratt, J. W., and Seidenberg, A. (1959), Intuitive probability on finite sets. *The Annals of Mathematical Statistics*, **30**, 408–419.

Krantz, D. H., Luce, R. D., Suppes, P., and Tversky, A. (1971), *Foundations of Measurement* (Vol. 1). New York: Academic Press.

Kripke, S. A. (1979), A puzzle about belief. In A. Margalit (ed.), *Meaning and Use*, pp. 239–283. Dordrecht: Reidel.

Laplace, P. S. (1774), Mémoire sur la probabilité des causes par les événements. *Mémoires de l'Académie royale des Sciences de Paris (Savants étrangers)*, Tome VI, 621.

Laplace, P. S. (1820), *Théorie analytique des probabilités*. Troisième édition, revue et augmentée par l'auteur. Paris: Courcier.

Laplace, P. S. (1829–39/1966), *Celestial Mechanics* (N. Bowditch, trans., 4 volumes). Boston: 1829, 1832, 1834, 1839. Reprinted by Chelsea Publishing Co., New York, 1966.

Laplace, P. S. (1951), *A Philosophical Essay on Probabilities* (6th French edn, translated by F. W. Truscott and F. L. Emory). New York: Dover.

Lewis, D. (1973), Causation. *Journal of Philosophy*, **70**, 556–567.

Luce, R. D. (1967), Sufficient conditions for the existence of a finitely additive probability measure. *Annals of Mathematical Statistics*, **38**, 780–786.

Luce, R. D., and Raiffa, H. (1957), *Games and Decisions: Introduction and Critical Survey*. New York: Wiley.

Luce, R. D., and Suppes, P. (1965), Preference, utility and subjective probability. In R. D. Luce, R. R. Bush, and E. H. Galanter (eds), *Handbook of Mathematical Psychology* (Vol. 3), pp. 249–410. New York: Wiley.

Mackey, G. W. (1963), *The Mathematical Foundations of Quantum Mechanics*. New York: W. A. Benjamin.

Manin, Yu. I. (1979/1981), *Mathematics and Physics*. (A. and N. Koblitz, trans.). Boston, Mass.: Birkhäuser, (Originally published, 1979).

Markel, J. D., and Gray, A. H., Jr. (1976), *Linear Prediction of Speech*. Berlin, Heidelberg, New York: Springer-Verlag.

Marschak, J. (1950), Rational behavior, uncertain prospects, and measurable utility. *Econometrica*, **18**, 111–141.

Martin, E. (1981), Simpson's paradox resolved: A reply to Hintzman. *Psychological Review*, **88**, 372–374.

Martin-Löf, P. (1966), 'Algorithms and random sequences', doctoral dissertation, University of Erlangen, Germany.

Mates, B. (1950), Synonymity. *University of California Publications in Philosophy*, **25**, 201–226.

Maxwell, J. C. (1892), *A Treatise on Electricity and Magnetism* (3rd edn). London: Oxford University Press.

McKinsey, J. C. C., Sugar, A. C., and Suppes, P. (1953), Axiomatic foundations of classical particle mechanics. *Journal of Rational Mechanics and Analysis*, **2**, 253–272.

Meehl, P. E. (1954), *Clinical versus Statistical Prediction: A theoretical analysis and review of the literature.* Minneapolis: University of Minnesota Press.

Mill, J. S. (1893), *A System of Logic* (8th edn). New York and London: Harper.

Miller, G. A. and Johnson-Laird, P. N. (1976), *Language and Perception.* Cambridge, Mass.: Harvard University Press.

Moser, J. (1973), *Stable and Random Motions in Dynamical Systems with Special Emphasis on Celestial Mechanics.* Hermann Weyl Lectures, the Institute for Advanced Study. Princeton, N.J.: Princeton University Press.

Needham, J. (1959), *Science and Civilisation in China* (Vol. 3): *Mathematics and the Sciences of the Heavens and the Earth.* Cambridge: Cambridge University Press.

Neurath, O., Carnap, R., and Morris, C. W. (eds) (1938), *International Encyclopedia of Unified Science* Vol. 1, Part 1. Chicago: University of Chicago Press.

Newton, I. (1946), *Principia.* Berkeley, California: University of California Press. Cajori translation.

Nisbett, R. E., and Wilson, T. D. (1977), Telling more than we can know: Verbal reports on mental processes. *Psychological Review*, **84**, 231–259.

Nussbaum, M. C. (1978), *Aristotle's De Motu Animalium.* Princeton, N. J.: Princeton University Press.

Oates, W. J. (1940), *The Stoic and Epicurean Philosophers: The complete extant writings of Epicurus, Epictetus, Lucretius, Marcus Aurelius.* New York: Random House.

Ornstein, D. S. (1974), *Ergodic Theory, Randomness, and Dynamical Systems.* New Haven and London: Yale University Press.

Peirce, C. S. (1891), The architecture of theories. *Monist*, **1**, 162–176.

Peirce, C. S. (1892), The doctrine of necessity examined. *Monist*, **2**, 321–337.

Pisoni, D. B., and Sawusch, J. R. (1975), Some stages of processing in speech perception. In A. Cohen and S. G. Nooteboom (eds), *Structure and Process in Speech Perception*, pp. 16–35. New York, Heidelberg, Berlin: Springer-Verlag.

Poincaré, H. (1890), Sur le problème des trois corps et les équations de la dynamique. *Acta Mathematica*, **13**, 1–271.

Ptolemy, C. (1952). *Almagest.* Translated by R. C. Taliaferro. Chicago, Ill.: Encyclopaedia Britannica.

Ptolemy, C. (1964). *Tetrabiblos,* Loeb edition. Translated by F. E. Robbins. Cambridge, Mass.: Harvard University Press.

Ramsey, R. P. (1931/1964), Truth and probability. In F. P. Ramsey, *The Foundations of Mathematics and other Logical Essays*, pp. 156–198. New York: Harcourt, Brace, 1931. Reprinted in H. E. Kyburg, Jr, and H. E. Smokler (eds), *Studies in Subjective Probability*, pp. 61–92. New York: Wiley.

Rawls, J. (1971), *A Theory of Justice*. Cambridge, Mass.: Harvard University Press.

Roberts, F. S., and Luce, R. D. (1968), Axiomatic thermodynamics and extensive measurement. *Synthese*, **18**, 311–326.

Rosen, D. (1978), In defence of a probabilistic theory of causality. *Philosophy of Science*, **45**, *604–613*.

Rosen, D. (1982/3), A critique of deterministic causality. *The Philosophical Forum*, **14 (2)**, 101–130.

Rutherford, E., and Geiger, H. (1910), The probability variations in the distribution of α particles. *London, Edinburgh, and Dublin Philosophical Magazine*, **20**, 698–707.

Salmon, W. C. (1980), Probabilistic causality. *Pacific Philosophical Quarterly*, **61**, 50–74.

Salmon, W. C. (1982), Further reflections. In R. McLaughlin (ed.), *What? Where? When? Why?* pp. 231–280. Dordrecht: Reidel.

Savage, L. J. (1954/1972), *The Foundations of Statistics* (rev. edn). New York: Dover, 1972. First published in 1954.

Scott, D. (1964), Measurement structures and linear inequalities. *Journal of Mathematical Psychology*, **1**, 233–247.

Semb, G. (1968), The detectability of the odor of butanol. *Perception and Psychophysics*, **4**, 335–340.

Siegel, L., and Moser, J. K. (1971), *Lectures on Celestial Mechanics*. New York: Springer-Verlag.

Simpson, E. H. (1951), The interpretation of interaction in contingency tables. *Journal of the Royal Statistical Society, Ser. B*, **13**, 238–241.

Smith, B. H., and Kreutzberg, G. W. (1976), Neuron-target cell interactions. *Neurosciences Research Program Bulletin*, **14**, 211–453.

Sneed, J. D. (1966), Strategy and the logic of decision. *Synthese*, **16**, 270–283.

Solomonoff, R. (1964a), A formal theory of inductive inference, Part I. *Information and Control*, **7**, 1–22.

Solomonoff, R. (1964b), A formal theory of inductive inference, Part II. *Information and Control*, **7**, 224–254.

Stegmüller, W. (1973), *Probleme und Resultate der Wissenschaftstheorie und Analytischen Philosophie, Band IV. Personelle und Statistiche Wahrscheinlichkeit. Zweiter Halbband, Statistiches Schliessen, Statistische Begründung, Statistische Analyse*. Berlin: Springer-Verlag.

Suppes, P. (1956), The role of subjective probability and utility in decision-making. In J. Neyman (ed.), *Proceedings of the Third Berkeley*

Symposium on Mathematical Statistics and Probability (Vol. 5), pp. 61–73. Berkeley, Calif.: University of California Press.

Suppes, P. (1957), *Introduction to Logic.* New York: Van Nostrand.

Suppes, P. (1966a), Concept formation and Bayesian decision. In J. Hintikka and P. Suppes (eds), *Aspects of Inductive Logic*, pp. 21–48. Amsterdam: North-Holland.

Suppes, P. (1966b), The probabilistic argument for a non-classical logic of quantum mechanics. *Philosophy of Science*, **33**, 14–21.

Suppes, P. (1970a), Probabilistic grammars for natural languages. *Synthese*, **22**, 95–116.

Suppes, P. (1970b), *A Probabilistic Theory of Causality. (Acta Philosophica Fennica*, **24**), Amsterdam: North-Holland.

Suppes, P. (1973a) Congruence of meaning. *Proceedings and Addresses of the American Philosophical Association*, **46**, 21–38.

Suppes, P. (1973b), New foundations of objective probability. Axioms for propensities. In P. Suppes, L. Henkin, A. Joja, and Gr. C. Moisil (eds), *Logic, Methodology and Philosophy of Science*, pp. 515–529. Amsterdam: North-Holland.

Suppes, P. (1974a), Aristotle's concept of matter and its relation to modern concepts of matter. *Synthese*, **28**, 27–50.

Suppes, P. (1974b), The essential but implicit role of modal concepts in science. In K. F. Schaffner and R. S. Cohen (eds), *PSA 1972*, pp. 305–314. Dordrecht: Reidel.

Suppes, P. (1974c), The measurement of belief. *Proceedings of the Royal Statistical Society* (Series B), **36**, 160–175.

Suppes, P. (1980a), Limitations of the axiomatic method in ancient Greek mathematical sciences. In J. Hintikka, D. Gruender, and E. Agazzi (eds), *Pisa Conference Proceedings* (Vol. 1), pp. 197–213. Dordrecht: Reidel.

Suppes, P. (1980b), Procedural semantics. In R. Haller and W. Grassl (eds), *Language, Logic, and Philosophy* (Proceedings of the 4th International Wittgenstein Symposium, Kirchberg am Wechsel, Austria 1979), pp. 27–35. Vienna: Hölder-Pichler-Tempsky.

Suppes, P. (1981a), *Logique du Probable.* Paris: Flammarion.

Suppes, P. (1981b), Scientific causal talk: A reply to Martin. *Theory and Decision*, **13**, 363–380.

Suppes, P. (1982), Rational allocation of resources to scientific research. In L. J. Cohen, J. Łos, H. Pfeiffer, and K.-P. Podewski (eds), *Logic, Methodology and Philosophy of Science, VI.* Amsterdam: North-Holland.

Suppes, P. (1983), Arguments for randomizing. In P. D. Asquith and T. Nickles (eds), *PSA 1982.* Lansing, Mich.: Philosophy of Science Association. pp. 464–475.

Suppes, P., Léveillé, M., and Smith R. L. (1974), *Developmental Models of a Child's French Syntax* (Tech. Rep. 243, Psych. and Educ. Ser.). Stanford, Calif.: Stanford University, Institute for Mathematical Studies in the Social Sciences.

Suppes, P., Léveillé, M., and Smith, R. (1979), Probabilistic modelling of the child's productions. In P. Fletcher and M. Garman (eds), *Language Acquisition*, pp. 397–417. Cambridge: Cambridge University Press.

Suppes, P., Smith, R., and Léveillé, M. (1973), The French syntax of a child's noun phrases. *Archives de Psychologie*, **42**, 207–269.

Suppes, P., and Winet, M. (1955), An axiomatization of utility based on the notion of utility differences. *Management Science*, **1**, 259–270.

Suppes, P., and Zanotti, M. (1976a), Necessary and sufficient conditions for existence of a unique measure strictly agreeing with a qualitative probability ordering. *Journal of Philosophical Logic*, **5**, 431–438.

Suppes, P., and Zanotti, M. (1976b), On the determinism of hidden variable theories with strict correlation and conditional statistical independence of variables. In P. Suppes (ed.), *Logic and Probability in Quantum Mechanics*, pp. 445–455. Dordrecht: Reidel.

Suppes, P., and Zanotti, M. (1980), A new proof of the impossibility of hidden variables using the principles of exchangeability and identity of conditional distributions. In P. Suppes (ed.), *Studies in the Foundations of Quantum Mechanics,* pp. 173–191. East Lansing, Mich.: Philosophy of Science Association.

Suppes, P., and Zanotti, M. (1981), When are probabilistic explanations possible? *Synthese*, **48**, 191–199.

Suppes, P., and Zanotti, M. (1984), Causality and symmetry. In S. Diner, D. Fargue, G. Lochak, and W. Selleri (eds), *The Wave-Particle Dualism*, pp. 331–340. Dordrecht: Reidel.

Tarski, A. (1951), *A Decision Method of Elementary Algebra and Geometry* (2nd edn). Berkeley, Calif.: University of California Press.

Tarski, A. (1959), What is elementary geometry? In L. Henkin, P. Suppes, and A. Tarski, (eds), *The Axiomatic Method*, pp. 16–29. Amsterdam: North-Holland.

Van Fraassen, B. C. (1982), Rational belief and the common cause principle. In R. McLaughlin (ed.), *What? Where? When? Why?* pp. 193–209. Dordrecht: Reidel.

Victor, S. K. (1979), *Practical Geometry in the High Middle Ages. Artis Cuiuslibet consummatio and the Pratike de geometrie*. Philadelphia, Pa.: The American Philosophical Society.

von Neumann, J., and Morgenstern, O. (1947/1953), *Theory of Games and Economic Behavior*. Princeton, N. J.: Princeton University Press.

von Plato, J. (1983), The method of arbitrary functions. *British Journal for the Philosophy of Science*, **34**, 37–47.

Wheeler, J. A. (1962), Curved empty space-time as the building material of the physical world: An assessment. In E. Nagel, P. Suppes, and A.

Tarski (eds), *Logic, Methodology and Philosophy of Science*. Stanford, Calif.: Stanford University Press.

Wittgenstein, L. (1969), *Über Gewissheit*. G. E. M. Anscombe and G. H. von Wright (eds), *On Certainty*. Translated by D. Paul and G. E. M. Anscombe. Oxford: Blackwell.

Yule, G. U. (1911), *An Introduction to the Theory of Statistics*. London: C. P. Griffin.

Zweig, A. (1967), (editor and translator). *Kant: Philosophical correspondence 1759–99*. Chicago, Ill.: University of Chicago Press.

Name index

Abraham, R., 128
Aharonov, Y., 112
Alimov, N.G., 229
Almog, J., 166
Anderson, J.R., 155
Anscombe, G.E.M., 58
Archimedes, 200
Aristotle, 3–9, 11, 14, 16, 35–38, 47, 66, 85, 94, 95, 104, 116, 123, 185, 187–189, 196, 198–201, 209, 221
Aumann, R.J., 203
Ayer, A.J., 104

Bailey, C., 17
Barrow, J.D., 19
Bayes, T., 3, 35, 36, 40, 43, 44, 46, 61, 62, 65, 184–187, 205, 210–214, 220, 222
Becquerel, A., 23
Bell, J.S., 24, 25, 72, 113
Bentley, R., 28
Bickel, P.J., 55
Bjelke, E., 49
Blackwell, D., 203
Bohm, D., 112

Cagan, R.H., 14
Cantor, G., 103
Carnap, R., 119, 120
Carterette, E.C., 14, 15
Cartwright, N., 56, 57
Chaitin, G., 31

Chang, W.W. and I.B., 189
Chao, B.Y., 190, 192, 193
Church, A., 162, 168, 169
Clauser, J.F., 25, 113
Cohen, M.R., 57
Collingwood, R.J., 8–10
Cover, T.M., 213

David, F.N., 32
Davidson, D., 204
Dawes, R.M., 219
Debreu, G., 204
Democritus, 17, 122, 123
Descartes, R., 11, 26, 28, 36, 76, 85, 101, 104–107, 109, 111, 116, 126
Dewey, J., 11, 116

Eddy, J.A., 21
Edmunds, L., 11
Einstein, A., 23, 25, 111–113
Ellis, C., 174
Epicurus, 12, 15–17, 28, 83
Estes, W.K., 114
Euclid, 7, 79, 102, 150, 165, 188, 189, 192, 193–197, 199, 200, 202
Evans, J.V., 21

Fant, G., 136
Fichte, I.H., von, 4
Fine, T.L., 31, 96
Finetti, B., de, 93, 96, 98, 205, 206, 216, 223, 228

Fishburn, P.C., 205
Fisher, R.A., 206, 211
Freedman, S.J., 25, 113
Frege, G., 103, 149, 152
French, T.E., 194
Friedman, M.P., 14, 15

Geiger, H., 23, 27
Girshick, M.A., 203
Gleason, A.M., 24
Gray, A.H., Jr., 138
Greenwood, M., 48
Gumowski, I., 129

Hammel, E.A., 55
Hazan, M., 191–193
Heisenberg, W.K., 77, 84–87, 90–93
Herodotus, 16
Herstein, I.N., 203
Hesslow, G., 58–62
Hilbert, D., 24, 216
Hintikka, J., 199
Hintzman, D.L., 57
Holt, R.A., 25
Horgan, T., 60
Horne, M.A., 25
Hume, D., 12, 35, 36, 38–41, 43, 46, 47, 87
Humphreys, P., 125

Ito, S., 200

James, W., 11
Jeffrey, R.C., 205
Johnson-Laird, P.N., 150

Kahneman, D., 219
Kant, I., 1–4, 7–11, 21, 22, 25, 26, 35, 36, 41, 46, 47, 81, 85, 93, 101, 105–107, 109–112, 116
Kaplan, D., 166
Kare, M.R., 14
Kelvin, W.T., 111
Kendall, M.G., 48

Kepler, J., 51
Keynes, J.M., 225
Kohlrausch, K.W.F., 23
Kolmogorov, A.N., 30, 222, 225
Koopman, B.O., 205, 206
Kraft, C.H., 223
Krantz, D.H., 164, 205, 225, 230
Kreutzberg, G.W., 121
Kripke, S.A., 161
Kutscher, H.W. and A.H., 189

Laplace, P.S., 17–20, 22–26, 35, 36, 40, 41, 43, 45–48, 58, 82–84, 100, 101, 110, 112, 125, 128, 185, 205, 220
Leibniz, G.W., 126, 127
Leucippus, 11
Léveillé, M., 148, 177, 182
Lewis, D., 53
Luce, R.D., 164, 205, 225, 229
Lucretius, 16, 17

Mackey, G.W., 138
McKinsey, J.C.C., 18
Manin, Yu. I., 201
Markel, J.D., 138
Marschak, J., 203
Marsden, J.E., 128
Martin, E., 57
Martin-Löf, P., 30
Mates, B., 166
Maxwell, J.C., 29, 83, 111
Meehl, P.E., 219
Mill, J.S., 100
Miller, G.A., 150
Milnor, J., 203
Moivre, A. de, 35, 42, 43, 47
Morris, C.W., 118
Moser, J., 19, 128

Nagel, E., 57
Needham, J., 32
Neurath, O., 118
Newton, I., 21, 26, 28, 29, 33, 40, 41, 46, 51, 125–127, 163

Nisbett, R.E., 155
Nussbaum, M.C., 198, 201

O'Connell, J.W., 55
Oates, W.J., 16
Ornstein, D.S., 19

Peirce, C.S., 11, 83, 84, 116
Pisoni, D.B., 137
Plato, 16, 33, 116
Plato, J., von, 33
Podolsky, B., 25, 113
Poincaré, H., 128, 129
Ptolemy, C., 51, 200, 201

Raiffa, H., 205
Ramsey, R.P., 203–205
Rawls, J., 193
Remes, U., 199
Roberts, F.S., 229
Rosen, D., 58, 59, 63
Rosen, N., 25, 113
Rutherford, E., 23

Salmon, W.C., 63–68
Savage, L.J., 204, 205, 225
Sawusch, J.R., 137
Scott, D., 151, 223, 224
Semb, G., 14
Shimony, A., 25

Siegel, L., 19
Simpson, E.H., 55–57, 82
Slovic, P., 219
Smith, B.H., 121
Smith, R.L., 148n, 177, 182
Sneed, J.D., 205
Solomonoff, R., 30
Stegmüller, W., 94
Stuart, A., 48, 100
Sugar, A.C., 18
Suppes, P., 5, 18, 28, 30, 48, 52, 54,
    68, 71–74, 91, 114, 115, 139, 148,
    164, 165, 167, 177, 182, 200, 204,
    207, 211, 213, 214, 219, 226, 230

Tarski, A., 102, 150, 195
Tversky, A., 219

Van Fraassen, B.C., 67, 68
Victor, S.K., 193

Wheeler, J.A., 111, 112
Wilson, T.D., 155
Winet, M., 204
Wittgenstein, L., 85

Yule, 48, 57

Zanotti, M., 68, 71–74, 226, 230
Zweig, A., 4

Subject index

action at a distance, 26, 40
algebra
  Boolean, 91, 92
  classical, 92
  of events, 91, 92
algorithm, 59, 62, 144, 145, 213, 216–218, 221
axiom of choice, 78, 103, 114, 115
axiomatization, 193
  of geometry, 140
  Kolmogorov's, 225
  Luce's, 225

Bayesian
  conceptions of rationality, 184
  expected-utility model, 220
  methods, 186
  theory, 187
  theory of decision making, 186
  theory of rationality, 213
  theory of subjective probability, 3
behavior, 19, 20, 25
  change in, 115
  of elementary particles, 115
  human, 36
  justification of normative goals of, 213
  linguistic, 149
  normative, 219
  optimal, 213
  of physical phenomena, 129
  prediction of, 65, 129, 134
  random, 128
  rational, 196
  rationality of, 99
  theory of rational, 215
  unpredictable, 210
behaviorism, 133
belief(s)
  as aspect of theology, 51
  in astrology, 51
  concept of probability as theory of subjective partial, 205
  degree of, 164
  and desires, 210
  expression of, 52, 98
  indirect discourse, 162
  and intentions, 210
  measuring the probabilities, 215
  probability distribution of, 204, 213
  problems of measuring, 213, 214
  process of changing, 212
  process of determining, 214
  propositional attitudes about, 168
  puzzles about, 161
  qualitative structure, 224
  rational, 2
  rationality of, 99
  realism of, 27
  Scott's axioms as a theory of, 224
  sentences, 162
  in spurious causes, 51
  statements about, 162

strength of, 164, 165
subjective, 164
substitute for, 51
theory of partial, 187
and values, 206
Boolean, *see* algebra

cause(s)
common, 25, 67–69, 71, 72, 74
determinate, 40
genuine, 50, 51, 55, 57
negative, 64
prima facie, 48, 50, 54, 55–57, 65, 66, 68
probabilistic, 25, 59
secret, 41, 42
spurious, 48, 50, 51, 55, 57, 65
true, 206
ultimate, 51, 56
certainty, 2, 8, 55, 148
analysis of, 77
asymptotic, 100
claims of, 76
concept of, 93
defense of, 93
demonstrative, 79
empirical, 82
Euler's three senses of, 77, 79, 82
fantasy of, 84
genuine, 82
kind used by Descartes, 85
of knowledge, 10
longing for, 99
method to achieve, 76
moral, 79, 80, 82
objective statements of, 93
philosophical analyses of, 82
philosophical search for, 85
a priori, 76, 77
retreat from, 87
in science, 84
search for, 76
sense of, 82
senses of, 79
strict, 88

Wittgenstein, 85
choice, 22, 25, 37, 103, 114, 115, 153, 169, 181, 190, 206, 210
closure condition, 226
completeness, *see* incompleteness
complexity, 14, 32, 83, 123, 136, 141, 179, 214, 220
characterization of randomness, 32
continuity and, 138
definition of, 31
degree of, 115
dependence of randomness on, 30
of experimental evidence, 112
as a general notion, 31
of phenomena, 21
of phenomena of speech perception, 137
of utterances, 140
computation, 24, 131, 145, 148, 175, 178, 207
arithmetical, 218
theory of, 131, 132
computer, 17, 31, 49, 123, 130–133, 145, 146, 151, 156, 159
current, 160
language, 195
model, 151
programming, 151
programs, 151, 159
science, 188
conditioning, 220
congruence
concept of, 165
degrees of, 168
hierarchy of, 169
of meaning, 161, 167
relation of identity, 166
relations, 154, 166, 167, 169
requirements of, 168
result-, 157–161
correlation
between cigarette smoking and lung cancer, 51

conditional, 67
negative, 72
phenomenological, and
common causes, 71
criterion, 32
for acceptance of grammar, 177
empirical, 80
of identity, 86
independent, 193, 194
judgment in decision making,
216
objective, 218
of performance, 218
prediction of a numerical, 219
of proof, 78
of rationality, 196, 216
syntactic, 80, 81

data
analysis of, 56
empirical, 31, 80, 111
decision(s)
Bayesian theory of decision
making, 186
choice of, 206, 210
consequences of, 206
decision making in modern
mathematical statistics, 216
economic, 207
expectation of, 205
inexplicit, 215
informal, practical, intuitive,
215
maker, 184
making, 219–221
optimal, 213
preference among, 204
rationality of, 207
recursive procedure for logical
truth, 102
role of intuitive judgment in
theory of decision making, 217
Tarski's procedure, 102
theory, 213

definition
of analysis, 199
Aristotle's, of matter, 7
of causal chains, 66
of causal concepts, 36
of classes for actuarial tables, 56
of complexity, 31
complexity, of randomness, 33
of 'discipline', 124
of matter, 5
of metaphysics, 10
probabilistic, of prima facie
causes, 66
of probability, 223
of randomness, 31
recursive, 144
recursive, in sentential logic, 144
of the set of computable
functions, 151
of spurious causes, 50
Tarski's, of truth, 150
determinism, 2, 8, 32
argument against, 12, 13
of common causes, 67
concept of, 12, 30
dichotomy between determinism and randomness, 32
Kant's ideas of, 25
Laplacean, 18
neo-Kantian and neo-Laplacean
views about, 26
prediction and, 129
strict, 87, 88, 100, 101
strict Laplacean, 83, 84
versus stability, 129
distribution
joint, 89
joint, improper, 90
joint, of position and momentum, 89
joint, of random variables, 89
joint, of spin and position, 89
marginal, 90, 92, 146

economics, 184, 201

error
  experimental, 25
events
  algebra of, 91, 92, 225, 226, 230
  sequence of, 64
evidence
  experimental, 112, 201
exchangeability
  in physics, 73
  principle of symmetry, 73
expectation
  and probability, 205

first-order
  logic, 101, 102
formula
  well-formed, 144
foundations
  of mathematics, 103, 123, 143,
    151
  of physics, 108, 110, 111
grammar
  context-free, 147, 174
  probabilistic, 139, 140–143, 147,
    173, 175, 177, 179

Heisenberg
  uncertainty principle, 77, 85, 87,
    90
  uncertainty relation, 93
hidden variables, 24, 25, 112, 113
  deterministic, 67
  search for, 88
  theorems about, 71

incompleteness
  of arithmetic, 102
  in Cartesian physics, 104–107
  Einstein–Podolsky–Rosen
    paradox, 112–115
  of geometry, 102
  in Kant's metaphysical founda-
    tions, 107–110
  in logic, 101
  of set theory, 103

unified field theory, 111, 112
indeterminism, 21, 22
indirect discourse, 161, 162, 168,
  169
  semantics of, 169
information
  and computation, 131
  processing, 216
intension, 166, 168
interpretation
  intuitive, 89
invariance
  problems of, 138

justice
  procedural, 193

kinematics, 109

language(s)
  babble of speech, 13
  competence versus perfor-
    mance, 143–147
  developmental models, 179–183
  formal, 140, 143
  informal, 80
  learning, 10, 144, 145, 149
  length of utterances, 140
  natural, 139, 141, 143, 144, 149,
    152, 168
  philosophy of, 135
  syllables, 136, 138
  words, 136, 138–140, 148, 150,
    152, 156, 159, 161, 163, 167,
    169, 172, 178, 186
  Zipf's law, 139
law(s)
  adequate probabilistic, 15
  basic probabilistic, 27, 35
  basic, of science, 35, 52
  biological, 119
  causal, 10
  of complex phenomena, 112
  deterministic, 23, 29
  exponential, 97

exponential, of radioactive
    decay, 15
foundational, 60
fundamental, of matter, 110
fundamental, of natural
    phenomena, 10
fundamental, of physics, 22
fundamental, of the universe, 22
general, 59, 60
of gravitation, 26
inadequacy of deterministic, 15
of inertia, 105
of motion, 104
natural, 129
of nature, 41, 83, 104, 105
Newton's, 33, 41
Newton's inverse square, of
    attraction, 28
objective probabilistic, 207
physical, 119
of physical phenomena, 7
probabilistic, of decay, 23
of quantum mechanics, 123
statistical, 35
of thought, 108
unity of, 119
Zipf's 139
learning
    all-or-none, 179, 180
    developmental models, 179–183
    incremental, 180–182
    language, 10, 144, 145, 149
likelihood
    maximum-, 174–176
    maximum-, estimate, 174, 175,
        177
linguistics, 141, 150, 177
    statistical methodology in, 135
logic
    classical, 91, 102, 186
    first-order, 101, 102
    nonclassical, 91
    of quantum mechanics, 91, 92
    sentential, 144

mathematics
    foundations of, 103, 123, 143,
        151
meaning
    congruence of, 161, 167
    synonymy, 169
measurement
    theory of, 214
mechanics
    classical particle, 18
    quantum, 6, 23–25, 27, 34, 68,
        70, 71, 77, 84, 86, 88, 89, 91,
        92, 112, 113, 122, 123, 138,
        141, 209
    statistical, 24, 34, 84, 152, 155
memory, 146
    core, 131
    human, 169
    limited, 213
    storage, 131
    visual, 158
modalities, 29, 30

N-body problem, 65, 127, 128

ordering, 225
    partial, 92
    weak, 225, 228

paradigm, 20, 49
paradox
    Simpson's, 57
phonemes, 138, 146
    analysis of, 137, 138
    distinctive features of, 136
plurality, 54
    of language in science, 120–122
    of methods, 124
    of political views, 122
    and reductionism, 120–125
    of science, 121
    of subject matter in science,
        122–124
prediction
    of behavior, 65

and instability, 129
theoretical, 63, 177
probabilistic
  grammar, 139–143, 147, 173,
    175, 177, 179
  learning, 149
  metaphysics, 3, 7
probabilistic laws, 35
  adequacy, 15–19, 23
  objective, 207
probability, 89, 173
  conditional, 49, 50, 64, 173
  distribution, 20, 69, 70, 72, 85,
    86, 89, 90, 92, 93, 99, 113, 173,
    174, 204, 210, 213, 220, 226
  joint, 70, 72, 89
  space, 74, 115, 222
  subjective, 3, 187, 204, 206, 213,
    220, 223
  theory, 35, 40, 41, 46, 48, 60, 86,
    89, 91, 93, 110, 120, 138, 187
procedures
  and communication, 155–159
  human versus computer, 160
  justified, 185, 187, 189, 196, 201,
    202, 221
  and meaning, 153–155
  and properties, 153
  result-congruent, 156, 157
  for semantics, 159, 160
proof(s)
  finding, 145
  mathematical, 79–82, 155, 200,
    217
proposition(s), 169
  general, 10
  metaphysical, 10, 11
prosody, 135

quantifiers, 150
quantities, 195, 214, 215, 223
  physical, 83, 84, 86

radioactive decay, 13, 15, 23, 27,
  40, 97, 209

random
  sampling, 211, 212
  sequence, 30, 31
  strategy, 210
  variable, 71–74, 86, 89, 90, 222,
    223, 225, 226, 230
randomization
  intentional, 212
randomness
  Aristotle on luck, 36–38
  babble of speech, 13
  common natural phenomena,
    12–15
  and complexity, 30–32
  intentional, 210–212
  process versus outcome, 32, 33
  smelling and seeing, 13
  and stability, 32, 33
  and stochastic equations, 21
rational
  behavior, 196, 215
  man, 185, 207, 208, 212
rationality
  concept of, 184, 196, 213
recipes, 189, 190, 192–195
reductionism, 120–125
reinforcement, 114, 115, 212
responses
  puzzle about, 154, 166–168

sample space, 50, 86, 114, 227
seeing, 15, 79
semantics
  and meaning, 135
  procedural, 160
sequence
  of events, 64
  finite, 30, 31, 114, 173, 175
  infinite, 114
  random, 30, 31
set
  cylinder, 114
  theory, 103, 123, 124, 150
set-theoretical methods, 149

space
  Hilbert, 24
  probability, 74, 115, 222
  and time, 11, 89, 100
standard deviation, 72, 86, 90
state
  of nature, 184, 204, 205
statistical
  independence, 175
  mechanics, 24, 34, 84, 152, 155
  methods, 124, 125
stochastic
  process, 143, 152, 195
strategy
  optimal, 210
  pure, 145
synonymy, 169
syntax, 80, 101, 135, 141
  of natural language, 149
  theory of, 143

theology, 1, 2, 29, 51, 186
theory
  of language, 150
  of probability, 28, 61, 214
  of rationality, 187
truth
  Tarski's definition of, 150
uncertainty, 187, 206
  appropriate concept of, 99
  chance and, 16
  concept of, 99
  fundamental principle of, 84–86, 91, 92, 97
  Heisenberg principle of, 77, 85–87, 90–93
  of mathematical knowledge, 77

probability and, 61
theory of rationality in situations of, 187
about the true state of nature, 184

unity of science, 118–125
utility
  expected, 184, 196
  maximizing expected, 198, 204, 210
  normative model of expected, 207
  theory of expected, 203, 206, 210, 219–221
  theory of probability and, 205
utterance, 137
  children's spoken, 149
  complexity of, 140
  grammatical acceptability of, 140
  grammatical type of, 175
  phonemes of a given, 137
  prosodic features of, 157
  purpose of a given, 140
  relative frequencies, 140–142
  sameness of, 156
  sequence of, 175
  spoken, 154, 167, 172
  surface structure of an, 148
  understanding of, 148

variance, 71, 86
  conditional, 72
  of a probability distribution, 85